The Last Village Smithy

The Last Village Smithy

Memories of a Small Town In the New England Hills

Ray Glabach

authorHOUSE®

AuthorHouse™
1663 Liberty Drive
Bloomington, IN 47403
www.authorhouse.com
Phone: 1-800-839-8640

First published by AuthorHouse 6/29/2011

ISBN: 978-1-4567-5899-8 (e)
ISBN: 978-1-4567-5900-1 (hc)
ISBN: 978-1-4567-5901-8 (sc)

Front cover image provided courtesy of Greenfield Recorder-Gazette and the Leyden Historical Society

Library of Congress Control Number: 2011908061

Printed in the United States of America

To my grandkids, Mikayla, Kyleigh, Chloe, and Cate
Lest they forget their past

I shall be telling this with a sigh
Somewhere ages and ages hence:
Two roads diverged in a wood, and I--
I took the one less traveled by,
And that has made all the difference.

Robert Frost

Contents

Foreword

Being asked to write the forward to a book of Leyden, MA memories is an honor and a privilege. The beauty, colors, and fresh air atop this small mountain town holds residents dear to this place, draws new residents from near and far, and entices others to return. Theirs are the memories shared in this book. While the title is *The Last Village Smithy*, this book is as much about the village, or town, and its people, as it is about the blacksmith and his shop. In numerous ways, the blacksmith, Henry Glabach, his blacksmith shop, and the town, were intertwined and interwoven for many, many years.

I have lived most of my 88 years in the small New England mountain town of Leyden. My husband, Wayne, and I raised four boys and a girl in Leyden starting shortly after WWII. I have known the author of this book, and his family, since before he entered grade school. My oldest son, Wayne, Jr. was a boyhood friend of the author. They attended school, played baseball, and participated in numerous activities together for many years. My husband and I were friends with, and worked on numerous church and town activities with, both Henry and Jessie Glabach as well as with most of the other residents mentioned in this book. Along the way I have been very involved with the town and its people. I have served as tax collector, school committee member, 4H instructor, and have been on every committee the church has had. I have even preached a few sermons in the town's only church.

Through the years, my family did a lot of business with Henry Glabach, the Leyden Blacksmith who is central to this book. We bought gasoline from him, had him do some car repairs, and fix broken farm machinery. Wayne was an original member of the first trained volunteer fire department which Henry organized and led.

Henry had a very low key way of doing business. I remember at various times asking him, or Jessie, how much we owed them. I never received an answer. We'd pay for a job being done and have a little extra to put toward our bill, but to no avail. Years later, I happened to think about the peas we gave to Henry and Jessie each year. Wayne always raised a big vegetable garden, and one year he found out that Henry and Jessie liked fresh peas, but that they didn't raise any. So, Wayne gave them a bushel each summer for a number of years. Maybe that's why we never received a bill.

I always used to enjoy attending the annual town meetings where much of the town's business was transacted. I especially enjoyed listening to the passionate, friendly, debates between some of the town's old-timers such as Louie Black, John Glabach, and Jimmy McDonald. I don't remember the specifics of these arguments, but they generally centered on taxes and roads.

Longtime, and returning, Leyden residents often comment about the many informal social gatherings that we used to have and that they miss them today. Some of these were Old Home Day, swimming lessons at Baker's pond, horseshoe tournaments at Barton's Garage, visits to sugar houses, and discussions at the blacksmith shop.

Many of the older, longtime residents are gone now, but children and grandchildren have stayed or are returning. Many are interested in carrying on some of the traditions and telling about the history that is forever etched in their minds. That speaks volumes about why Leyden is a unique small New England town where people want to live, raise a family, and retire.

I think that everyone will enjoy reading this book of Leyden memories. The stories that follow will surely bring back memories of your own.

Edith Fisher
Chairman of the Leyden Historical Commission, 1975 - 2006

Acknowledgements

I owe a big "Thank You!" to Edith Fisher of Leyden. Edith was a good friend and neighbor of Henry Glabach, the Leyden blacksmith, and his wife, Jessie, for many years. Like them, she was always highly involved in all aspects of the town. Her sons, Wayne (Junior), and Bobby were boyhood friends of mine in school and on the ball fields. Many years after the events recorded here had passed into history, Edith contacted me asking for stories about the blacksmith shop. In her position as chairman of the Leyden Historical Commission, she was hopeful of raising funds to purchase the vacant blacksmith shop for the town to use as a museum. That effort failed, partly because it took me far too long to comply with her request. Throughout the process of creating this book, Edith has acted as a terrific resource, offering suggestions and searching out information. She kindly accepted my request to write the foreword to this book.

I want to thank my wife, Joan, for her proofreading, ideas, and ongoing encouragement during the times I was questioning the value of this effort.

Recent conversations with several longtime Leyden residents contributed to some of the stories in this book. Among these were Edith Fisher, Dottie Howes, William Glabach, and June Barton Damond. I am indebted to Katie Ainsworth for her detailed information regarding the food booth at the fairgrounds.

The very talented artist, and Leyden resident, Richard

DiMatteo, kindly gave his permission to reproduce several of his images in this book. Some are from a series of sketches he made of Leyden scenes for note cards in 1984, and the cover of the 1985 Leyden Town Report. At my request, he created, especially for this book, a sketch from a photograph I took years ago. It is of the blacksmith shop anvil, and is on the title page.

Chapters 1, 5, 11, 16, 21, 25, 28, and 34 begin with a stanza from Henry Wadsworth Longfellow's famous poem, *The Village Blacksmith*, written in 1841. It, along with Rudyard Kipling's *IF*, was a favorite of Henry Glabach, Leyden's Village Blacksmith.

I want to thank Jock Dempsey, of anvilfire.com, for his permission to reprint the poem, *A Blacksmith's Prayer*.

Most of all, I want to thank all the people who lived in Leyden, and surrounding communities, in the 1940s, 1950s, and 1960s. Through living their daily lives, they each helped to create the stories and memories I have recorded here.

Ray Glabach
Windsor, Colorado
rayglabach@yahoo.com
May 2011

Introduction

This book is based largely on my personal memories of people and events that occurred in the small western New England town of Leyden, Massachusetts, while I was growing up there in the middle decades of the 20th century. It is not intended to be a pure history book, although everything herein is based on history in one fashion or another. Every event described, or story told, actually happened. I was involved in some, witnessed others, and a few I heard about shortly after they occurred.

Leyden was, and is, small in both area and population. Located in the hills north of Greenfield, Leyden shares a border with another small New England town named Guilford, Vermont. It consists of 18 square miles of wooded hills and lush valleys that are geologically the southern end of Vermont's Green Mountains. In the early 1950s, the town's total population was a little less than 400 people, living in about 200 homes. Initially settled before the Revolutionary War, the town's population peaked at around 1000 in the early 1800s, followed by a slow decline beginning around the time of the Civil War. The town had once boasted a couple of inns, several grist mills and sawmills on the larger streams, and a cheese factory, all of which were gone long before I was born.

In the mid-20th century, many town residents made their living by operating small dairy farms, or working in Greenfield, down the partially paved road from Leyden Center. Even those residents with out-of-town jobs, often raised a few milk cows, a hog or two, and a brood of chickens. A vegetable garden behind the house often fed the family through the summer, with the surplus bounty preserved against the coming winter. Here and there, logging was still active using portable mills, powered by gasoline or diesel engines, that were moved from place to place following the tree cuttings. In 1950, the only other businesses in town were a small grocery store, a slaughter house, and a single village blacksmith shop.

A century earlier, when Longfellow published his poem, *The Village Blacksmith*, the blacksmith and his shop, or smithy, was an essential component of all communities large and small. Many of the iron items required by the advancing civilization, and growing population, were made from iron that was heated glowing hot in a blacksmith's forge and hammered out on his anvil. However, within a few short decades following that poem's publication, the factories of the industrial revolution increasingly took over responsibility for most of the manufacturing. The ringing tones of the blacksmith's anvil were gradually replaced by the puff-puffs of steam power, and the roar of the internal combustion engine. Yet, there was an ongoing need, especially in smaller communities, or those remote from the large industrial centers, for someone with the skills to form metal into whatever shape was needed, repair tools and machinery, or provide advice and assistance with the project of the moment.

This book is, in part, a biography of my father, Leyden's last village smithy, both the shop and the man. Both were quite possibly the last in a long line of traditional New England village blacksmiths and their shops. Henry's, and his wife Jessie's, lives were thoroughly woven into the fabric of life in Leyden during the 1950s and 1960s, just as they had been for several decades before and after the events described herein. They were involved in one fashion or another, with nearly every aspect of the town. They were simply known as Henry and Jessie to all Leyden residents (and to numerous residents of neighboring towns as well.) Henry's trade was from an earlier time as were many of his principles, habits, and interests. For example, all his life he shaved with a straight razor, long after everyone except barbers had abandoned them in favor of disposable blades or electric shavers.

By trade, Henry was a blacksmith and wheelwright, but he was much more. In many ways, and for many years, he was immersed in the lifeblood of the town. For example, he was the town's first fire warden/fire chief, a position he held without pay for 48 years. He was a key member of every town and church construction committee from the 1930s through the 1970s. This included the new Town Hall, church restoration, the new consolidated school, church addition, food booth at the fair, and the fire station. He was also a church trustee, Town Hall janitor, winter road boss, Old Home Day chairman, and in many other ways, a very involved citizen of the town. Possibly his finest trait was that he was a person that anyone in town could call upon for help or advice at any time for any reason. He was always among the first in line to help the town, or any of its residents, with whatever the problem of the moment might be.

Jessie's traits were very similar to Henry's, which made them a great team. In addition to being a wife and mother, she was a school teacher, church treasurer, newspaper reporter, fair booth chairperson, school board member, Civil Defense coordinator, Red Cross first-aid instructor and provider, and downright great cook. She was quite superstitious, and possessed considerable psychic capability as you will see in the chapter devoted to her. Like Henry, she took a very keen interest in everything and everyone in town. Anyone in need of help for whatever reason needed to look no further than Jessie.

Material for this book came mostly from sifting back through the decades of my dusty memories of growing up in that little New England town in the hills. A major resource was the voluminous scrap books and photo albums that my mother, Jessie, had kept most of her life. It's been at least 50 years since the happenings described herein took place, so I'm sure that in some instances my memories deviate a bit from what others may remember of the same or similar events. All of our memories may deviate somewhat from what really happened, or who was actually involved. Such is the course of aging and the passage of time.

Where my recollection is clear, I have used the actual names of the people involved, unless I felt the material might be a bit sensitive to them or their descendants. A few other names have been changed, not to protect the innocent, but because in reaching back over a half century or more, I simply cannot clearly remember the names of everyone involved in everything I have written about. So, here and there, I have manufactured a few names, something unforgivable if this was intended to be a totally factual history tome. When I first introduce a character with a name I have created, I have indicated that it is a pseudonym. I hope the reader will excuse me if missed one or two.

Although the book is best read in the order given, I have tried to write chapters that can stand on their own and will prove stimulating to readers with a variety of interests. The type of content varies from chapter to chapter. Some are descriptive, or somewhat technical, others are simply interesting stories. The chapters are arranged by topics, and are not in any rigid chronological order. The reader who likes to jump around shouldn't get too lost.

Following the final chapter, titled *The Anvil No Longer Sings,* I have included four appendices. Each contains additional information about a specific topic, beyond what will be found in the main text:

- Appendix A, *At the Forge and On the Anvil,* provides additional information about the village blacksmith's essential tools, the forge and anvil, and describes how Henry used them in his shop.
- Appendix B, *We Used to Say...,* lists some of the hundreds of colorful sayings and colloquialisms that added a lot of flavor to the typical backwoods New Englander's language of decades past.
- Appendix C, *Leyden and the 1704 Deerfield Massacre,* steps backward to a major historical event of the early 18th century in Western Massachusetts. This appendix presents a logical alternative to the

generally accepted route of the Indians and their captives across Leyden on their way to Canada following the raid on the Deerfield settlement to the south. It is very relevant to this book because it describes a logical route which passed by, or through, the future location of many of the places mentioned in the main text including homes, schools, the Old Home Day field, and Henry Glabach's farm.

- Appendix D, *A Few Leyden Recipes*, contains an original Leyden recipe for blueberry pie, and another for blueberry muffins, as served in the town's annual blueberry suppers. It also contains the 70+ year old recipes for beef stew and clam chowder that are still served at the Leyden Church food booth at the Franklin County Fair.

I feel that I was very lucky to have experienced a way of life that will never exist again, and was quite rare even then. I was fortunate to experience first-hand, the transformation away from a way of life in which much of the power was generated by the muscles of people and animals just as it had been for hundreds of years. My grandparents lived in harmony with the land without benefit of electricity, using living horsepower as their only locomotive force, and reading by the light of oil lamps. Although my father was a blacksmith with ties to the long ago, he also recognized the importance of adjusting to changing technologies over which he had no control.

My grandchildren are growing up in a totally different world than I did. Their world of satellite TV, Smart Phones, texting, GPS, and Facebook, with "Made in China" on nearly everything they see and use in their daily lives, bears little resemblance to what I experienced at their ages. Packaged food from around the world, ready for the oven or microwave, is now purchased at huge stores, with little thought as to how that food came to be, or the creatures that gave their lives in order for us to survive. Things were not always this way. I know. I was there.

Now, *The Last Village Smithy*.

Chapter 1

THE ANVIL'S SONG

Under a spreading chestnut tree
The village smithy stands;
The smith, a mighty man is he,
With large and sinewy hands;
And the muscles of his brawny arms
Are strong as iron bands.
                              Longfellow

The cool early morning autumn air was so still that the leaves on the centuries old maple trees, that stood alongside the road between the house and the blacksmith shop, hung as unmoving as if weighted down with the hundreds of years the same trees had spread their roots in that location. They were there when the Deerfield captives were herded along the valley floor below (Appendix C.) It's very likely that, they already had their roots in the soil of the future town when the Pilgrims landed at Plymouth. Later, they had reached young maturity when the town was founded and named for the Pilgrims' refuge in the Old World. If the shots fired at Bunker Hill really were heard in these hills, those trees were home to forest wildlife that heard them. Still vibrant in the 1950s, but showing the effects of their age, they had witnessed all the history of the little New England hill town of Leyden.

The first rays of sunrise peeked over East Hill and caressed the little cluster of public buildings, the Town Hall, the tiny library, the only church, the blacksmith shop, and the eight or ten houses which made up Leyden Center. Awakened by the dawn of a new day, a grey squirrel left its nest and cautiously headed down one of the ancient maples. Sensing no danger in the stillness, it scampered across the road and headed up the hill intent on another day of gathering and hoarding acorns for the coming winter. Most trees in the Center, as the heart of town was called, were maples, but a row of mature oak trees grew along the west side of the Town Hall providing the winter food supply for every squirrel and chipmunk within a half mile.

It was the start of Indian Summer, that glorious time of year in New England that exists between the first frost and the onset of the seemingly unending, harsh winter season. Here and there a few trees had begun to trade their green coat of summer for their colorful autumn cloak which would be short-lived before being abandoned for the bare limbs of Old Man Winter.

Soon, a handful of cars would head down the road to Greenfield, driven by town residents who earned their living elsewhere. For the moment, nothing but the squirrel moved in Leyden Center. The only sounds were faint noises coming from down the hill at Casper Zimmerman's farm as he turned his dairy cows out to pasture after their morning milking. As if in protest of the stillness, a single crow took off from the top of a pine tree behind the white church on top of the hill. Cawing loudly, it flew low over the shop before flying downward into the valley below in search of its breakfast.

Suddenly a puff of pure white smoke emerged from the chimney on Henry Glabach's blacksmith shop as if a new Pope had been elected within. Soon the puff was followed by a column of dense white smoke that rose straight up in the still, crisp air. Finally, after rising many feet above the building as it had for decades, the column of smoke began dissipating, slowly drifting to the east.

"The Shop" as it was known by everyone for miles around, had been built by Ed Howes, the next-to-last Leyden village blacksmith. Howes' original shop had been located behind his house (later Henry's) down the hill just a bit toward Zimmerman's farm. A blacksmith shop had stood on that site since long before the Civil War. In the 1870s, a cheese factory was located across the road and together they had formed the tiny industrial center of the town. One night in the early 1920s, that original blacksmith shop burned to the ground. Howes and his teenaged apprentice, Henry Glabach, had been setting iron tires on some wooden wagon wheels that day. That task required building a ring of fire large enough to heat the iron rims enough so that they would expand and fit over the wood wheels, shrinking on tightly as they cooled. The speculation was that Ed and Henry had not fully extinguished the flames before ending their long work day, and slowly walking up the hill to their well-deserved supper. The town had no fire department, no fire equipment, and no trained firefighters to extinguish the flames. The shop and everything combustible inside was a total loss. Townspeople using burlap sacks, shovels, and hoes managed to keep the flames from climbing the hill through the dry grass to the house. With morning's first light, Ed and Henry were walking through the still smoking ruins of the source of their livelihood, salvaging horseshoes, smithing tools, pieces of iron, and most importantly, two heavy anvils which were the symbols, and essential tools, of their trade.

Never one to be discouraged in the face of adversity, Howes immediately began plans for a larger, more fire resistant, new shop. There used to be a fairly widespread superstition that it was bad luck to erect a new building in the same location as one that had burned, so a different location was selected. The new shop was built of concrete blocks to make it more fire proof and farther from the house just to be safe. The floor was poured concrete, except in the inside horseshoeing area which was formed from thick, wide, knot-free, wood planks. Wood was used in that area to provide greater traction for the horses while wearing their iron shoes. As portions of the shop were completed, Ed and Henry gradually moved their work inside out of the weather. Finally, in 1925, the building was completed and in full operation.

Since all the wooden items in the old shop had been lost in the fire, Ed and Henry attended several weekend auctions searching for used benches, and storage items for their new building. A prize acquisition was an antique, swivel, octagon cabinet with 72 pie-shaped drawers. In the new shop, it became the prime storage location for small nuts, bolts, and washers. Larger items were stored in several neat rows of wooden horseshoe calk boxes. As the years passed, a number of antique dealers and collectors tried to purchase the cabinet from Henry, but he wouldn't sell. "I'd just have to buy something else to store my small nuts and bolts in," he would say. That cabinet provided an excellent example of Henry's fantastic memory. None of the 72 drawers were labeled. And, items were not stored in any particular system of organization. Yet, whenever Henry needed a particular bolt or nut, all he needed to do was to pull out any one drawer and observe what was inside. He then knew in exactly which other drawer he would find the item he needed. It was rarely necessary for him to pull a third drawer.

This brisk, fall morning, inside the shop he had purchased from Howes' widow many years earlier, Henry was preparing several sets of horseshoes for another day of shoeing at farms just across the state line in Vermont. As he worked at his forge, Henry smiled as he breathed in the mixed odors of hot iron, hardwood, horses, and time. "That was the smell of honest work," he would tell me in later years. Unlike in 1920 when he was apprenticed to Ed Howes at the age of 15, few horses were now brought to the shop for shoeing. Instead, by the 1950s, Henry mostly made "barn calls." Normally the shoes would have been prepared the day before so that he could get an early start on the road, but yesterday, fate had given him a higher priority. An early season chimney fire at a house in West Leyden had required his full attention as Fire Warden/ Fire Chief which consumed all the previous day's afternoon and evening.

To fire up his forge, Henry had gathered a huge double handful of hardwood shavings from the pile that always accumulated on the floor beneath his antique wood planer.

The planer was probably 100 years old, but it still saw frequent service whenever a logging sled or truck body was to be built or repaired. A cavity was dug out in the coke or soft coal that filled the forge pot and the shavings were piled in. After lighting the shavings Henry began turning the crank on the rotary air blower with his left hand while the right scooped coal over the shavings until they were totally buried. Henry preferred the hand-cranked blower over the traditional bellows because it gave a steady air flow and the heat of the fire was easily adjusted by how rapidly he cranked. This produced a dense, pure-white smoke which was pulled up the chimney by natural draft. Henry kept a fast rotation on the blower and soon flames burst through the pile immediately eliminating the smoke.

Today Henry would be shoeing several large working, or draft, horses that were still a common source of power on numerous farms and logging camps in the area. With winter coming on, each iron shoe would need sharp toe and heel calks to improve the horses' traction on ice and frozen ground. Once the fire was hot enough, Henry pushed the heel end of each of four large horseshoes down into the glowing coals. He continued to turn the handle on the blower for several minutes pulling a shoe frequently to check its color. When the heated end of a shoe had turned to a bright yellow, it was ready for the blacksmith's hammer on the large anvil. Using a set of handmade, long handled tongs, he removed one shoe from the forge and held it on the anvil. Grasping a smithing hammer in his right hand and with a tight grip on

Henry Glabach, working at his big anvil in 1957.

the tongs with his left, he began reshaping the shoe with powerful blows.

Everyone in or near the Center could always tell when Henry was working at this forge. On a cool, crisp, autumn morning, the ringing song of the anvil carried for at least a half mile. Under the right conditions, it could sometimes even be heard far across the valley on top of East Hill. At first, the anvil sang loudly, but in a low key in response to heavy hammer blows on the hot, soft, glowing iron, sending glowing sparks of hot metal in all directions like a 4th of July sparkler. As the horseshoe quickly cooled and the iron became harder, the tone changed to a higher note with a louder ringing tone. To keep the hammer's beat as he repositioned the shoe the hammer would come down lightly on the bare anvil which would respond with a weaker, but higher pitched, ringing, bell-like tone.

This was the same anvil's song that had followed the march of civilization worldwide for centuries. Less than 50 years earlier at the dawn of the automotive age, the anvil's song was still being heard daily in every town, village, and city. However, in the last few decades, as gasoline and diesel engines had increasingly replaced living horsepower, it had become a song heard less and less frequently. By the 1950s, it was a song that large numbers of people, maybe the majority, had never heard. But in the small town of Leyden, it remained a song that was still sung almost daily. It said that the blacksmith shop was in operation and all was well in that small part of the world.

Henry Glabach was born in September of 1905, at his parents' farm at the end of the road on the north end of East Hill. It was across the valley from where he would work in his blacksmith shop for more than six decades. He was second oldest of 12 children born to John B. and Marie Glabach. John B. had immigrated to the US from Minden, Germany, and worked as a cigar maker for a few years in Greenfield. Marie Buntemeyer was also a German immigrant though they met on this side of "the pond." When she and John B. were married, they decided that they wanted their children raised on a farm. They agreed that it would be a big family and it was. I never met my grandmother, Marie, since she died of cancer long before I was born. John B. always had a strong German accent, but when his children were growing up, he insisted that English was to be spoken in their home. "We are Americans now, and Americans speak English," he said. For the Glabachs, English was not a second language, it was the language.

Although he gave up the cigar making trade, John B. never gave up his love of smoking cigars. He was seldom without a White Owl, lit or not, clenched between his teeth. The aroma of cigar smoke always hung closely around him and in his home. He sometimes had severe attacks of asthma to which the cigars may have contributed. Actually, he claimed that his asthma attacks often came on when he was stressed, or worried about something, and smoking a cigar calmed him down. In spite of the cigars, and a diet rich with fatty German foods, John B. outlived two wives, dying in 1968 at the age of 92.

As a boy, Henry attended the one-room East Hill School walking or skiing to and from school every day. All the formal education Henry ever received was in that one-room school. He would often claim that he received his higher education in the School of Hard Knocks. Many days, on the way home from school, he would stop and help a neighbor with the milking, earning a few dollars a month to help support his younger siblings. At the age of 13, he was expected to provide full-time help on his father's farm, so his formal education ended with the 8th grade. Actually it would have been very difficult, in 1918, to attend high school since the town had none. After working on the family farm for a couple of years, John B. arranged for Henry to be apprenticed to the blacksmith down in the Center. So Henry went to live with Ed Howes and his wife. Room and board represented a large portion of his compensation. Of his remaining earnings, all but $10 of his monthly paycheck was collected by John B.

During his years as an apprentice, Henry learned not only the finer points of working with hot metal and shoeing horses, but also fixing farm machinery and repairing horse drawn wagons and especially wood-spoked wagon and buggy wheels. One of his first iron working tasks was to supply the main power in many forgings. This was a standard teaching technique that blacksmiths had used with their new apprentices for centuries. Ed Howes would heat the item to the proper temperature and lay it on the anvil. Using a small hammer, Ed would hit the piece lightly to show Henry where to then strike with the heavy sledge. This not only showed the apprentice the proper way of forming the piece, but relieved the blacksmith of a lot of hard work! Once Henry became adept at forging, he began to create his personal set of blacksmith's tongs whenever the workload in the shop permitted. A blacksmith needed a wide variety of sizes and shapes of tongs to hold the various shapes of metal he needed to work with. Henry forged over a dozen different sets of tongs, most of which were still in regular use when he retired decades later.

After Jessie and Henry were married in 1929, he told his father that from then on he would be keeping all of his earnings. They rented what, in future years, became the Beaudoin house on the south end of Leyden Center, just a short walk from the shop where Henry was employed. Later, they bought a farm down in the valley below the Zimmerman farm, where Jessie's parents were to later live.

Ed Howes and his wife liked to travel to places they had never been. Every time they visited a new place, they brought back a stone with them. These stones were used to pave a walkway beneath a metal rose arbor outside the kitchen of their home. Eventually their travels took them to New York City where Ed, more used to the ways of horses and small towns, than to automobiles and a big city, was struck and killed by a taxi cab. Henry bought out the widow and became owner of the house and business. He and Jessie moved into the former Howes house near the shop, but also kept the farm for many years. Sometime, probably in the late 1930s or early 1940s, Jessie's parents, Frank and Bertha Wood, relocated from Charlemont, or Hawley, to Henry's farm.

Realizing that the future belonged to engines, not horses, Henry never took a blacksmith apprentice saying that it wouldn't be fair to teach a kid a trade that was going to disappear. His younger brother, Wilhelm (Bill), assisted in the shop part time for many, many years in addition to his full-time employment at a tool manufacturer in Greenfield. From time to time, a neighbor down on his luck and in need of a job, or a freshly discharged veteran, would be welcomed in the shop as a temporary assistant. Following the end of WWII, several local young men earned a few dollars working for Henry while they reestablished their lives.

In the 1950s, and long before, the shop was not only a place to get a horse shod, machinery repaired, or buy some gas. It also served a very important social function for informal gatherings. Local residents would often drop in for some need, and end up staying for several hours chatting with Henry and anyone else that might appear. Topics ranged all over the map, but town politics was a very popular subject. The discussions in Henry's shop about who would make a good selectman candidate at the coming election probably had as much to do with the ultimate selection as did the actual voting.

Phil Koshinsky was a daily visitor to the shop, as it was the terminus of his mail delivery route. The Leyden Post Office had been shut down in 1935 after more than 100 years of service. From then on, mail delivery was by way of either Greenfield or Bernardston, depending on where in town you lived. Phil was the mail carrier for the portion of Leyden that was served by the Greenfield Post Office, called the Leyden Star Route. Phil's route basically ran from the Greenfield line to the shop. The rest of the town was served out of the Bernardston Post Office by an RFD carrier. Phil was a diabetic and in the summer months, even while delivering mail, he rarely wore a shirt because exposure of his skin to sunlight reduced his need for insulin. By Labor Day his skin was as brown as old leather shoes. In the late 1950s, when the fire department was being officially organized, Henry, as chief, and Phil, as assistant chief, held many long talks around the forge about how the department should operate and how to obtain sufficient funds to pay for the necessary equipment and training.

Old photos of the shop show the name LEYDEN in huge letters on the roof. I remember them well. The letters must have been at least four feet high. The story was that the name

Horses outside the shop, in winter, waiting to be shod.

of the town was painted there as a guidepost for early aviators who might be flying over the hills and not know quite where they were. I remember hearing once that at one time the roof had been painted as part of a "sprucing up" of the shop. In spite of the new paint, the letters continued to show clearly until new shingles were installed years later.

At the center of the T-shaped shop were two forge setups made of brick and concrete surrounded by heaps of horseshoes, tools, scrap iron, and other metal items that might be needed some day. The scrap iron overflow area was at the top of a small hill just south of the shop. Old horseshoes, worn-out tools, broken farm equipment, etc. were all thrown into the pile. When the size of the pile got out of hand, Henry would start paying close attention to the scrap iron price being paid by Kramer's Junk Yard in Greenfield. When the price was right, I would help him load up his truck and we would head for town. Sometimes we would haul three or four loads in a single day. Usually the very next day, the pile would be born again like weeds in a vegetable patch.

One forge setup, no longer in use, was originally equipped with a DC powered electric blower. That position was the one used by Ed Howes' and was never been operated after his death. Henry preferred to continue to use the hand operated setup that he had learned on as a teenager. Near the forges were wooden benches mounted with old style, long blacksmith's vises. Of course each position had a large anvil and water quenching trough close by. In the 1950s, the bench behind the forge Henry used was also set up for electric welding which Henry admitted was a huge improvement over the old-fashioned forge welding that he had learned as an apprentice.

Adjacent to the forges was the horseshoeing area. When horses were brought to the shop for shoeing, they were led inside onto the wood floor and tied to metal rings fastened to the concrete block walls. Over the decades, the hundreds of horses that had been shod in the shop left their marks on those wood planks. Decades later, when Henry finally retired and sold everything at auction, the planks from the floor of the shoeing area were one of the most sought after items.

At the shop, a horse would be hot shod which was the best fitting and longest lasting way of shoeing. The hoof was trimmed just as it would be for cold shoeing and then the hot horseshoe was pressed against it to burn away small irregularities creating a perfect fit. Of course the horse felt no pain from the trimming and hot shoe since a horse's hoof is much like a person's fingernail and contains no nerve endings.

During the 1950s, a major activity at the shop was repair work for local farmers and of the town's road maintenance equipment. It was just about a daily event to have to repair broken parts or make new ones from scratch if they were beyond repair. Henry's pricing structure for repairs was very flexible just as it was for shoeing a horse. He never had such a thing as an hourly labor rate. Frequently the cost of materials that were purchased for a project was passed along to the customer without a markup. If the required parts could be made from scrap metal located in large piles both inside and outside the shop, only a very minimal materials charge was made. Very often the bill was based more on what Henry felt was proper and fair rather than the number of hours it took him to do the work. Sometimes when a customer would stop in to pick up a repaired item Henry would pencil out a bill and then look at it and say, "That's too much. Give me half of it and we'll call it square." Or he might say, "Just pay me whatever you think it's worth to you." Many a time a farmer who was low on funds, but very much in need of a repaired piece of equipment, paid with a promise to come back when he had the money. They always did.

Henry always enjoyed a challenge to do something he had never done before. Sometimes it was to improve on the design of a piece of farm equipment to make it more effective or reliable. Other times it might have been to fabricate a duplicate antique to replace one that had been lost from a pair or set. Sometimes a particularly challenging project would sit around the shop for many weeks while Henry thought through the optimum process for completing it. Suddenly, one day, it would occur to him how to go about doing it and everything else would be postponed until that job was completed.

I can only recall one time that Henry was stumped by a project requested of him. One day, somebody brought into the shop a millstone, the kind used in an old water-powered grist mill. It must have been 100 years old or more. The stone was less than three feet in diameter, and maybe eight to ten inches thick. Someone had cut a shallow groove in the center of the edge all the way around the circumference. The owner wanted Henry to cut the stone into a pair of discs following that groove. Henry told him that he had never worked with stone, and had no idea how to go about it. All his tools were for cutting iron or wood, not stone. He was reluctant to try anything for fear of breaking the millstone. He had a reverence for anything old, and did not want to risk destroying the stone. However, the owner was insistent, telling Henry that he was confident that he could do it. Every day for several weeks, Henry would spend a few minutes looking at the stone, touching it, and measuring it. But, nothing came to him. Finally, he called the owner and told him to come and get it and take it to a stone cutter or mason. The owner said he would, but he never came. For at least the next 30 years, that stone sat around the shop, gradually being moved farther away from the busy working areas. The stone can be seen leaning against the right end of the iron tire-making machine in a photograph in this chapter. As far as I know, it was sold in the auction when Henry finally retired.

The west end of the shop was the woodworking area. Many of the tools housed there had been salvaged from the ruins of the old burned shop. Henry once described to me the processes by which he and Ed Howes had straightened and retempered the cutting portions of the tools that had been excessively exposed to the heat of the fire. In addition to the specialized wheelwright hand tools, this area contained a large table saw with an 18-inch blade, an edger-joiner, a huge band saw, and the ancient planer which I'm sure dated from the mid-19th century. All were driven by an overhead flat belt and pulley system. The first power source that I remember for the system was the engine, clutch, and transmission from a 1928 Model A Ford with an electric starter. The exhaust was piped outside through a hole in the block wall. That was an improvement over the hand cranked Model T power plant that it had replaced. Sometime in the early '60's the Model A engine was sold to an antique car restorer and was replaced with a 240-volt, 5 horsepower electric motor of only slightly more recent vintage.

No matter what power tool was to be run, the Model A engine would be fired up and the overhead belt system started turning the idler pulley above each tool. To start a tool, a wooden handle would be pushed to one side in order to move the appropriate belt off its idler pulley and onto the tool's drive pulley. As a boy, I always was quite scared of that system with all its moving belts and no guarding. Although I did it frequently, I was always nervous helping Henry to plane or rip boards.

Jessie was a nervous type and it always bothered her when Henry, or Bill, was using the woodworking equipment with all its turning, unguarded belts. There often would be a heated discussion between Henry and Jessie on the subject of safety. Henry always claimed that the best safety system was simply staying alert. "Knowing you can't get hurt can cause you to be dull and do something stupid," he would say. Finally, to end the arguments, he agreed to buy an insurance policy that would cover medical expenses for anyone who might get injured by the equipment.

The ancient, belt-driven, planer in the wood-working area of the blacksmith shop.

One day an insurance salesman arrived at the shop. He was there to look things over and decide how much to charge for the insurance premium. After a quick look around, and with an astonished look on his face, he informed Henry that there was no way he would write an insurance policy with all those exposed moving belts and pulleys everywhere. "You will need to enclose all those belts inside guards before we can even talk about insurance," he said.

"If all those belts are enclosed, why would I need insurance?" Henry replied. "With everything that moves totally enclosed nobody could get hurt." That was the end of the insurance issue.

In spite of the scary nature of the woodworking system and its very frequent use by Henry or his brother, Bill, there was only one serious injury that ever occurred as far as I know. Sometime before I was born, the edger clipped off Henry's right index finger at the center joint. Ever after, that half-length finger with its small round knob of a finger nail was sort of Henry's trade-mark.

One of the most interesting activities at the shop was the wheelwright work. It was even more of a dying art than blacksmithing and often attracted an audience when a major job was being worked on. Henry was one of very few people left in New England who had the tools, knowledge, and experience to repair and restore old wooden spoke, iron tired wheels from wagons and buggies. In the early 1950s, many of the wheels he worked on were from local farm wagons that still saw daily use. By the '60s, the focus had largely shifted to restoring wheels from antique wagons and buggies for show purposes, museums, or collectors. Wheels would be shipped to him for repair from all the eastern states. He did not have the facilities to build wooden wheel hubs from scratch. If the original hubs were beyond repair, he would obtain new ones from a source in the Amish area of Pennsylvania. Everything else, the wood spokes, wood rims, and iron tires, he could make from scratch.

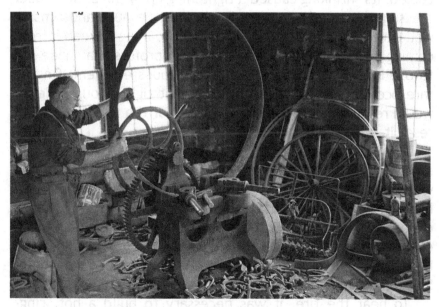

Henry Glabach forming an iron tire for a wooden wheel.

In one corner of the shop, adjacent to the horseshoeing area, was a massive machine operated manually by what looked like a ship's wheel. This was the device used to bend a straight band of iron into a perfect circle to make the tires for wagon wheels. The ends would then be welded together and ground smooth to complete the circle. Most people didn't realize that it was the shrinking of the iron band, or tire, that held the entire wood spoke wheel together. Setting the iron tires onto repaired wood wheels often drew a crowd of observers, and more than once was the subject of a feature article in the *Greenfield Recorder-Gazette* and other newspapers.

To ensure a tight fit, and hold the wheel together, the inside diameter of the iron tire was made a little smaller than the outside diameter of the wood wheel. In order to get the tire onto the wheel, the circle of iron needed to be heated to a high temperature. Heating caused the iron to expand, increasing the tire's diameter enough to fit it snugly over the wood wheel. The trick was to heat the iron tire very uniformly. Then, after it was fitted over the wood wheel, and the iron cooled, its shrinking caused a tightening up of the entire wheel pressing the wooden spokes firmly into the hubs and rims. A well-fitted iron tire never needed any tire bolts to keep it from coming off. Henry saw it as a matter of professional pride not to use tire bolts unless a customer requested them. On the rare occasion that a fitted tire was not tight enough, Henry would remove it, reduce the diameter of the tire slightly and reset it.

The heating of the iron tire increased its diameter only slightly. Thus, it was essential that, the diameter of the wooden wheel was only slightly greater than that of the tire prior to heating. For example, a tire for a large wheel, say 4 ½ feet in diameter, would only increase its diameter by about 0.4 inch even if heated to a dull red, or about 1300 degrees F. That's less than a quarter inch of tolerance on each side of the wheel. Smaller tires and wheels would have even less to work with.

To heat the tire, it was necessary to build a hot, ring-shaped fire outside just south of the shop. The tire was laid on the ground supported by a few small rocks. Then, hundreds

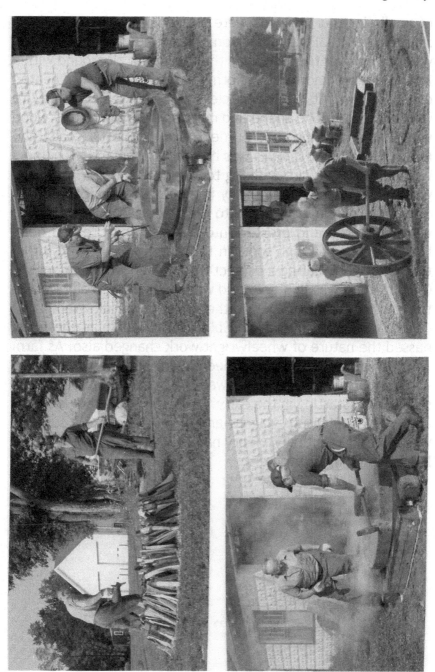

Henry, his brother Bill, and Art Beaudoin,
setting the iron tire on a large ox-cart wheel.

of small pieces of firewood were stacked teepee-style on both sides of the tire. Finally, a gallon of used motor oil or kerosene was poured over the wood and the fire was lit all around with a torch. The fire had to be uniformly hot so that the tire heated evenly to retain its perfect circle. An uneven temperature tire would lose its round shape and not fit properly over the wood wheel. After the fire had burned down to mostly coals, and Henry judged that the tire was hot enough, he and his helpers would lift the hot tire with big tongs and set it over the wood wheel. One man would quickly hammer around all the edges of the iron forcing it down onto the wheel. Bit by bit the tire was hammered and pressed into place. If the tire had been hot enough, small high spots in the wood were burned off by the hot metal creating a perfect fit between wood and metal. Once the tire was in place, cold water was poured all over the tire causing it to shrink on, rather like iron shrink wrap.

As with horseshoeing and blacksmith work, as the years passed the nature of wheelwright work changed also. As farm wagons with wood-spoked wheels were replaced by wagons with rubber tires, fewer and fewer wheels were repaired at the shop. Then, starting in the early 1960s, the interest in restored horse drawn pleasure wagons and buggies created a surge in wheel work. Eventually, Henry had to turn away work from all but his longtime customers.

Chapter 2

SHOEING ON THE ROAD

When Henry Glabach started shoeing horses in 1920, at the age of 15, nearly every New England farmer and logger still used living horsepower as a primary locomotive force, even if they owned a new-fangled tractor. Two to four times a year, each draft horse needed to be reshod and they were nearly always taken to a local blacksmith shop. In Leyden, the horses were driven to the Center to Ed Howes' shop. If the shoes were heavily worn, new ones would be needed. Other times, if the shoes were still in good condition, but the horse's hooves had overgrown them, just a trim and reset might be required. Riding and pleasure buggy driving horses needed similar treatment and with all the metal work and equipment repairs being made, the Leyden shop was a busy place for Ed Howes, his apprentice, and a helper or two.

By the mid-1930s, tractors and trucks were causing working draft horses to be less common and the automobile had all but eliminated the pleasure horse in many areas. There were still quite a few horses around, but they were being trucked to the shop from a lot farther away. Henry decided that the future of the blacksmith's trade (he never called himself a farrier) was to become mobile and take "the shop" to the barn or logging camp. This quickly became a big hit with the horse owners because they no longer had to take a day off to travel with their animals to and from the shop. Now they could get their horses shod right where they were kept or being worked. Phone calls would come into the shop or house all week making appointments. Some of Henry's bigger customers set up a standing three month schedule. Henry never worked on a strict "first come first served" plan because it made more sense to do all the customers in the same general area instead of wasting a lot of time traveling back and forth.

When he first began shoeing on the road, Henry would work at it, or in the shop, seven days a week. However, after having a few close calls and injuries while shoeing on Sunday, he decided that Sunday would be his day off

The first vehicle I remember our family owning was a gray 1938 Chevrolet four door sedan, although I know Henry owned a 1927 Model T Ford before that. Jessie and he had driven the Model T from Leyden to Niagara Falls and back, without a map, over mostly unpaved roads, for their honeymoon in 1929. Jessie still talked about that trip in the 1950s. For his part, Henry still talked about that Model T, and its two speed Ruxell rear end. He said that it would stall out if he tried to drive it up the steepest part of the road up East Hill, but that if he went up in reverse it would go up easily. I think Henry always missed that Model T.

The '38 Chevy was our only vehicle, so it did on-the-road horseshoeing duty as well as being the family car. During most weekdays, Henry would load his horseshoeing equipment into the trunk of that car, including his 150 pound anvil, and head out. About once every other week, Jessie would get the car for about a half day to drive to Greenfield for groceries and other errands. The 1938 was later replaced by a 1946 and around 1950 Henry obtained his first pickup truck, a used GMC.

By the late 1950s, he was traveling as far south as the middle of Connecticut and into northern Vermont and New Hampshire. If there were more horses to be shod at a farm than could be done in one day, he would sometimes spend the night, often in the barn with the horses, and continue shoeing the next day. For a while he had a contract to do all the shoeing for the equestrian department at the University of Massachusetts, in Amherst. However, after a couple of years he dropped them. "They never shod a horse in their lives, but they think they know more about it than I do," he said.

Henry possessed a phenomenal memory. Not only could he drive just about anywhere in New England without consulting a map, once he had shod a horse he could always prepare the correct size and shape of shoes for the animal the next time it needed to be shod months later. The horseshoes were prepared at the forge in the shop a few days in advance. On the road, he used his 150 pound anvil to make minor adjustments to the cold shoes at the barn as needed. He never liked pounding cold iron because the metal did not respond well. "The sure road to Hell for a blacksmith is to pound cold iron," I often heard him say.

The process of shoeing a horse was started by closely tying the horse's halter to something solid, or having it held tightly by a trusted helper. It was always tied short so that the horse's head couldn't move side to side very much which helped to make the animal stand more still. Restricted side to side movement also minimized the biting tendency that some horses had. It even helped to reduce kicking if the animal could not see its target.

Much of the shoeing operation required one of the horse's feet to be lifted off the ground and held there trapped between Henry's knees. Henry blamed the terribly painful knees that he developed in later years on "all the tons of horseflesh I supported on them for so many years."

To remove the old shoe, Henry would first bend upward the ends of the cinched-over nails by driving a small wedge he made especially for the job, between the end of each nail and the hoof. Next the shoe would be loosened slightly by holding a metal block against the shoe and striking it with his shoeing hammer. Finally the shoe was grabbed with large tongs and twisted off. Although the rim of a horse's hoof has no blood vessels or feeling, the center portion is quite sensitive and can be easily damaged if the shoe is not removed properly.

Once the old shoes were off, Henry would trim the hooves. Like a person's fingernails, a horse's hoof is always growing. Before an iron shoe was nailed on, the hoof was trimmed

Henry, shoeing horses at Louis Black's farm in Leyden, mid-1950s.

to the same size as the shoe. However, as the hoof grew, it would extend past the metal shoe, sometimes an inch or more. The part of the hoof that extended past the shoe was very vulnerable to breakage if the horse stumbled or stepped just right on a rock. A broken hoof could take a long time to heal properly and the horse might be out of commission for several weeks. That is why it was important to have a horse reshod about every three months even if the iron shoes were not very worn. Henry used a large set of pinchers to cut off most of the overgrown hoof before trimming it with a special shoeing knife.

If there were any dogs hanging around near where a horse was being shod, they would often dart in and grab pieces of the smelly cut off hoof and chew it like a bone. "They think it is dog candy," Henry would say. He used to have a dog, named Chum, that was never far from him. In those days, most of the horse shoeing was still done at the shop, and Chum would follow Henry there every morning, stay all day, and return home with him in the evening. One icy winter morning they were walking to the shop together when Chum was hit by a car and killed. Henry was heartbroken. His plans for the day were cancelled. Instead, he used some of his best lumber to build an elaborate coffin for Chum. Henry never allowed himself to become attached to another animal.

A proper shoeing job produced no pain for the horse. However, just because there was no pain, didn't mean that every horse enjoyed being shod. A few would kick, some would bite, and sometimes one would do both. Usually Henry could calm a horse down enough to get it shod without any trouble. Often, gentle techniques would work such as feeding the horse an apple or scratching it behind an ear. A common trick was to give the horse a scoop full of grain to divert its attention away from what was going on with its feet. If the "I'm your friend" techniques failed, it was time to let the horse know who was boss. A firm rap on the ribs with the handle end of a shoeing hammer often did the trick.

From time to time there would be a horse that just would not cooperate, no matter what Henry and the horse's owner tried. If the uncooperative horse was a kicker, Henry had a technique that worked almost every time. He always carried a well-used 1-inch thick manila rope in his truck. He would tie one end around one of the horse's legs just above the foot, and then pass the rope over its back to a helper standing on the other side of the animal. The helper pulled on the rope while Henry lifted the foot to begin shoeing it. The rope restricted the horse from kicking with the foot being shod, and with one foot held up off the ground the horse could not lift a second foot in order to kick.

Probably the worst injuries Henry received while shoeing were while he was nailing on the new shoe. He always wore a thick leather shoeing apron, but the sharp nails could penetrate it easily. To do the nailing Henry stood behind the horse's leg with his back toward the animal's head. Then he bent over and lifted the foot off the ground. Stepping over the hoof he would support the foot between his knees while working. The iron shoe was nailed onto the trimmed hoof while holding the foot in this position. The proper sized horseshoe nails would protrude out of the hoof a half-inch or more, be twisted off, and then clinched over to hold the shoe firmly in place. If the horse pulled its foot away while the nails protruded, Henry could get some nasty wounds in his legs. Whenever this happened, Henry always finished shoeing the horse before seeking medical attention. One horse did this to him twice and he refused to ever shoe that horse again.

It would usually take Henry between 20 and 40 minutes to shoe a horse start to finish. If a horse was troublesome, it might take over an hour. Of course the actual amount of time consumed depended a lot on how often he stopped to talk with people that were watching him work. "I learned a long time ago that it was a mistake to talk and shoe at the same time. You need to concentrate on what you are doing so you don't get hurt or make a mistake," he said. Henry never charged for shoeing by the hour, just by the horse no matter how long it took.

I remember one time when a customer with a very large riding stable needed to have 27 horses shod. The stable owner had put off calling Henry to make arrangements until it would be nearly impossible to get the horses all shod by the date they were needed. Because the customer was one of his largest clients, Henry rearranged his schedule in order to give it a try. When he arrived at the stable, he found out that there were actually 34 horses that needed to be shod, not 27. And, all the horses had to be fully shod within three days' time. To make matters worse, he had received such short notice that he had not had time to make up all the proper shoes in the shop. Most of the shoes would have to be made up cold, on site, from standard blanks, all 136 shoes. Fortunately everything went smoothly and by the evening of the third day Henry was headed for home and some much needed rest.

Over the years he had developed considerable skill in making up corrective shoes for horses. Just like people, some horses had a tendency to roll their foot to one side, so he would build up the metal on that side of the shoe to correct the horse's gait. Other horses had an especially sensitive frog, or center portion of the foot, so he would make special shoes with a metal bridge in the center for protection. If a show horse was supposed to be a Tennessee Walker, he would add weight to the toe ends of the front shoes to enhance that special stepping motion.

From time to time he would be called in to assist a veterinarian in diagnosing and/or correcting a horse's foot or leg problem. One time a veterinarian asked Henry to examine the foot of a horse that the vet had been treating for quite some time without success. The horse had a severe limp and acted as if the foot was very tender. The vet had tried antibiotics, a splint, and several other remedies to no avail. Henry examined the foot closely and told the vet that he had seen something very similar before. Although there was no outward sign of an infection, other than the reluctance to put weight on the foot and an overly sensitive frog, Henry was sure the foot was heavily infected deep inside. The vet disagreed because he had been treating the animal with antibiotics and had seen no improvement.

"Well, let's have a look-see," Henry said. Holding the sore foot tightly between his knees, Henry took his shoeing knife and started carefully carving away the inner part of the hoof near the frog. Being very careful to stay away from areas with feeling, he carved much deeper than he normally would if he was going to shoe the foot. Bit by bit, he carefully dug deeper and deeper.

Finally, as he made his last cut, a crack suddenly opened near the center of the foot. A gusher of hot puss and fluid surged out. After cleaning up the foot, he told the owner to soak the foot in a pail of hot water with Epsom Salt several times a day and that soon he should see a marked improvement. The next day Henry returned with a special protective shoe he had made for that foot.

As times changed the horses changed with it. While the majority of the shoeing work prior to about 1955 was large draft horses, fewer and fewer of those existed in later years. However, there was resurgence in the popularity of smaller riding and driving horses that more than made up for the decline in large horses. Henry always missed the big horses however.

Henry always enjoyed working at the various fairs, shows, and horse pulls around the area. He would often be hired by the event coordinators to setup for shoeing in the horse area and deal with the occasional thrown or loose shoe. Sometimes he would be busy shoeing throughout the event, other times things were pretty slow. In any case, his shoeing setup always attracted a lot of attention from fairgoers and he loved to talk with strangers about what he did as they took photos. Many thought that his setup was part of the show.

One time a group of young men showed up, beers in hand. They were having a good time talking with Henry about blacksmithing. Finally, the discussion came around to the anvil sitting on an upended wooden horseshoe keg.

"How do you get that thing in and out of your truck?" someone asked.

"I pick it up and carry it," Henry replied, surprised that they even asked. "It only weighs about 150 pounds."

"Can I give it a try?" another asked.

"Help yourself, but don't drop it on your foot!"

Three of the young men took turns lifting the anvil, carrying it a short distance, and exclaiming about how heavy it was. The fourth could not get it off the keg.

"Here's a challenge for you," Henry said. With that he set the anvil on the ground and then tipped it back onto its heel so that the horn pointed toward the sky. "Now try to lift it by gripping just the horn with both hands."

This was an ancient test of a man's strength. If he could lift a heavy anvil by gripping only the tapered horn, he was indeed a strong man. The first young man wrapped the fingers of both hands around the horn, gripped as tightly as he could and lifted. His hands simply slid off the sharply tapered horn. Each of the young men tried several times, but each time the anvil remained firmly planted on the ground.

"That's impossible," all three agreed. "Nobody could lift that much weight by holding just the horn. Has anybody ever lifted this anvil that way?"

"Yes, I've seen a few guys do it, but not many," Henry replied. With that he approached the anvil, knelt down, and interlocked the fingers of both hands around the horn. With a mighty upward heave, he lifted the anvil at least two feet off the ground and sat it back down. "How about a couple of you fellas setting that anvil back on the keg for me," he said.

Chapter 3

THE OX SHOE INCIDENT

By the 1950s, the days of using oxen as working draft animals were pretty much over in the U.S.A. There were a few teams of oxen around western New England, but their main function was to appear in fairs, parades, and other events, rather than doing any real work. Apparently the shoeing of oxen at the shop had been a common occurrence up until about 1930, but it dropped off drastically after that. I can remember Henry shoeing only one pair of oxen while I was growing up and that attracted a lot of attention from townspeople as well as the Greenfield and Brattleboro newspapers. He always claimed that a pair of oxen was often superior to a pair of horses because they could pull a heavier load, could subsist on just grass without need for special food such as grain, and could live outside year round without need for a barn. These were reasons that so many oxen pulled Conestoga wagons during the westward migrations of the 1800s. On the downside, they were slow, sometimes uncooperative, and could be "downright dumb."

When shoeing most horses, it was simply necessary to reach down, pull up on the fetlock, and the horse would usually obligingly lift the foot allowing the shoeing to proceed. Not so with any ox. Anyone messing with an ox's foot was asking for a kicking, biting, goring, or all three. In order to safely shoe an ox, it was necessary to firmly restrain all the moving parts of the animal.

Outside, and a little to the south of the shop stood the ox shoeing device, also called an ox sling. The ox sling resembled the framework for a narrow barn stall, but it was much more ruggedly constructed. The animal would be led into the device and tied very closely at the front by its nose ring. A pair of wide leather belts were passed under its belly and attached to rollers high on each side of the frame. The rollers were about six or seven feet off the ground and when turned with a long lever they would act as a winch and lift the ox totally off its feet. Each of the animal's legs was then secured to one of the corner posts and all the ox could then do was bellow and complain. If it swished its tail too much, that got tied off too. The shoeing could then proceed in perfect safety, until the ox was released that is!

Shoeing an ox took considerably longer than shoeing a horse. In addition to the time required to restrain and release the animal, it was necessary to shoe each foot twice. Unlike a horse which had a one piece hoof and was shod with a single U-shaped shoe, an ox had a split hoof requiring each half to be shod with a separate shoe. And, of course there were two types of ox shoes for each foot, inside shoes and outside shoes. On top of that, it was necessary to be much more careful in trimming and nailing to the hooves of an ox compared to the more robust hooves of a horse.

Henry had several interesting stories from his younger years of shoeing oxen, and he loved to tell them to visitors at the shop. One of the best concerned an ox that was especially uncooperative. Luckily for Henry, it occurred when he was quite young and could run pretty fast! The gist of the story (possibly enhanced with the retelling over the years) was more or less as follows: The ox had protested its shoeing the whole time, but thanks to the ox sling it had proceeded without incident. When the shoeing was over, the animal's legs were untied and it was lowered back onto its feet. The unsuspecting owner untied the nose ring rope, expecting to have to encourage the ox to back slowly out of its confinement. Instead, the animal lunged backward yanking the lead rope out of the owner's hands. Then the loose ox took a couple of quick turns around the open space in front of the lumber shed looking for something, or someone, to heap vengeance upon. Soon, it spotted Henry standing nearby still wearing his leather shoeing apron, wiping the sweat from his forehead. The ox lowered its head, snorted, and the race was on.

One of the large sliding doors on the south side of the shop was wide open and Henry went through it on a dead run followed closely by the angry ox. Henry ran completely through the shop and out an open door on the garage end. Luckily, the ox was slowed somewhat by its new iron shoes which didn't provide much traction on the hard concrete floor. But, it knew where Henry went and charged out the door after him. Henry always said that in any given situation, there was always something that was the best thing to do under the circumstances. These circumstances seemed to call for some solid protection from the oncoming ox, and soon! Henry rounded the corner of the shop and with the ox gaining ground he jumped into the outdoor vehicle repair pit located directly behind the gas pumps. The ox, possibly surprised at Henry's sudden disappearance, cleared the corner of the open pit and kept on going across the road and downhill through the apple orchard celebrating its new found freedom and bellowing curses in ox language. Afterward, Henry admitted that jumping into the pit probably wasn't the best idea he ever had. "What if that ox had jumped in after me?" he said. "He would have had me trapped in there!"

One day many years later, a representative from Old Sturbridge Village showed up unannounced at the shop. Henry wasn't terribly busy at the time and as always he was more than willing to gab especially about old times and old tools. The purpose of the visit was to try to convince Henry to help set up the blacksmith shop exhibit at the museum. Part of the deal was to sign him up to put on a series of blacksmithing and horseshoeing demonstrations. Henry always liked to publicize his trade, so a deal was struck on the spot.

A few days later, Henry received a phone call from the representative. He told Henry that the museum was also very interested in obtaining the ox shoeing device that had been observed on his recent visit. Having not used the thing in years, and not expecting to ever again, Henry was glad to sell it and clear some space for his ever increasing scrap iron pile. A number of years later on a visit to the museum, I saw Henry's ox shoer sitting outside one of the buildings. I imagine it is still there, but I wonder how many people know what it is and how it was used.

Between the shop and the Town Hall was an old carriage shed that probably predated the shop by quite a few years. I imagine it originally went with whatever was on the site of the shop before the shop was built there. It is possible that it was one of the carriage houses that were located near the church for use by church goers in the 1800s. It was open on the south side with space to park several buggies and wagons inside, out of the elements. Henry called it his lumber shed. Inside were an old farm wagon and a very old sleigh that looked like something out of Currier & Ives. The sleigh was up high supported by the roof rafters. I never heard the story behind the sleigh, but I believe the farm wagon was once used by my Grandpa Frank Wood down at Henry's farm.

Most of the space in the lumber shed was taken up by inside storage of a good supply of hardwood lumber needed for all sorts of wagon and truck body projects. Whenever Henry came across a supply of well-seasoned ash or hickory at a good price he would add to his supply. One hardwood he rarely used was oak. About the only thing he would use oak for was the flooring boards in a truck body or wagon. Oak has a grain structure such that when it is cut, strains are often released that can cause a perfectly straight piece to bow, twist, or develop longitudinal cracks.

One bay of the lumber shed was entirely taken up by cut firewood which was the winter fuel supply for the shop, the house, and the library across the road. We would accumulate logs and branches from a variety of sources all summer and fall. These would be piled in the open space in front of the shed. Before winter set in, Henry would hire a farmer or lumberman with a large tractor powered circular saw to cut all the wood to stove length. Henry pointed out that this was the same process that had been used on his father's farm when he was a boy. The only difference was that back then, instead of a tractor, the saw was powered by a horse walking on a treadmill. For several days after the sawing, my job was to throw all the pieces of firewood into a huge pile in the lumber shed.

Attached to the east end of the lumber shed was a small, fully enclosed portion. I have no idea what its original purpose was. There was a long, narrow workbench along one side that had two of the old-fashioned blacksmith vises attached. Henry simply used it for storage. That was where he kept his supply of odd sizes and styles of horseshoes, ox shoes, mule shoes, and other seldom used items. Many of the unusual horseshoes were of the type that he referred to as drive calks. They were a type of factory-made shoe for draft horses which had a number of tapered holes built into them. When preparing to use one of these shoes, the blacksmith had to hammer tapered, hardened calks into each hole. These were supposed to provide superior traction for the horse compared to a smithy prepared shoe. Some owners would always request these shoes for the winter and Henry would provide them, but he never recommended them. For one thing, the shoes could not be adjusted to accurately fit the exact shape of a horse's foot. For another, the tapered calks would not always stay in place.

Mules were not that common, but occasionally someone would ask to have one shod. Henry would poke around in the little shed to see if he had any prepared mule shoes that might fit. If he did not, he could easily make mule shoes from a slightly larger sized horseshoe. A mule shoe resembled a horseshoe except the heel ends of the shoes continued straight back with a little outward flare at each end instead of continuing the rounded shape as for a horse.

That little shed was the scene of my first encounter with paper wasps, and the worst bee stinging that I ever received. I was maybe eight or ten years old at the time. I always had the run of the shop and town buildings, but Henry had told me to stay out of that little shed, never telling me why. Being forbidden territory made it all the more tempting to me to go inside and find out why I wasn't supposed to be in there.

32

The shed was never locked and on a very hot day when Henry was off shoeing I decided that it was time to investigate the mystery.

The latch opened easily, but it was necessary to lift up on the squeaky-hinged door rather firmly in order to push it open. The inside was quite dark due to the never-painted, aged wood and the fact that the only light was that which came in from the opened door and through the cracks between the boards. For a minute or so, I stood looking in while my eyes adjusted to the darkness.

Slowly and cautiously, I entered, expecting to see something scary, mysterious, or exotic. Looking around I saw only a lot of horseshoes, tools, and many pieces of metal, the functions of which I had no idea. I began poking around trying to locate what it was I wasn't supposed to see. I was so absorbed in doing what I wasn't supposed be doing that I was unaware of the buzzing and flying that was going on. Suddenly I was stung on my neck, face, and hands simultaneously. Looking up I noticed numerous paper wasp nests hanging from various locations. The air was thick with wasps, most of which were headed my way. I lunged for the door and flew out it as fast as my legs could carry me. I didn't stop until I was at the far side of Henry's garden where I fell down and rolled in the fresh dirt and moist grass in an attempt to relieve the stinging pain.

Later at the house, Jessie doctored my stings with a baking soda paste that really didn't seem to do much good. It was several hours before the pain was lessened. It was several more hours before I had the courage to face Henry who, lucky for me, returned home rather late that evening. He showed me no sympathy. "Now you know why I told you to stay out of there," he said.

Chapter 4

A DOLLAR'S WORTH

The north end of the shop building contained a concession to the modern era: two bays for automobiles. It was pretty much an ordinary auto repair shop/gas station. These bays were reserved strictly for automobile repairs and operated as the Leyden Garage. While still a teenager, Henry foresaw the inevitable replacement of the horse by the internal combustion engine. As Model T's and A's became increasingly common, he decided to learn how to repair them, and devised several unique maintenance techniques that eventually became standard in the industry. Even in the 1950s, these early Fords were still sometimes seen on the roads in Leyden, although they were 20 to 30 years old. Others had been converted into substitutes for factory-made farm tractors and could be observed pulling formerly horse drawn implements through the fields. Their high clearance and low power made them more effective than many newer vehicles during winter snows and the spring Mud Season. It wasn't until sometime in the early '60s that the mailman who crossed East Hill every day from the Bernardston Post Office abandoned his trusty Model A for a pickup truck.

A pair of gas pumps stood out front of the garage along with one for kerosene. Kerosene was sold in the winter for use in portable space heaters. Between the pumps and the shop was the outdoor pit which allowed a mechanic to work underneath

Leyden's "Main Street," showing the garage part of Henry's shop.

cars while standing up. The Leyden Garage operated as a Gulf gas station from 1935 to about 1960. After that it was a Phillips station and finally Amoco. For many years it was the only place in town where gasoline and oil could be obtained. It was always Henry's policy to give a 2-cent per gallon discount to Leyden citizens. When I was about 10 years old, it became my job during the summer and other school breaks to "tend the pumps." I usually didn't have proper change in my pocket to give customers their discount, so I came up with the idea of simply pumping them a little extra gas instead. If a local resident wanted, say, $2.00 worth of gas, which amounted to about 10 gallons, I would pump them $2.20 worth for their $2.00.

Henry approved of my scheme, but instructed me that this was to apply only to town residents. Strangers were to receive only the amount of gas they paid for and no discount. One day, a man I didn't know stopped and asked for $3 worth of regular. The most common request in those days was "Gimme a dollar's worth," so I was impressed. I ran the pump up to three dollars and stopped. That evening at supper (the noon meal was called dinner in those days) I was telling about the huge sale I had made. As I was describing the man and his car, Henry interrupted, telling me that it sounded like a man that had recently moved into a house in West Leyden. When we had finished eating, he loaded me into his truck and we drove to the man's house where Henry apologized and gave the customer his 30-cent discount. That man became one of our best gas customers for many years afterward.

In the 50's the Commonwealth of Massachusetts required all cars to have a safety inspection twice a year, in April and September. The Leyden Garage was official state inspection station 1121, and those months were kept busy with residents stopping by to "get a sticker" at the cost of 50-cents. I wasn't an official inspector, but Henry was away shoeing frequently, and I became quite skilled at forging his signature on the state-required stickers. The inspections were quite thorough including brakes, wipers, lights, etc. Each car was required to be tested for headlight alignment which often required adjustment, something unheard of these days. Turn signals had to be working, if a car was so equipped, but they were not required. The state's policy was that hand signals were the preferred method of indicating a turn. The only hand signal seen these days is when one driver cuts off another!

Repairing cars was never Henry's favorite pastime. For a few years he leased the automobile portion of the shop to Doug Barton. Barton sold gas and repaired cars there for several years before opening his own garage on Brattleboro Road down in the valley at the base of East Hill. Henry was glad to get his whole shop back for his own use again, and I believe he loaned Barton some money to help get him started in his new location. Gas sales dropped a little for a while because now there were two places to buy it in town.

As long as somebody was at home, the shop was kept open and the gas pumps on, even if nobody was working there. Long before the days of credit cards and self-serve pumps, Henry's pumps often operated on the honor system. Numerous Leyden residents would routinely pump their own gas and then stop by the house to pay or would leave a dollar or two on the anvil inside the shop. There was never a concern that someone might not pay for their gas or that they would pump more than they paid for. If someone needed gas and didn't have the money, they were simply asked to pay when they could. No records were kept because they were not necessary. Crime was nearly nonexistent in Leyden in those days. I suspect it isn't too prevalent there today either. I understand that the town now has an official police force. Unless things have changed a lot since the 1950s, I imagine that they don't have a whole lot to do.

Conversely, one of the very few less savory incidents that I heard about while growing up was Henry's seldom-told story of the day three tough looking guys stopped at the shop under the pretense of buying some gasoline. No matter how busy he was inside, whenever Henry heard a car pulling up to the gas pumps he stopped what he was doing and walked out front to find out what was needed. I'm sure he also saw it as an opportunity to chat with the customer, nearly all of whom were locals, about the issues of the day. On this day he was inside alone repairing something and, as usual, walked out front to the gas pumps when he heard a car drive up. The car was unfamiliar to Henry, as were its occupants. It was an older model and sported numerous areas rusted out from the road salt of many winters. Inside were three rather large, scruffy looking men. As he approached, the driver said curtly, "Gimme a dollar's worth."

As Henry began pumping the gas, all three men got out of the car and walked up the incline and through the open door of the garage. Henry thought nothing of it, and, in fact, he liked to show strangers around his place of business. When the dollars' worth was in the tank, he returned inside and noticed that the drawer to the old cash register that always sat on a bench in the garage area (but was never used) was standing open. The three customers were in the shop area searching drawers, shelves, and bench tops.

"Lose something?" Henry asked.

"Just lookin' 'round," one replied.

"That'll be a dollar for the gas and you can be on your way."

"Where's the money?"

"The only money I know about is the dollar you owe me for the gas I just put in your car."

"There must be a cash box around this place somewhere. Let's see what's in it."

"There's no cash box here. You better give me the dollar you owe me and hit the road," Henry offered as he turned slightly and entered the forge area through the small door that connected it with the garage. Concerned about the intentions of his three visitors, Henry wanted to get his back to the forge, the big anvil to his left, and the workbench between him and the three tough looking customers. Just as he entered the doorway, the three toughs started toward him.

"Well," one said, "in that case we'll just see what's in your wallet."

Now Henry was normally a very peaceful man. But if somebody cheated or threatened him, or his, they soon found out they had quite a bit more trouble on their hands than they had anticipated. He was not an especially large man, but due to a lifetime of hard work, wrestling horses, hammering iron, and carrying his heavy shoeing equipment around daily, he possessed tremendous upper body strength. When he was a retired old man he could still easily beat me in arm wrestling.

In his younger years, Henry had been a pretty good baseball pitcher for the Leyden men's team. The stories were that his fastball was unhittable. It had to be, it was the only pitch he could throw! As he reached the workbench, his right hand grabbed a large horseshoe and in one smooth sidearm motion, he threw it as hard as he could at the nearest tough who was just reaching out to grab him. The horseshoe struck below the belt and doubled the first tough over in pain. Seeing what had happened, the second tough dropped back, but the third kept coming.

Meanwhile, Henry's left hand had gripped the handle of a shoeing hammer and passed it to his now empty right hand. A shoeing hammer resembled a carpenter's hammer, but the head was a little smaller and the claws on the rear were shorter, stuck our straighter, and had less of a curve. Henry raised the hammer shoulder high with the claw end facing forward.

Lunging toward Henry, the third tough reached a hand out for a long piece of iron bar that was lying on top of the big anvil. That was a mistake. Down came the shoeing hammer, claws first, directly on top of the back of that hand. The claws completely penetrated the hand, striking the anvil beneath with so much force that one of the claws broke off of the hammer head and remained imbedded in the hand.

With all the fight out of them, all three toughs ran out the open garage door toward their car followed by the broken shoeing hammer flying through the air behind them.

Henry rarely talked of the event and very few people ever knew that it had occurred. He didn't think it was that big a deal, and besides, he felt it didn't portray the proper image for his business or the town. Sometime later a resident who had somehow become aware of the incident asked Henry if in hindsight he wished he had done anything differently when confronted by those three "gentlemen." His reply was, "Yes. I wish I had grabbed something else. That was my favorite shoeing hammer."

Chapter 5

THE WATER WITCH

His hair is crisp, and black, and long,
His face is like the tan;
His brow is wet with honest sweat,
He earns whate'er he can,
And looks the whole world in the face,
For he owes not any man.
                                    Longfellow

"Henry, I need to have a new well drilled for the barn and I need you to tell me where they should drill." That was not an uncommon request from farmers and townspeople in and around Leyden in the 1950s, and 1960s. Most of the easy water had been found years before, so now when a new well was required it was most often drilled through solid rock by a professional well drilling company. Sometimes a reliable water source was struck within 30 to 50 feet. Other times it was necessary to drill down several hundred feet. Whenever a hole was drilled, there was no guarantee that water would be found no matter how deep the hole. Whether the result was a good well, or a dry hole, either way the drilling company would be paid. It was important to increase the chances that something resembling a water supply would be the result.

Sometime in the early 1950s, Henry added the skill of dowsing for water to his extensive repertoire. These days dowsing is often associated with the occult and/or people thought to be at least one brick short of a load. However, 50 years ago or more in the New England hills it was taken quite seriously, because it often worked.

Dowsing to locate underground water, or minerals, had been practiced in New England since at least the 17th century and at least 200 years before that in parts of Europe. The art of locating water with a forked stick, or divining rod, is also known as water witching. The scientific community scoffs at claims that dowsing for water actually works, yet very few scientific studies of a realistic nature have been conducted. Most of the studies have been very flawed in significant ways. I've read of one "test" in which a container of water was buried and dowsers were challenged to find it. In another, a water hose was run along the first floor of a building and dowsers on the second floor were challenged to identify where it was. Neither test remotely resembled the real world of water flowing downhill through cracks in solid New England rock. Sometimes the scientific community simply goes along with whatever thinking is politically correct or popular in government/media circles, so as not to jeopardize any potential grants that might come their way.

Dowsing for water wasn't something Henry set out to learn to do. He simply stumbled into it one day while shoeing horses and discovered that he had the skill. For several years he had been shoeing horses for someone I will call Bruce Hammond, somewhere in New Hampshire. Mr. Hammond had a dowsing-for-profit sideline and had earned quite a reputation for his talents. One hot, dry, summer day as Henry was finishing up the last shoe on one of Hammond's mares, he and Henry began talking about the ongoing drought. Bruce told Henry how he had recently dowsed a well for someone that came in at nearly 10 gallons per minute, a very large flow for a New England drilled well. Being a very inquisitive, but skeptical sort, Henry asked for details as to how it was done. In response, Mr. Hammond took Henry over to an apple tree and showed him how to select a small branch for making a dowsing rod. It had to be from a fruit tree and larger in diameter than a pencil, but thinner

41

than a finger, so that it was easily bent without breaking. "New grown twigs full of sap work the best," Hammond said.

Cutting a Y-shaped branch from the tree, he explained that the shape was very important. He trimmed the two equal arms of the Y to about 2-feet in length and the stem to about 1-foot. Other than sharpening the ends, he left all the bark on.

With the newly-made dowsing rod in hand, Hammond took Henry behind his house to demonstrate how it worked. He pointed out where he had located an underground stream flowing from up on the hill past his house and into a low area. Then he proceeded to demonstrate the process he had used to find it.

Bruce stood with both feet together holding one branch of the Y-shaped stick in each hand with the stem of the Y facing upward. He explained that it was essential that his hands hold the stick with the fingers curled upward, the stick exiting his hands beside his little fingers. He twisted his forearms while moving his fists slightly toward each other. This created a bend in each branch of the Y until the upward facing stem began to quiver from the tension. Then he began to slowly walk. As he approached the location of the underground stream he had pointed out, the stick started to quiver more and soon it started tipping forward. Continuing, the stick ended up once again nearly vertical, but this time instead of pointing toward the sky, the stem of the Y pointed toward the ground.

After demonstrating a few more times and defining the direction of the stream, Hammond asked Henry if he would like to give it a try. Henry was very skeptical. He wasn't at all sure that Hammond hadn't himself somehow made the stick twist downward. He was not ready to believe that there was some mysterious force due to an underground running stream that had pulled on the stick.

"Before I try it," Henry said, "I want to see if the stick finds the same spot if you do it blindfolded. If it does, then I'll give it a try."

A rag was procured and Henry tied it in place over Hammond's eyes. He then led the man around in a few circles so he didn't know exactly where he was. "Okay, now show me where that stream of yours is located," Henry said.

After a few minutes of aimless wandering around, suddenly the stick dipped toward the ground. It was a little farther up the hill, but it was directly in line with the other spots that defined the direction of the supposed stream. Henry was impressed. He had to keep his promise and give it a try although he still felt a little foolish. Hammond helped Henry select and cut a new stick. When ready, Henry did everything exactly as Hammond instructed and walked exactly where Hammond had walked, but, alas, the stem of the stick simply continued to point toward the sky.

After several more tries with no luck Henry was convinced that somehow Hammond had tricked him. He was ready to go pack up his tools and stop wasting time. Hammond encouraged him to try once more, but this time he told Henry that he was going to walk very closely behind him and reach forward, holding each of Henry's wrists tightly. Feeling rather foolish for even trying in the first place, Henry finally agreed to just one more try. At least nobody was watching.

This time as they approached where Hammond said the hidden stream was located, Henry felt the stick begin to move just a little. Hammond told him to hold the stick very tightly as they walked slowly forward. When they reached the "magic" location, the stick twisted downward with such force that even Henry's strong grip could not stop it. Needless to say, Henry was very impressed. He then tried it several more times on his own and to his surprise now it worked every time with no help from Hammond.

That night over supper, Henry related to us in detail his experience with "the stick." Being of a scientific bent even at a young age, I was far from convinced that a branch from an apple tree could locate flowing water underground. "Why not?" Henry asked. "A tree's roots grow underground toward where there is water, don't they? How do they know which way to go?" I never knew Henry to exaggerate or lie about anything, so I decided that somehow Hammond's enthusiasm had simply boiled over onto my father without anything real actually occurring.

Several days later, I was helping Henry put something together in the shop when the conversation again turned to water witching. I was debunking it with my best, but very limited, scientific knowledge. Soon, without speaking, Henry took a shoeing knife and walked across the road to an apple tree where he cut and trimmed a Y-shaped branch. Using the branch he proceeded to demonstrate dowsing for an underground stream he said he had located near the shop the day before. When nobody was looking, he had cut a stick and decided to see if he still had the talent. He had soon located a stream and had marked the location using several old boards. This day, as he walked up to the boards, the stick sure enough pointed downward. I was still far from convinced and accused him of making the stick go down wherever he wanted it to just as Henry had initially accused Hammond.

Never a man of words when actions spoke louder, he handed me the stick and told me exactly what to do. To humor him I held the stick the way he said, and walked where he told me to, but the stick simply pointed skyward with hardly a quiver everywhere I went. Looking at my shoes, a pair of rubber soled sneakers, Henry remembered that Mr. Hammond had said it was necessary to be barefoot or wear leather soled shoes. He went into the shop and returned with an old pair of his high topped, all leather work shoes of the type he always wore. I put them on and repeated my former moves with the same lack of positive results. Then, just as Mr. Hammond had done with him, Henry came up behind me, firmly grabbed my wrists and said "Try it again." This time as I approached the area marked by the boards I could feel the branch start to quiver. "It's moving a little!" I said

"Grip it as tight as you possibly can with both hands," Henry told me, "and don't be in a big hurry."

As we crossed the stream location the stick bent forward from vertical stopping when it pointed down at about a 45 degree angle. I could not grip tight enough to stop it. I gripped so tightly that the bark twisted off in my hands. I had to admit that there was something to it. However, unlike Henry's experience following Mr. Hammond's help, I was never able to make the stick move unless Henry held my wrists tightly. Whatever the mysterious talent was, it seemed that Henry had it, but I did not.

For at least the next ten years, Henry had the dowser's skill and it seemed to improve a bit with use, or possibly with his age. He could trace the course of underground streams by walking in a zigzag pattern. Substantial streams could be differentiated from minor ones by how strongly the stick pulled downward. A minor stream would cause the stick to bend downward from vertical only a few degrees. A strong flowing one would cause it to point nearly straight down. Sometimes he could even estimate how deep the water was below the surface of the ground by the number of times that the stick would go down and then back up as he rocked forward and back at a fixed location.

Word began to spread of Henry's skill after several very successful wells were drilled at locations he had suggested. He didn't come up with a winner every single time, but his successes far outweighed his failures. I don't think he ever took any payment for this service. Among the successful well sites he located was the place where the well was drilled for the Town Hall when the town finally decided that hauling in water for church suppers and other events was a tad old-fashioned, not to mention hard work.

One of his most impressive dowsings was the location of a new water supply for our home. Water at Henry and Jessie's house was often an iffy thing during the dry days of summer. The original water supply was a natural spring close to the road and about 75 feet west of the boundary between their property and the Zimmerman farm. It was adjacent to where the original blacksmith shop had burned, and probably was the water supply for the old shop as well, and maybe the cheese factory. Lifting the spring's cover often revealed a frog living inside. Henry saw the frog as a good sign that the water was safe to drink. Although it was a good water supply most of the year, the spring often went dry, or nearly so, in

August or early September almost every summer. In addition, as the nearby road was improved and built up, road runoff would sometimes find its way into the spring making the water unusable. Something had to be done about a new source of water. Although Henry had dowsed several promising sites on his property, none seemed to be especially strong. And, drilling a deep well through solid rock was costly, requiring money he just did not have at the time.

During discussions at the shop about the summer drought, several long-time residents of the town recalled that they had heard stories about a hand-dug Town Well located somewhere in the Center where long ago residents would come for water in the summers when their own supply failed. They claimed that the well wasn't terribly deep, yet it had the reputation of never going dry in the hottest of summers. For some unknown reason, the location of the well had been lost many years ago.

Most of the stories claimed that the Town Well was located somewhere in the vicinity of Henry's blacksmith shop, but nobody knew just where or even on which side of the road. One Sunday, Henry decided he would use "the stick" to try and locate that well and asked me if I would like to go along and give him a hand. Knowing that dowsing worked only for water that is flowing through rock underground, not still water resting in a hole or well, he knew the stick would not find the well directly. However, if it was as reliable a well as the legends claimed, he reasoned that it must be located on a substantial underground stream or possibly at the junction of two or more streams. If he could locate and follow enough streams, he reasoned that one of them might lead him to evidence of the lost well.

Henry and I criss-crossed much of Leyden Center that Sunday wearing out several apple sticks in the process. My job was to place a small stake in the ground wherever he found a good response from the stick. After we had a lot of stakes in the ground, it became a life-sized game of connect-the-dots to plot the courses of the underground streams. He located several streams all flowing generally from the direction of the top of the hill downward toward his shop and beyond. One stream started west of the Town Shed, crossed the west end of his garden, and passed near the south side of the shop. It then crossed the road and passed near the north side of the small Robertson Library before continuing on downhill toward Zimmerman's barn. A second stream began near the Town Hall and appeared to cross the first stream near the library. A third, but much weaker stream, passed to the north of the shop and then also angled toward the library before coming very close to where the first two intersected.

All three streams passed under the short slope that began at the south end of Henry's apple orchard near the library. We examined the area closely, but found no surface evidence of a well, just a smooth slope. Nevertheless, Henry thought there was a good chance that the well might have been located at, or near, where the three streams essentially crossed. If it wasn't the location of the old well, it sure looked like it might be a good place for a new one. Best of all, it was on his own property. Encouraged, Henry walked over to the shop and returned with a long heavy pry bar. He sunk the bar into the ground in a more or less grid pattern and soon struck something solid. "That could be the capstone over the well," he said.

Several days later Henry, his brother Bill, and a couple of very curious helpers started digging with picks and shovels near where Henry said the streams crossed, and he had struck the solid object. They didn't really know what they were looking for, but were hoping to find some evidence that would suggest there used to be a well at that spot.

After removing a foot or so of soil, they struck a flat piece of slate about three or four feet across and two to three inches thick. They anxiously dug around the slab, and with the use of several large pry bars lifted it to discover a hand-dug well complete with rock lining. They tossed in a stone and a very satisfying splash was heard from below. They speculated that for some unknown reason, the well had been capped over and covered in 1913 when the library was built. The short slope that had hidden the well all those years was probably created from dirt that had been removed when the library's basement had been dug. Somebody came up with a pail and rope and soon everyone was tasting the well water and pronouncing it very drinkable. About a week later we ran a plastic pipe from the well to the pump in our cellar and our water problems were over.

Am I convinced that dowsing is for real? I sure am. I have had it proven to me. I heard numerous people tell Henry how they had located a good water supply exactly where he had told them to drill. I have felt the bark of a dowsing rod twist off in my hands. I helped locate that lost well. However, I was never able to do it by myself, only if Henry held my wrists. I have read numerous accounts of tests that "proved" that dowsing does not work. Sorry. I know that it does, but I don't know how, and neither does anyone else.

I accept the fact that "water witching" does not work everywhere. For example, some of the land in the West, and much of the Midwest, lies above huge aquifers of geologic water. These are gigantic underground deposits of gravel and sand that are saturated with water. In those areas, you can drill a well almost anywhere and strike water, sometimes within ten feet or less of the surface.

In New England the underlying geology is totally different. There is a relatively shallow layer of soil covering solid granite and other types of igneous rock. Quarrying and road cuts provide ample evidence that this underlying rock contains numerous fractures that run in any and all directions. It is not difficult to envision surface water penetrating down to the underlying rock and finding its way to these cracks and fissures. From there the water would flow downhill by the path of least resistance creating the underground streams that some "experts" claim to not exist.

Unfortunately, much of the debunking of dowsing has been brought on by some of the dowsers themselves. Not satisfied with just locating water, some convinced themselves that they, and/or "the stick," had some kind of magical powers that could answer all sorts of questions. In fact, in his later years, Henry's mentor, Mr. Hammond, started giving advice for marriage, investments, predicting weather, etc. all by "asking the stick" for answers. He charged a healthy fee and some gullible people paid it. Henry stuck only to finding water, never bragged about it, and accepted only a "Thank You" as payment. It always pleased him no end to have someone stop by the shop and tell him how they had a well drilled where he said and that it struck water at about the depth he predicted.

In his later years, Henry's dowsing powers gradually weakened to the point where eventually he no longer had the touch. He attributed it to the severe arthritis that developed in his hands, possibly a result of all those decades of hammering iron and horseshoe nails. "You have to be able to grip the stick really tight in order for it to work," he would say. "My hands hurt so these days I can't squeeze something that small anymore." But, he still liked to tell stories about the many successes he had had helping people find water.

Chapter 6

A LEAD PIPE PINCH

In the 1950s, we were totally unaware of all the dangerous materials that surrounded us and have been identified in the last 50 - 60 years. Yet, somehow most of us not only survived the 1950s, but many of us are still around many decades later to tell about it. For that matter, how did all of our preceding generations make it to their childbearing years so that we could be born? Maybe it's true that "what you don't know won't hurt you."

Based on today's standards, we lived very dangerously in 1950. Not one automobile had seat belts, air bags, anti-lock brakes, third brake light, automatic headlights, a crumple zone, video backup camera, tire pressure alarms, or any of the many more safety gadgets deemed important today. Even turn signals and a heater/defroster were options and not standard equipment. Child car seats, if used at all, were mainly to contain a child in an area of the car so as to not bother the driver. Of course nobody wore a bike helmet because they hadn't been invented. If they had, we probably wouldn't have worn them anyway. We drank whole milk, ate red meat, and consumed processed foods (although we speculated about what hot dogs were really made of.) Our new-fangled electric refrigerators had compressors charged with a very poisonous gas, and the interior wire shelves were plated with cadmium, a metal that is quite toxic at very low levels. We played with the little balls of mercury from a broken thermometer and rubbed a little of it onto a copper penny to make it shine like a mirror. The heating pipes in our homes were often insulated with pure asbestos which also lined our car's brake shoes, was in the siding on some houses, and was the primary component of nearly anything that was fireproof or fire resistant. Whenever we opened a new bottle or jar of food, medicine, or cleaning chemical, we simply unscrewed the lid without having to fight our way past one or two safety seals. The cellphone hadn't been invented so we couldn't be in constant contact with others no matter where we were when something went just a little bit wrong. On the other hand, we didn't have to worry about whether or not the little devices cause brain cancer. In the small towns and rural areas such as Leyden, the water we drank in our homes and schools came straight from wells and springs without benefit of filtration, chlorination, fluoridation or any other 'tion.

Near the top of the list of materials to be avoided in today's world is lead, the same metal that for centuries was an essential component of the progress of civilization. Today we know that there are some very legitimate health concerns associated with exposure to lead. For example, studies have shown that exposure to lead can cause learning disabilities in some children. Certainly some risks have been avoided by transitioning our thinking about lead from an essential component into a deadly poison, but as I suspect is true with some other modern day hazards, history suggests that the danger might be just a bit over blown.

Today every trace of lead is being systematically removed from our lives. Lead shot can no longer be used in shotgun shells to hunt the migratory fowl that fed generations of our ancestors. Lead has been removed from gasoline where it helped to usher in the automotive age by cushioning the valves in Henry Ford's Model T and later by keeping higher compression engines from knocking and destroying themselves. Lead-based solder was used to repair leaking utensils and to connect copper water lines in millions of homes, but it is no longer allowed. Once a boy was old enough to be trusted to safely melt solder, a common pastime was to increase the size of one's army by casting more and more soldiers from 50/50 lead/tin solder. Our parents' concerns were about the molten metal and flames, not the lead we were exposed to.

Lead was removed from paint in 1978 by government edict. Lead oxide had been the primary pigment used to make paint for centuries. Today if we sell a house built before that date, we have to sign a document disclosing if there is any lead paint in the house. We are warned to never sand or scrape old paint because we might create dust containing a little lead. If a speck of lead paint is detected on a child's toy made in China, it is all over the TV and internet news. I'm sure that every toy I had while growing up was totally covered with lead paint, as were all the walls in the house, my crib as a baby, and much of the furniture throughout the house. The latest target for lead removal from the environment is wheel weights. When you buy tires, the tire shop balances them by attaching small weights to the metal wheels to minimize vibration. For about 100 years those weights have been made mainly of lead. Now several states have banned the use of lead in wheel weights and more states are on track to do so. Apparently there have been just too many cases of lead poisoning due to people chewing on wheel weights. As kids in the 1950s, we were all exposed to those and other sources of lead as were our parents and generations before them. Yet, here we are.

I would wager that many readers do not know that back in the days before the invention of plastic pipe for underground water piping, one of the most common piping materials to bring water from the well, spring, or brook to the house or barn was lead, 100% pure lead. In order to move water from its source to where it was needed, some sort of pipe was needed. Iron pipe was straight and rigid requiring fittings every time there was a change of direction. And, over time it rusted resulting in leaks or blockage of the flow. Copper was superior to iron, but was generally too expensive for use in long runs. In the 1950s, lead water piping was still very much in use. Lead had several advantages as a water pipe material: It was relatively inexpensive, it was quite flexible lending itself to easy bends and turns, it did not rust, and it was easy to join pieces of it together and to repair.

The biggest disadvantage of lead pipe was that it was not at all resilient. It was so soft that if pressed hard, or bent too sharply, it easily kinked or flattened and didn't bounce back. Once damaged, it could reduce the water flow or even shut it off all together. Hilly Leyden's soil isn't very thick so the lead pipe was often laid in a rather shallow ditch close to bedrock. If a large rock was placed above the pipe, over time the lead pipe could be reduced in cross section due to the weight of the boulder. Or, if the pipe was laid through a wet or swampy area, cattle or horse's feet might sink deep enough to pinch it off. Once a lead pipe was pinched shut it stayed shut.

When the water flow through lead pipe dropped way off or stopped, it was necessary to find the bad section, cut it out, and replace it with a new piece. A lot of the water lines didn't use a pump in those days and depended on gravity to carry the water from its source to the house or barn where it was needed. Often a siphon was set up to carry the water up over a ridge or hill before dropping down to the point of use. A siphon is a very simple system requiring no pump or other mechanical device to make water flow, just gravity. All that is required for a successful siphon is for the point of discharge to be at a lower elevation than that of the water where it enters the submerged pipe. It doesn't matter that in between, the pipe may have to rise over a hill considerably higher than the pipe's inlet and outlet. That's right, with a siphon you can make water flow uphill without a pump! The greater the difference in elevation between the inlet and outlet, the greater the flow rate of water. However, if a crack or hole developed in a siphon pipe allowing air to leak in, the pipe would quickly fill with air and the water flow would stop. Once the pipe was repaired and airtight once again, it was necessary to flush out all the air and fill the pipe with water before the flow would resume.

The trick to starting a siphon flowing was to push out all the air and get the pipe completely filled with water. Filling the siphon pipe required the use of a force pump. It was a hand operated device greatly resembling an old bicycle tire pump. The bottom of the force pump was set into a large pail of water and the pump's hose attached to the discharge end of the water line. The pump's handle was then worked up and down pushing water backward up the pipeline all the way to the water source flushing air out ahead of it. That could be a lot of work because the pipe was often long and always went uphill. Once the line was completely filled, and if there were no more air leaks, when the hose from the force pump was removed, water would immediately start flowing again and keep flowing. If air could still leak in, all the water that was forced into the pipe would run out and flow would stop. After locating and eliminating the other air leak, the hard work of filling the line needed to start all over again.

If getting the water flow started was a lot of work in the summer, it could often be many times more difficult in the winter. Sometimes when there was a cold winter with little snow to insulate the ground, the water in shallow buried pipes would freeze forming an ice plug and water flow would stop. Flowing water can tolerate a lower temperature than standing water, so knowledgeable owners, and especially those who had experienced frozen pipes before, would often keep the water flowing a little on cold nights to help prevent freezing. Once the pipe was frozen in one location, it would often freeze in other spots also, because the water was no longer moving.

It was not unusual for Henry to get calls during the winter to come to some house or barn and help thaw out frozen water pipes. If the frozen pipe was lead (or some other metal) it could usually be thawed using an electric current. If the pipe was plastic, the only recourse might be to wait for spring. I seem to recall that for a while you could buy plastic water pipe that had a couple of metal wires molded into it during manufacture. Those wires were for use in thawing if you followed the manufacturer's directions exactly. Of course, not everyone bothered with directions and some learned the hard way that connecting those wires directly to 115 volt AC was a quick way to melt a hole in your water pipe, give yourself a first class zinger, or burn your barn down if you were having an especially bad day.

The trick to thawing water lines was to carefully control the flow of electricity. You needed high current, but low voltage. This was most easily done by using an electric welder as the power source. Henry had a big green Lincoln arc welder that was nearly the size of a small refrigerator. When he received a thawing out call, he would wrestle that beast into the back of his pickup truck along with a spool of about a thousand feet or more of single strand insulated copper wire. To prepare to thaw the pipe, Henry would take one end of the long wire and unroll it from the spool as he walked with the property owner along the route of the water line. It was necessary to locate the pipe beyond the point at which it was suspected to be frozen. He would try to find the pipe as close to the water source as possible if his wire was long enough. After exposing a short section of the pipe, Henry would solidly clamp the wire to the metal pipe making sure there was good electrical contact.

Back at the house or barn, the other end of the wire would be attached to one lead of the welder. The second lead from the welder was then connected to the pipe at the barn or house. The only remaining connection was to feed the welder with a reliable supply of 240 volt AC electricity. Hmm, water and 240 volts. If you are thinking this sounds a bit risky, like using an electric hair dryer while you take a bath you are not too far off the mark!

The underlying theory was that running a large enough electric current through the pipe would warm the metal creating sufficient heat to melt the frozen area. After turning the welder on, the current was slowly increased. Hopefully, after a few minutes, water would start to flow. Finding the correct current setting was the tricky part. If the amperage was set correctly, the current flow would warm the lead pipe, thaw the ice, and water flow would be restored. If the current was too low, insufficient heat would be generated to do the melting. If it was too high for too long, one or more sections of the pipe might melt. Henry admitted to melting a few pipes the first few times he tried it. After a while he got "the feel of it."

Many houses and farms did not have an outlet for the necessary 240 volts to feed his welder, but this usually did not stop Henry. He had learned that in most electric installations, there was 240 volts available at the meter or fuse box even if there was no proper outlet installed for it. He would simply remove the plug from his welder cord and attach its wires directly to the electrical bus often using clamp-on pliers. Sometimes it got interesting when he needed to be creative about hooking up the welder to the 240 volt supply when there was no way to disconnect the power. In such cases the connection had to be hooked up live. He had learned the electrician's safety trick of working with one hand in his pocket so that if he touched a live part the current would not pass totally through his upper body from one hand to the other, passing through his heart on the way. Nevertheless, he did get a few zingers.

I remember one time when I went with Henry on one of these thawing out calls. It was in the barn of a very old farm that had been retrofitted with electricity fairly recently by someone who obviously didn't know too much about what he was doing. There was no 240 volt outlet and no obvious way of turning off the juice to make a temporary hookup. Undaunted, Henry proceeded in preparing to make a live connection. Suddenly there was a loud bang and a shower of sparks flew around Henry from all sides. From where I stood, it looked like he was holding a huge 4th of July sparkler. There was also the smell of burned metal like when a piece of iron in Henry's forge had been heated too hot.

"Dad, are you okay?" I shouted not daring to get closer. Henry stood still for a moment and then turned around with dark smudges on his hand and face.

"I think I'm okay," he said, "But I need you to go out to the truck and get me another screwdriver." That's when I noticed Henry was still holding the plastic handle of what had been a large screwdriver. The metal blade and shank were totally gone.

Another time I went along with Henry when he had been called upon to thaw the water line that supplied water from a spring to another of the oldest farmhouses in town. He had made all the electrical connections and had a good 240 volt power source. But, no matter how he tried, he could not get any electrical current to flow. He checked and rechecked all his connections to no avail. Finally Henry and the farmer decided that there must be a break in the lead pipe somewhere disrupting the electrical continuity.

Armed with picks and shovels, the three of us proceeded to dig down to the water line about half way from the house to the spring. Henry relocated his copper wire to that point, but again he could not get any electricity to flow. So we dug another hole halfway between that one and the house with the same result. Finally, as we were digging our fourth hole along where the water line was believed to be, we struck what appeared to be a large dark tree root.

"Maybe the real problem is that this tree root has grown so big that it pinched off the pipe underneath it," Henry said.

Further inspection of the "root" however didn't support his theory. The wood obviously wasn't alive. It was very dead and in places showed signs of rot. In addition, it looked as if the wood might have, at one time or another, been treated with tar or creosote to preserve it. It appeared to be a log about six or seven inches in diameter. The ground wasn't terribly frozen, and our hole wasn't all that deep, so we dug along the wood for a ways in each direction trying to locate the water pipe.

Suddenly Henry stopped digging and exclaimed, "Good God! This IS the water pipe. It's the old-fashioned wooden water pipe! I helped replace some of it up at my Dad's farm many years ago!"

The reason that we could not get electricity to flow was that some of the water pipe was still the original wood. That wood pipe had probably been in the ground, and in use, for going on 100 years or close to it. There was lead pipe at the spring and at the house, but in between was some of the old wood pipe, still in use. Several weeks later when the weather was much warmer, Henry and I stopped by that farm to see if the water problem had been solved. The farmer told us that for the rest of the winter he had had to obtain water for the house and barn by filling milk cans at the spring and hauling them on a bob sled behind his tractor. Recently, however, he had used a single bottom plow to dig up the water line in the area where we had found the wood pipe. He had then replaced the wood with modern plastic pipe. Showing us a section of the wood pipe he had removed, he pointed out how about a one-inch hole had been bored along the center of a log to create a water pipe. The thing that amazed us all was that the wood had lasted many, many years underground reliably carrying water. Henry speculated that the pipe had been made from locust wood which had the reputation of lasting a very long time in the ground when used for fence posts.

It has been another five or six decades since the wood pipe episode, and I suppose by now the last of the wood pipe in Leyden has rotted away and been replaced by plastic. However, I'd bet anything that there is a lot of lead water line still in use, and I'd also bet that some of the current property owners don't know it.

Chapter 7

JESSIE

In the days before TV, and with no movie house in town, there was a group of Leyden residents that often put on plays in the church or at the Town Hall for the entertainment of all. The productions were usually held during the fall or winter when the time demands of farming were lessened somewhat. Residents looked forward to these plays with great anticipation. The acting was several notches below what would have been expected from professional thespians, but that often added to the entertainment when an actor stopped in mid-sentence and admitted "I have no idea what my next line is!" Or, if someone accidentally skipped ahead a page or two in the script, another actor might say "Hey, you're not supposed to say that yet!" In about 1925, Henry Glabach and Jessie Wood met when both had parts in a production of "Aaron Slick from Pumpkin Crick." Henry played the lead role of Aaron. Someone once commented "Aaron couldn't have been very slick, it took him four years to get her to marry him!"

Jessie was one of five children born to Frank and Bertha Wood of Hawley, Massachusetts. Frank was born in 1877 and immigrated to the US from Nova Scotia. As far as I know, there has never been any record unearthed of the reason that Frank left Canada, but apparently he signed onto a ship's crew and sailed from Halifax to Boston, never to return. Bertha was nine years Frank's junior, and was from a branch of the Parker family that may have already been in Massachusetts in the mid-1600s. I recall once hearing a family story of an ancestor of Bertha's who fought at the Battle of Bunker Hill. I never heard any statement as to whether that ancestor was behind the stone wall on top of the hill, or wearing a red coat while climbing up.

Frank was sort of a "jack-of-all-trades." After marrying Bertha and starting a family, he worked in a furniture factory in Charlemont, did some farming, and worked at various other jobs to make money to support his increasing responsibilities.

Jessie studied teaching at North Adams Normal School and was pursuing that profession in Leyden when she met Henry. She taught in the one-room school on East Hill and later in the Beaver Meadow School. The schoolmarm married the village blacksmith; sounds like a script from a western movie!

When my sister Orilla and I came along, Jessie stopped teaching, but started again when we were approaching high school in order to help pay for our college educations. For several years, she taught at the one-room school at Weatherhead Hollow in Guilford, VT. She rarely helped with anything at the shop, but she handled most of the paperwork for Henry's business. He always kept detailed ledgers showing the jobs he had worked on, and horses he had shod. Jessie would convert these into invoices to be sent out as needed.

Very confident in herself, Jessie was always willing to take on any task (as long as it didn't involve horses or alcohol.) Jessie was a nervous worrier about real or imagined dangers to others in the family or to close friends, but never worried much about herself. At times she could be a little crusty and seldom shied away from expressing her opinion. She was a world-class back seat driver except that she would never sit in the back seat. "I need to sit in front so I can help the driver if I need to," she would say.

She would be quite nervous when there was a strong thunderstorm. I remember many a storm in which Jessie would pull Orilla and me close to her on the living room sofa and read to us loudly to distract us from the storm. I actually think she was more frightened of it than we were. If the lightning was

*Jessie, using her adding machine to check the figures
in the Town Report.*

quite close she would have us all lie down flat on the floor in
the center of a room. She said that we needed to keep our
heads as low as possible and we were forbidden to touch any
animal, water, or be near a window.

Her fear of thunderstorms began one night when Jessie
was in her late teens or very early 20s. She was driving home
through a violent thunderstorm in a Model T Ford or similar
vehicle. Lightning was flashing all around her and rain was
pelting down hard, making it very difficult to see. The Model
T wasn't all that watertight, but it was far better than being
outside.

After a short time she approached a metal bridge. It was
the type that looked like it was built using a giant Erector set.

It had iron on the sides that provided much of the structural support as well as protecting cars from going over the edge into the water below. The top of each side of the bridge was a continuous horizontal iron beam that went from one end of the bridge to the other. Just as she began to drive onto the bridge, there was a terrific thunder clap and the Model T's engine abruptly stopped.

Sitting there, trying to summon enough courage to get out in the rain and lightning to crank the engine to try and restart it, she suddenly became aware of a very unusual phenomenon. Much of the darkness had faded away and suddenly she could see everything around her car in a strange flickering blue light. The entire bridge was giving off a bluish glow that seemed to vibrate up and down in intensity. Soon a ball of pure white lightning larger than a beach ball came out of nowhere and settled on the top of the horizontal beam on the right side of the bridge at the far end. It began rolling along that beam at the speed of a slow walk until it reached the end of the bridge behind her where it disappeared as suddenly as it had appeared taking the bluish glow with it.

Fearful and confused as to what she had just seen, she sat very still for a few minutes. Finally, summoning up the courage to get out in the weather, she jumped out and cranked the engine which started on the first turn. She then continued on toward home without further incident. It was several weeks before she told her family what had happened because she thought her brothers would laugh and make fun of her.

Her fear of horses stemmed from an incident that happened when she was a child in Hawley, Mass. She and her family were all riding in their horse drawn wagon heading into Charlemont for supplies. As they were crossing a narrow one-lane bridge, a large black horse came galloping toward them pulling a driverless buggy. The buggy was totally empty as it bounced along behind the galloping horse. Being half way across the narrow bridge, it was impossible for her father to get their horse and wagon out of the way and the black horse kept on coming. It knocked their horse down and dragged its buggy over the top of their wagon. Fortunately the whole family had seen the danger coming and had gotten down flat on the bed of their empty wagon. Nobody in the family was seriously hurt, but the family's only horse was killed. From that day on she no longer wanted anything to do with a horse. Rather ironic that she should marry a man whose livelihood depended on horses for nearly 70 years.

Jessie accepted Henry's shoeing of horses, but was never comfortable with it and worried about him constantly. Many days, Henry would leave home early in the morning to go off somewhere shoeing horses and would return sometime in the evening. Jessie always started openly worrying about 4:00 p.m. Supper was always planned for 6:00 p.m. and she expected him to be there well before that time. If he had not appeared by 7:00 p.m., she would start making phone calls to the customers he had been planning to shoe for that day. Most of the time she would find out that he had recently left for home, but a few times it turned out that her worries were well founded. On occasion she would ask Uncle Bill or George Howes to go looking for him. Other times she would drop us kids off with a neighbor or relative and go looking for him by herself.

I remember one time that she was totally beside herself when Henry could not be located and it was after 9:00 p.m. She called the Franklin County Hospital and discovered that he had been in their emergency room, but had been treated and released. Luckily Henry arrived home shortly thereafter. He said that he had been shoeing a horse when the horse suddenly yanked its foot away before he had clipped off all the new horseshoe nails in that hoof. One nail stabbed into Henry's right leg and ripped its way through the calf muscle. Anyone who knew Henry would not be surprised to learn that he first made sure the horse understood that its recent behavior was not to be repeated. After the horse had apologized, Henry simply got a clean towel from the owner of the horse, wrapped it tightly around the wound, secured it with electrical tape, and proceeded to finish shoeing the now very cooperative horse. Later, on his way home, he was near the hospital, so he decided he should stop in to have the leg looked at. After several stitches, a tetanus shot, and another of penicillin, he continued his journey home.

Jessie was a serious believer in superstitions and would go out of her way to avoid breaking a taboo. Although she was a very religious person, and an active member of the Leyden Methodist Church, Jessie had dozens of superstitions. She believed in most of them very strongly and did not feel that they in any way interfered with her Christian beliefs. Some were quite common. For example, she would never walk under a ladder. Jessie actually carried it a bit further in that she wouldn't even walk near one if she could help it. If a mirror was broken, it meant that the breaker would have seven years of bad luck, but the curse might be lifted if the broken pieces were buried deep in the ground after sundown on the same day that it was broken. Nobody was allowed to ever place a hat on a table because that foretold a death in the family. And, bad things always happened in threes.

I don't know if Jessie's avoidance of having her picture taken stemmed from a superstition or not. Whatever the reason, she always greatly disliked having her photo taken. Sometimes if it was a special occasion, she would permit it. However, at a party or family gathering, if somebody approached her with a camera, she would walk away or turn her face. There are numerous family photos of the back of Jessie's head.

Not all her superstitions predicted bad things. A lucky penny found on the ground was a good sign. However, if you saw a penny and did not pick it up, that was bad luck. One time she and I were crossing Main Street in Greenfield through a short gap in the traffic. Right in the center of the street, with traffic coming at us from both directions, she stopped, bent over and picked up a penny. Lucky pennies were never to be spent. Over the years, Jessie had collected a good quantity of lucky pennies and kept them in jelly jars on her dresser. Safety pins were treated similarly to pennies. If a pin was found on the ground unclasped, it was bad luck. If the point was secured, it was good luck. In either case, it was bad luck to leave it on the ground.

Crows were always considered to be a good sign. It wasn't

that the crow would cause something good to happen right away. Rather, the presence of a crow indicated that there was a good chance that things were going to go well for a while. I remember one time that we all went to visit a relative who had just had a new baby. As we visited, a crow suddenly landed in a pine tree just outside the window of the room. The crow started cawing loudly and the father of the new baby started toward the window to scare the bird away. Jessie took his arm and stopped him saying, "That bird is a wonderful sign for the child's future. Let it be."

Although crows were considered to be good luck, Jessie believed that owls were the opposite. It was considered very bad luck to gaze directly into the unblinking eyes of an owl. If a person was ill and an owl could be heard hooting, it was a sign that the person was going to get worse or even die.

She always insisted on exiting a building by the same door that she entered. I don't remember what was supposed to befall a person if they went out the wrong door, but it did lead to some amusing situations. One time we arrived at Aunt Leta's place late one afternoon and immediately went around back to visit with her in her vegetable garden. After a while we headed into the house through the basement door and up the stairs into the house. Our visit lasted several hours and when it was finally time to head for home, it had gotten dark. Orilla and I went out the front door to the car. However, Jessie went downstairs into the unlit basement, poked around in the dark and found the back door that she had entered through. All the way home, Orilla and I were admonished for not doing the same.

I remember another time when I went with her to deposit some checks at the bank in Greenfield. I always liked to go to the bank with her because they gave out candy. The bank was on a corner and we entered through the door off of Main Street. While we were doing our banking, the janitor roped off the Main Street entry and began mopping the floor just inside that door. Turning to leave, Jessie saw the doorway roped off and she came to a sudden halt as if she had hit a wall.

"I'm sorry," the janitor said, "you folks will have to go out the side door, this floor is very wet."

I knew there was no way we would be going out a different door than we had entered, so I was curious as to what her strategy might be. Grabbing my hand, she said, "The floor doesn't look too wet to me," as she ducked under the rope and out the door.

Jessie always eyed every cat with suspicion although we usually had one or two hanging around the house mostly to deal with the ever present mice. Stray dogs and cats showed up at our house frequently and were always welcomed unless it happened to be a black cat. Black cats were to be avoided at all costs. George and Dottie Howes owned a black cat, as did the Zimmermans. One day, when I was about 8 or 10 years old, Jessie and I left the house to drive to Greenfield for groceries. We got about 200 yards from our house when the Howes' black cat ran across the road in front of us. She stopped the car, turned it around, and drove back past the house and down the hill planning to take a different route to town. As we approached Zimmerman's, their black cat came out of the barn and slowly walked across the road toward their house. She stopped the car again, turned around, and went home. Groceries could wait for another day.

I suppose that Jessie picked up many of her superstitions from her mother, Bertha Wood, who was also very superstitious. However, it was perhaps odd that the two of them didn't share all the same beliefs and Aunt Leta, who lived with her mother much of her adult life, didn't seem too superstitious at all.

I remember once I was with Grandma shopping in Greenfield. We were walking along the sidewalk headed for Wilson's Department Store which was on the same side of the street as we were. Suddenly she made a sharp turn and started to cross to the other side of the street more or less ignoring the traffic. "Where are we going, Grandma?" I hollered catching up to her. "You're going the wrong way!"

"We can't go that way right now," she responded, "there is a cat on that sidewalk."

Sweeping the floor after dark was claimed to cause all sorts of bad luck. Sweeping dirt along the floor and out the door was said to be sweeping your luck out the door with the dirt. By the time my sister Orilla was about 10 years old, she had already developed into a first rate cook, especially of baked goods. One evening when Grandma Wood and Leta were at our house, Orilla decided she was going to show off a bit and bake some cupcakes. Grandma said she would give her a hand and the two of them headed off to the kitchen. Everything was going well until in the course of assembling the dry ingredients, Orilla spilled about a half cup of flour on the floor. She reached for a broom to sweep it up.

"Orilla, STOP!" hollered Grandma. "It's getting dark outside. You can't sweep that up until morning." So the cupcakes were made while the two of them tracked flour all over the kitchen floor.

Henry didn't take all of Jessie's superstitions seriously, but he did believe in a few. It was quite common in those days to nail a horseshoe over the front door of a house or barn. It was supposed to bring good luck and was said to be especially powerful if the horseshoe was one that had been found lying in the road or in a field. Henry believed that the shoe had to be nailed onto the wall with the two ends pointing upward "to hold the luck in." Nailing the shoe with the points down would allow the luck to run out.

Many of Henry's customers paid him in cash, so he frequently would have several hundred dollars of folding money in his wallet. He told me once that when he was younger, he used to not pay any attention to how the money went into his wallet. Some presidents faced one way and some the other. While going through some tough financial times, for some reason he decided to arrange his money with all the presidents facing the same way and with the denominations in order. Soon after, his financial situation improved and from then on his wallet was always very orderly.

Jessie's psychic abilities were often amazing. I am not aware that she could identify playing cards such as in any of those so-called psychic tests, but on the other hand, I don't remember her ever participating in the pitch card games that were always an after-the-meal staple at family functions. She said that she just didn't see the point in it.

The most memorable demonstrations of her psychic abilities were associated with tragedy, death, or danger. One day, Jessie was cooking in her kitchen humming along to a song on the radio as was her custom. Suddenly she dropped everything and yelled out "Oh, God help us!" Telling Orilla and me to stay in the house, she ran out the door and over to the shop. Henry's shop was over 100 yards away and across the road from the house. When he was building or repairing a truck body, the project was always on the south side of the shop facing away from the house making it virtually impossible for anyone at the house to hear what was being done to the truck. Rounding the corner she discovered Henry unconscious and trapped in the scissors-like grip between a fallen truck body and the truck's frame. Apparently he had been working on the underside of the body with it in the raised position when it suddenly fell. Somehow Jessie summoned super human strength and lifted the downed truck body off Henry and pulled him to safety.

Another day Jessie, Orilla, and I went down to the farm to visit Aunt Leta, Grandma Wood, and Grandpa Wood. It was our custom to visit them every few days especially since Grandpa had turned ill. Frank had had a bad stroke a year or so earlier and was confined to a hospital bed which had been set up for him in what originally was the parlor of the old farmhouse. His physical abilities were very impaired, but he always knew us and tried hard to participate in conversations. Everyone had accepted that he was never going to get any better. As we visited that day, he seemed to be in the same state of health that he had been in for quite some time.

After a while we went back home. We had only been home a few minutes and I was down the hill in the side yard. Suddenly, I saw Mom's car coming from the front of the house. As the car turned down the hill, she slowed and yelled out the passenger side window that she was going back down to the farm because something had happened. Orilla and I were to stay home and wait for her to return. Giving no explanation, she continued on her way. When she arrived at the farm, Grandma and

Aunt Leta were cooking as she entered the house through the kitchen door. They were surprised to see her back again having left just a few minutes before.

"Did you forget something?" Leta asked.

Without answering, Jessie said, "It's terrible. I'm so sorry."

"What's so terrible?"

"Dad! He has died!"

The three of them hurried across the dining room into the parlor and up to the bed. Just as Jessie had foreseen, Frank Wood had died.

Once I asked Jessie how it was that she knew of things that others did not. At first she denied that she had any such ability. After I pestered her for a while, she would only say that sometimes she just knew things. She said she didn't hear voices or see mental pictures she just suddenly knew something as if she had just read it in a book. When I asked her how she learned to do it, she told me that it wasn't anything she did. "It just happens," she said, "but sometimes it is stronger than others." I tried and tried to develop the talent, if I had any, but I made little progress.

It wasn't always something that had already happened that Jessie became aware of. Sometimes she envisioned something that was going to happen in the future. In about 1955 the four of us went on a short vacation to the White Mountains in New Hampshire. We did all the touristy things, including traveling the cog railway to the top of Mt. Washington, rolling the car "up" the magnetic hill, and rode the aerial tram up Cannon Mountain. Jessie was enjoying it all as much as any of us until we stopped at Polar Caves.

Polar Caves was located in central New Hampshire. They were not really caves in the sense of Mammoth Cave or Carlsbad Cavern which were formed by limestone dissolving in water. Polar Caves were formed by an ice age glacier that piled gigantic boulders on top of each other over a considerable area. The "cave" is the space between and beneath these huge chunks of granite. Tourists pay a fee for the privilege of roaming the narrow passageways and wiggling through tight spots, one of which is called the Lemon Squeezer.

Jessie was immediately reluctant to enter the caves, but decided to give it a try. Suddenly, when we were about halfway through, she would not continue. The rest of us insisted on going all the way through. Jessie turned around and returned to the car, probably to the considerable annoyance of other tourists who were correctly following the one-way route. As we drove away she simply commented that she got a funny feeling about it and had to get out of there.

A few weeks after our visit to Polar Caves, there was a small article in the Greenfield newspaper about three tourists being trapped for a while in Polar Caves when a few of the boulders suddenly moved, boulders that had probably last moved over 10,000 years earlier.

One of Jessie's numerous civic responsibilities was as Leyden's Civil Defense Coordinator. For many years following WWII, the US government and news media were quite paranoid about the possibility of the USA being attacked by the Soviet Union. I've often wondered if the danger was actually all that real or not and whether the government influenced the media or if it was the other way around. I often wonder that same thing about some issues today. It certainly gave the government an excuse to keep the citizens in line and taxes high. The newspapers and fledgling TV news shows fell all over each other with updates as to the latest perceived Soviet threat. That government/media attitude existed until the mid-1980s when the Soviet Union collapsed like a wilted lettuce leaf. Of course, other "threats" just happened to come along just in time to replace those from the former Soviet Union.

In the 1950s, larger communities had air raid siren and radio warning tests on a regular basis. School kids were taught to "duck and cover" under their desks if the sirens went off. Leyden had no siren, but we practiced the duck and cover drill in school anyway, just in case. I remember when I was in the first or second grade someone in a very official looking uniform coming to the Center School to instruct us as to what to do in case of an air attack. When I asked him what there was in

Leyden that the Russians might want to destroy, Peter Snow loudly said, "Your father's shop!" The resulting laughter cost both of us our next recess.

In some parts of the USA it was not uncommon, if not encouraged by the government, for individuals and organizations to prepare bomb shelters. While the perceived threat was the A-bomb or the H-bomb, nearly all the shelters were constructed and equipped based on effects of conventional ordinance as used in WWII. Most were stocked with non-perishable food supplies and bottled water. Some of the more elaborate ones had first aid supplies, blankets, cots, and a few had hand operated blowers to filter radioactive particles out of the incoming air. I never knew of any air raid shelter, public or private, in Leyden. Greenfield had the basements of several large downtown buildings, banks, and schools identified as shelters. Entrances from the street were marked with the once common yellow and black signs.

Part of the overall plan was for each community to have a Civil Defense plan overseen by a local coordinator even in small towns like Leyden. It is doubtful that anyone really believed the Russians might fly thousands of miles to bomb Leyden, but we were still required to participate in the program. The Office of Civil Defense supplied Leyden with a few stretchers, several boxes of first aid supplies, and about a dozen fire extinguishers. The fire extinguishers went to the Town Hall and Town Shed and maybe the church. The rest of the material ended up in the big closet off my bedroom to never be used for anything worse than when somebody stopped by for a bit of first aid help.

There was an off-shoot of Civil Defense in Leyden for several years called the Ground Observation Corps (GOC) or Operation Skywatch. The program originally existed during WWII. It consisted of civilian volunteers who visually searched the skies along American coasts to try and spot incoming enemy airplanes that never came. With the destruction of German and Japanese air power late in the war, airplane watching was disbanded in 1944. However, in the very early 1950s, the program was reinstated due to fear of an attack on the US by the Soviet Union as an outgrowth of the Korean War. Although radar installations were becoming more common, there were still a lot of gaps in that coverage and human eyes were recruited to fill the holes. In 1951 there were over 8000 observation posts and this time much of the focus was along the northern border in addition to the coasts. One of those posts was in Leyden.

The high hills and clear air made Leyden a natural location for a GOC post. The post location was just off the old County Road, about a half mile past the Center School in the area known as the Old Center. It was on the hill just west of Charlie Bolton's house, also known as the Old Stage Coach Inn, and originally known as the Carpenter Tavern. The tavern was built in 1830 soon after the first tavern on the site burned. It still exists today and is one of the oldest buildings in town. The GOC post consisted of a small wooden building, not much more than a shack, a little larger than a 2-holer outhouse. A couple of men could have built it in a day and probably did. It held a commanding view to the north, east, and south, but the view to the west was somewhat obscured by trees and the top of the hill. Inside the shack were several pairs of binoculars, two or three stacks of cards containing black silhouettes of US and Soviet aircraft, and a telephone. The job of the volunteer(s) on duty was to scan the sky for any and all aircraft. When any type of airplane was spotted, even a single engine two-seater, the observer was supposed to make an identification of the type of plane if they could, note the direction of its travel, and then make a phone call to the regional filter center to report the observation.

As Civil Defense Coordinator, Jessie was responsible for maintaining the station and recruiting volunteers to man it during daylight hours. There were always a lot of hours that were not covered and many of the ones that were covered had Jessie and me as the observers. It wasn't that Leyden residents were not patriotic. However, they were putting in untold hours working their jobs and farms and didn't have a lot of spare daylight time to be spent gazing at the sky for a threat that they were certain was never going to appear over

Leyden. They had recently suffered through the depression, and WWII, and many didn't see what business it was of the USA to be involved with Korea or the Soviet Union on the other side of the world. It just might be that Leyden residents were just a little stronger on common sense than the average government bureaucrats that setup the GOC program. As was pointed out by several volunteers, the program only operated during daylight when planes could be seen. Were Soviet planes not capable of flying at night, or on overcast, stormy days when planes all flew above the clouds? The program was officially canceled in 1959, but many stations including Leyden's were out of action long before.

Leyden was far too small to have any kind of medical facility. If someone had a medical emergency it was necessary to transport the victim to Greenfield. From many parts of town that could be a 30-45 minute trip or more. Following a heavy snowstorm, or during mud season, it might be an impossible trip. Over the years, Jessie had taken numerous Red Cross courses and became a first-aid instructor. From November 15, 1941, to February 18, 1942, she taught a first aid class to a group of 26 Leyden residents as part of the "Community Preparedness for National Emergency" program. Most residents were aware of her training and took advantage of it when there was a severe injury. In fact, there was a sign posted near the house indicating that Red Cross first aid was available there.

One time a farmer appeared at our door with a bad cut on his arm just above the wrist. The farmer had removed the sickle bar from his mowing machine and was sharpening the blade sections when his grip on the file slipped and one of the triangular blades sliced his arm open for several inches. His wife had been driving him to the hospital in Greenfield and wisely decided to stop at Jessie's on the way to ask her to try to stop the heavy bleeding. Always incredibly calm in an emergency, Jessie distracted the farmer with conversation as she inspected and cleaned the arm. With each heartbeat, blood spurted out of the wound. The man's wife was pretty much a nervous wreck, so Jessie enlisted my aid.

"Take off your belt and wrap it as tight as you can around

his upper arm," she instructed me. "Watch the bleeding and if it still spurts, wrap the belt tighter until it stops. I have to make some pressure bandages." Soon we had the bleeding slowed down, but no matter what we did it would not stop.

"Go get into my car," Jessie told the wife. "You're in no condition to drive and we need to get this man to the hospital before he bleeds to death. Your job is to hold his hand as far above his heart as you can." Off they went. When she returned home a few hours later Jessie told me that the emergency room doctor had told her that she had saved the man's life.

About a week later, the farmer and his wife knocked on our door once again.

"We just had a couple of hogs butchered and we want to share some of the meat with you," the farmer said.

"That's very nice," Jessie said, "but there's no need. I'm happy to help when I can." He wouldn't take "No" for an answer, so for quite a while we ate prime pork out of our freezer.

Another time a local logger had a tree fall in the wrong direction and a large limb hit him squarely on top of the head as it fell. His helper brought him to Jessie in a semi-conscious state. Application of ice packs and ammonia smelling salts did little to improve his condition.

"He has a bad concussion, maybe a fractured skull," Jessie told the helper. "There's nothing I can do for him. We need to get him to the hospital. I'll drive."

Jessie always insisted on driving even in the slightest of emergencies. I don't think it was that she thought she was a better driver than anyone else. Rather I think she felt she was doing something important instead of just sitting and worrying. At the emergency room, they were told that the logger would have to wait his turn because there were more serious cases ahead of him.

"How do you know he isn't badly hurt?" Jessie asked, "Just because you don't see any blood? He could be bleeding inside his skull and if he is, the pressure needs to be relieved."

Getting nowhere with the emergency room staff, Jessie began searching for someone who would help. Just then she spotted Dr. Milton Sisson, who was our new family physician. Dr. Sisson was an old style medical doctor who was more interested in helping the sick and injured than he was in their insurance cards. He had become our doctor one night when I was six years old and had a severe attack of asthma. Our regular doctor would not make a house call, but Dr. Sisson did.

Dr. Sisson took one look at the logger and immediately consulted with a surgeon who rushed the victim into the operating room. Just as Jessie expected, the logger did have a fractured skull with internal bleeding, but within a few weeks he was doing just fine. A few months later he arrived at the shop with a huge truckload of prime firewood, cut to length and split to fit our stoves.

There was, however, a limit to Jessie's sympathy and helpfulness. She wanted absolutely nothing to do with alcoholic beverages or those who consumed them to any degree. If she attended a party or other event and it turned out that alcohol was being served, she would find some excuse to leave or at least stay as far away from the goings on as possible. She wasn't a Carrie Nation going around smashing up drinking establishments with an ax, but more than one host took alcohol off the menu when it was learned that Jessie would be in attendance.

I remember one time when she was tending the gas pumps from the house and a resident who was well known to be a frequent imbiber stopped for a fill up. As she approached his car she could smell the beer on his breath. On the seat beside him were several empties and at least one full six-pack.

"The pumps are closed for you," she told him.

"Whada ya mean closed," he replied, "it looks to me like yr open. Fill 'r up"

"You're already filled up. You're not going to go have an accident and kill yourself or somebody else on my gas. No way."

The driver became rather meek in the face of Jessie's best schoolmarm sternness. Finally he agreed to stagger into the shop and use the phone to call his wife to come and get him.

Meanwhile, Jessie took possession of his car keys and held them until the wife arrived.

Another time, a young boy, about 10 years old, suddenly entered Jessie's kitchen. He was obviously very scared of something. After getting him calmed down a bit Jessie learned that his father, a frequent drinker, was drunk and smashing things around the house. The boy said that his mother was not home, so he had run away. Not knowing what to do next, he came to Jessie seeking safety. She fixed him a big bowl of strawberries with sugar and cream and told him to stay with her as long as he wanted and at least until his mother returned home.

An hour or two later, a man, presumably the father, was seen staggering across Jessie's front lawn, bottle in hand as he approached the kitchen door. Oops, major mistake. Fumbling with the screen door latch, the man yelled out "Send him out here! I know he's in there. I'm gonna give him the whippin of his life!"

"You stay right where you are in that chair. I'll deal with your father," Jessie told the boy. Removing her apron and drawing herself up to her full height, she stepped onto the porch. "Is there something I can do for you?" she asked.

"Ya can send that boy out here," the father stammered. "You got no right to keep him. I'm his father and I can do whatever I want with him."

"He came to me asking for protection from you and that's exactly what he's going to get," Jessie replied. "Now sir, you get yourself and your bottle off my property and out of my sight."

"I don't take no orders from no woman."

"As long as you're drunk you'll take orders from this woman or there'll be Hell to pay, mister." With that Jessie grabbed his bottle with one hand and gave him a shove with the other ending up with a bottle of booze in her hand and a drunk flat on the ground in front of her. After emptying the bottle's contents near the door, she handed the empty bottle back to the drunk, helped him up, grabbed him by the shoulders and turning him around, she pushed him toward the road.

"Tomorrow after you are good and sober, you'll be back here replacing the petunias in my flower bed that you just tramped through. Don't cross me or you'll find you've bitten off more than you can chew."

That evening as Henry was coming in for supper the odor of all that dumped whiskey by the kitchen door was unmistakable. "So, Jess," he said, "it smells like you have an interesting new recipe for me to try."

One of Jessie's greatest claims to fame was her reputation as a first rate cook. She didn't prepare fancy French or Italian dishes with lots of sauces and such. Rather she stuck mainly to old-time New England menus with a few German dishes thrown into the mix. I don't recall seeing her ever use a written recipe; they were always stored in her head. Very often she made recipes up as she went along. She had a strict rule that she would not "go to the street" (her term for shopping in Greenfield) more than once a week and often it was closer to two weeks. Her talent for putting together delicious meals using whatever happened to be available was the envy of many of the women in town. Supper was the big meal of the day. It didn't always have meat, but it nearly always had potatoes in one form or another.

Orilla and I were always expected to eat whatever was set before us. If we protested, instead of being provided with something different, we were informed that tomorrow's menu might be more to our liking. Actually, I thoroughly enjoyed Jessie's cooking about 99% of the time, but there were one or two meals that appeared on the table from time to time that I just could not deal with. One of these was something she made from elbow macaroni and canned tomatoes. No matter how hungry I was, I could not make myself partake of that meal. One day, I knew in advance that the macaroni and tomato dish was planned for lunch. Somehow I managed to get invited to my friend Wayne Chapin's house that morning and to stay for lunch. I figured that I had pulled a good one until Wayne and I went into his house for lunch. "Ray, you're going to really enjoy what I have for you," his mother said. "It's a recipe I got from your mother." You guessed it: macaroni and tomatoes.

As growing kids, Orilla and I consumed a lot of milk. Not only was it whole milk, it was raw (unpasteurized) and very fresh. Every second evening I would walk down to the Zimmerman's barn with a one-gallon metal container while they were doing the milking. The milk had been in the cow moments before it was in my container.

There was no milkman, but we did have a bread man. I think he made his rounds in Leyden about twice a week. Although she cooked and baked nearly everything else, Jessie never made regular bread, so most of our bread was supplied by the bread man. He would stop and bring in a loaf or two and almost always hung around talking for at least a half hour. I often wondered how long it took him to drive his route if he spent that much time talking everywhere he stopped.

During the summer months, the produce from Henry's garden was the central feature of most meals. However, before the cultivated plants started to produce, Jessie looked to several wild native plants to help fill the larder. Early spring was dandelion season. While today the lowly dandelion is the hated weed in everyone's front yard, in 1950s New England, it was a very tasty vegetable that could be obtained for free and with little effort. We would go dandelion digging in the apple orchard or some other location that had damp soil and where dandelions grew profusely. To have the best flavor, dandelions had to be harvested before the blossoms opened. Plants with unopened buds were okay, but not if they had opened their yellow flowers. Once a plant was in bloom, it became tough and had a very bitter taste.

We would take a sharp knife and cut the root off just below ground level. When we got them back to the house, the plants were washed to remove the dirt. Then we soaked them in cold water for several hours to remove some of the bitterness. Finally, they were boiled with a chunk of salt pork or some uncooked bacon. If it was getting late in the dandelion season the boiling water might be changed once or twice. If blossomed plants could not be avoided, some pudding plant would often be included in the boil. It was a short growing wild plant with thick leaves that grew near the ledge outcropping just north of the shop. As with most greens eaten in back woods New England, the dandelion greens were sprinkled with a dash of apple cider vinegar just before eating.

A little later in the year the wild vegetable of choice was often milkweed. As with dandelions, they needed to be harvested before the flowers bloomed. Only the very top three or four leaves of the newest growth were snipped off. Milkweeds were prepared in much the same way as dandelions, but the flavor was totally different. Sometimes, if other greens were in short supply, and Henry had a nice crop of young weeds in his garden, we would have a meal of pigweed, but I never really cared for that.

Other wild contributors to Jessie's menus were nuts and wild mushrooms. We knew of several stands of shagbark hickory trees back in the woods and there was a nice butternut tree growing along the north side of the barn down at the farm. In the fall of the year we would head out to the trees with our pails and baskets to collect whatever prime nuts the squirrels and chipmunks were kind enough to have left for us.

One season the butternut crop was smaller than usual and the squirrels had beaten us to most of the prime nuts. One day Orilla and I sat and watched a large gray nut-gatherer rummage around for a few nuts he might have missed. Whenever he found one, he would carefully check it over and then scurry along the side of the barn where he would suddenly disappear, always in the same location. Upon investigation, we found a good sized gap between the barn boards. Checking inside the barn we discovered a hoard of butternuts up on a beam near the hay mow. A few minutes later Orilla and I entered the farmhouse kitchen with a large pail of butternuts. Grandpa was at the sink washing his hands.

"Where did you get all those?" he asked. "I thought the squirrels got all the nuts this year."

"They did," Orilla said. "But we discovered where they were hidden."

"Did you now? And what do you suppose the squirrels think of you stealing their winter food supply?"

"But they are our nuts," she said. "They came from our tree."

"That tree belongs just as much to the squirrels as it does to us." Frank said. "The squirrels are counting on those nuts. I think you better put them back where you found them."

We were never totally confident of our ability to distinguish between wild mushrooms that were safe to eat and the poisonous varieties. However, our neighbor, Lee Gerry, had the knack and so we seldom went mushrooming without Lee going along. Besides, he always seemed to know the best locations. Sometimes he would take us to a high rocky pasture which seemed like an odd place to find mushrooms, but find them we did.

I remember that most of the mushroom varieties we picked differed in appearance from what was found in the grocery stores. One type was an almost perfectly round ball that had no stem and would grow to several inches across. These we called puff-balls because when the plant matured and turned dark, a firm stomp on it with a well-directed foot would release a large cloud of mushroom spore to drift off in the breeze like a puff of smoke.

Sometimes if the 'shroom huntin' wasn't going well we would head into the woods in or near a low, wet, swampy area in search of what we called tree mushrooms. They were a shelf-like fungus that grew out horizontally from the trunk of a tree usually several feet above the ground. Sometimes we'd find them growing on downed, decaying logs as well. If picked while young, they could be sliced thin and sautéed with a little butter and garlic.

In June, 1954, Henry and Jessie celebrated their 25th wedding anniversary. All the many family members, and everyone in town, were invited to our house for a big party hosted by Orilla and me. Invitees were told that beer and ale would be served, (root beer and ginger ale.) In those days, silver dollars were common 25th anniversary gifts (the silver anniversary) and Jessie and Henry received over a hundred. You could walk into any bank and exchange a paper dollar (silver certificate) for an honest silver dollar. After the price of silver increased, and silver dollars became worth more than a dollar, for a while banks gave out little packets of silver granules instead of a silver dollar. That ended after 1964 when the last silver coins were minted and the dollar bill joined the larger denominations as a Federal Reserve note, just a government promise.

It was Jessie's life-long dream to own, operate, and be the "chief cook and bottle washer" for a restaurant. Every so often she would bring it up in a conversation with Henry, but he would never hear of it. She never pushed hard for it, but clearly it was something that she really wanted to do. Sometimes she would talk about wanting to convert the garage portion of the house into an eating establishment. Other times she had her eye on part of Henry's shop, especially after he stopped doing car repairs and the automotive bays were no longer used for much of anything except storage. Even when they were well into their 70s, and Henry was getting ready to retire and sell the shop and all its contents, she wanted to keep the shop the way it was with all the old tools and equipment. She said she would just clean it up, add a kitchen, and scatter tables around so that people could eat where the last village smithy had worked. She was convinced that people would come from far and wide to eat in the Blacksmith Shop Restaurant. She was probably correct. It was her dream, but it was too late, and it never came true.

Chapter 8

FRANK WOOD'S MUCK-LAND
POTATOES

After they were married in 1929, Henry and Jessie rented a house just a short walk from Ed Howes' blacksmith shop where he was employed. It was the last house in a short line of buildings that included the only store in town. In the early 1930s, they bought a 120 acre dairy farm which sat in the valley to the northeast of the Center. The farm's hilly pastures adjoined those of the Zimmerman farm uphill and to the west. In the valley bottom, the hay field extended along both sides of the Brattleboro Road from close to its intersection with today's Zimmerman Hill Road, northward to where it begins to slope downward into Beaver Meadow. The farm was bounded on the east by the steep hill that bordered the valley.

Two small brooks flowed through the meadow. One began at a small pond behind the rocky ridge just south of Beaver Meadow and flowed south along the eastern edge of the valley. Henry used to tell stories of how that pond used to be much larger and how in the winter some of the men in town used to play hockey there. The second stream flowed down the hill from Zimmerman's pasture, past the farmhouse, and joined the first stream in a swampy area along the eastern edge of the meadow. The combined brook formed the beginning of the stream that fed Leyden Glen. This was the very valley, and the very stream, that the Deerfield captives struggled along in the cold and snow of the 1704 winter as they traveled to Canada (see Appendix C.)

After Henry's employer, Ed Howes, was hit and killed by a taxi on a visit to New York City, the widow sold the house and business to Henry in about 1935. Jessie and Henry then moved into the former Howes home near the shop where they lived, until moving to Northfield in 1986. With the farm vacant, and in need of a caretaker, Jessie's parents, Frank and Bertha (Parker) Wood moved in. The Woods had been living in the Hawley, Charlemont area, where Jessie and her three brothers (Alvin, Rolland, and Howard) and her sister (Leta) were born and grew up. Leta was the youngest of Frank and Bertha's children. Like her brothers Rolland and Howard, Leta enlisted in the military during WWII serving as a nurse in the Navy. Her third brother, Alvin (who coincidentally had exactly the same date of birth as Henry) did not enter the military, being a bit too old at the start of the war. Leta was discharged from the Navy at Long Beach, CA, and remained there working as a nurse in a doctor's office.

Soon after her employer committed suicide, Leta decided to return to New England and moved into the farmhouse to live with her parents. There was a certain amount of hush, hush speculation that there may have been something more than an employer-employee relationship in California. Leta was very upset by his death, but seldom talked about it except to say, "He was a wonderful man." She didn't marry, or even date anyone, for many, many years. Instead she totally immersed herself in the operation of the farm and caring for Frank and Bertha as they grew old and feeble. When Frank was very ill from a stroke, she polished up her nursing skills, took care of him and replaced his lost income by working as an LPN at the hospital in Greenfield. After both parents had died and she no longer had anyone to take care of, she finally did marry late in life. It was not for love, but rather as a financial necessity for both parties.

On the farm, Frank milked a few cows and raised chickens and pigs with a lot of help from Bertha and Leta. For several years after Leta's arrival, the three of them pretty much totally supported themselves with the farm supplying nearly all their needs, either directly, or indirectly by the proceeds from the sale of milk, butter, and eggs. Every spring, Frank planted a big garden behind the house. In addition to over 30 varieties of vegetables, he always had a large raspberry patch and another for strawberries. In dry weather, his plants were nourished by water he diverted from the small brook running nearby.

The only thing he couldn't get to produce well in that location was potatoes. The spuds, as he called them, always turned out very small although there were a lot of them. Bertha refused to deal with those "peanut potatoes" so they usually ended up being cooked into a mash and fed to the hogs. Finally, Frank concluded that the soil behind the house was just never going to grow good spuds. After trying his luck in several other locations near the house and barn, and having similar luck, one year he decided to try growing potatoes in the rich soil at the east edge of the hay meadow, adjacent to the swampy area. The soil there was black as coal, always moist, and was composed largely of peat-like organic matter. "It's too wet down there to grow potatoes." Berta warned. "Your seed potatoes will just rot. We won't even have little ones for the hogs."

For once, Bertha was totally wrong. She even admitted it. Potatoes thrived in that black muck producing far more that the three of them at the farm could use. Sensing that he had a cash crop on his hands, the next time he had a ride to Greenfield, Frank took along two or three bushels of his best spuds and cashed them in at one of the grocery stores. They were a big hit with the store's customers. "Frank Wood's Muck-Land Potatoes" quickly became a highly sought after item by anyone lucky enough to sample them. Word quickly got around about the source, and soon customers were stopping at the farm to buy, making it unnecessary to haul potatoes to town. Bertha never did feel comfortable around strangers. If Frank or Leta was not at the house, she wouldn't answer the door when a potato buyer knocked. And, Bertha complained that she still wasn't any better off for potatoes because Frank was selling all the big ones leaving her with the small ones. After a couple of years, Frank reverted to only growing enough potatoes for use by the family. "There's too danged many people making a fuss," he said.

Frank and Bertha never owned a motor vehicle of any kind. I don't believe Leta had one either until she started working at the school cafeteria. The sole non-human source of power on the farm was a dapple gray draft horse named Pat. Pat pulled the plow, the mowing machine, the hay rake, the wagon, and anything else that needed to be moved. He was a strong, but very gentle, animal and was dearly loved by the entire family. One summer when both Pat and Frank were getting along in years, Frank leased a portion of his hay field to another farmer. Failing to heed Frank's warning to not get his tractor too near to the swampy east edge, the farmer proceeded to bury his Farmall's rear wheels up to its axle. After locating Frank in the barn, the farmer asked him to bring his horse down to the field and pull the tractor out. "That horse is all the horse I've got. And he's my best friend. I'm not going to risk him getting hurt pulling out your machine after you ignored what I told you," Frank replied.

Sometimes it seemed as if Pat had almost human characteristics. I remember one time when I was quite young; Grandpa Frank sat me on the wagon seat beside him as Pat pulled us up the steep hill behind the house to gather a quantity of large rocks to be used to repair a stone wall down below the house. Grandpa wrestled the rocks into the wagon until it contained all the weight that he felt the horse should be made to control on the steep downhill return trip. When we approached the steepest part of the decline, we stopped and Grandpa tied up the left rear wheel of the wagon with a chain so that it would not turn. We then proceeded down the hill with three wheels turning and the steel tire of the fourth wheel simply skidding along across the ground. This improvised brake permitted Pat to pull slightly as we went downhill instead of having to hold back and keep the heavily loaded wagon from overtaking him.

Frank and Bertha Wood, their horse Pat, and dog Tex, at Henry's farm prior to 1953.

However, on a curve in the path, the chained-up wheel struck a large section of protruding ledge rock and the chain either broke or came loose. The sudden loss of the brake caused the entire weight of the wagon, the load of rocks, Grandpa, and me to slam into the rear strap of Pat's harness. Some horses might have panicked, lunged down the steep hill with us and the wagon bouncing along behind. Not Pat.

Immediately, he squatted on his hind legs, stiffened his front legs in front of him and brought everything to a quick and safe stop. He remained in that posture until Grandpa rechained the wheel so we could proceed safely to the bottom of the hill.

As a young boy, I loved my grandparent's farm and spent as much time there as I could. I doubt that the farm had changed much in the previous 100 years or more. I have seen a photo from the 1870s that shows that farmhouse looking exactly as it did in 1950. The farm buildings that I remember from the late 1940s, and early 1950s, were more or less clustered around the large 2-story house with attached wood shed. Across from the house was the main barn. The barn's lower level contained stalls for the horse and a few milk cows. There was a ramp outside leading to the upper level which was used mainly for storage of loose hay. The hay was arranged so that it could be pitchforked down a hole to land just in front of where it was needed on the lower level to feed the animals. Attached to the barn on the south side was a small barnyard with a pigsty.

I remember Grandpa Frank having no more than about 10 or 12 milk cows, but they pretty much ruled his life. No matter what the day of the year, holiday or not, the cows had to be milked early in the morning and again in the late afternoon or early evening. A vacation or even a day off was unheard of. If a cow was not properly milked, it could result in considerable pain for the cow and resulted in a big decline in her milk output. After a few years, a cow's milk production declined with age and she was converted to a beef animal, always a sad occasion.

In the spring, summer, and fall, the cows spent most of their time high on the pasture north of the house and barn. As milking time approached, Frank would go out to the corner of the barn near the big butternut tree and call out loudly, "Come Boss, Come Boss, Come Bossy, Bossy, Bossy." This cattle call would be repeated several times until he saw the cows on the trail coming down the hill, or he heard the bell ringing around the neck of the lead cow, Bessie. Once the cows started for the barn, Bessie was in charge and would lead them all down the hill and into the east door of the barn where each cow would find its personal assigned stall. If a newcomer cow entered the wrong stall, a considerable ruckus would break out until the intruder moved along to an unclaimed location.

Once all the cows were in place, each was given its allotment of grain and the milking would begin. All of Frank's cows were always milked by hand for a couple of reasons. First of all, milking machines were expensive, and second, even if he had a machine there was no electricity in the barn to operate it. So, Frank would sit on a short three-legged stool, press his head against the cow's side and begin. The hand milking process was pretty simple. After giving the udder a quick washing, Frank held the empty milk pail between his knees underneath the cow's udder, grasped a teat in each hand and began a pulling squeezing action, alternating hands. A good milker would get a strong stream of milk with each pull until the udder was empty.

Below the barnyard, in the shade of the huge maple trees, was a small milk house where the milk was cooled and stored. Much of the milk was passed through a hand cranked centrifugal separator that separated out some of the cream that would later be used to churn butter. The milk was poured into 40-quart milk cans which were set into a rectangular concrete trough resembling a narrow bathtub. Water from the brook behind the house was diverted through a pipe to this trough and provided the cooling medium to chill the milk and keep it cold. Once a week, the milk truck would arrive to pick up the week's production.

When enough cream had been accumulated, it was time to make butter, usually once a week. The cream was taken up to the kitchen in the house and poured into the wooden butter churn. The churn was operated manually by a hand crank on one end which turned a large gear. That gear in turn rotated other smaller ones which caused the paddles inside the churn to turn in opposite directions. As a young boy I was often drafted to churn the butter, which I enjoyed immensely. That butter churn has retired to one corner of my dining room today.

After the soft butter had formed, a plug in the bottom of

the churn was removed allowing the buttermilk to be drained off. Then the soft butter was pressed by hand into a small rectangular wooden mold with removable top and sides. The mold was just the right size to create one pound of butter with a fancy flower design embossed on top. After it was packed full, the top and sides were removed and the brick of butter was wrapped in special butter paper. The finished butter was placed in the icebox to cool. The next day the butter would be taken to the IGA store in Greenfield by a neighbor or relative. There it was exchanged for flour, salt, and whatever supplies were needed.

Just past the milk house were two chicken houses. Frank always had a pretty large contingent of chickens along with a rooster or two. In addition to supplying eggs, most of which were sold locally or in Greenfield, the chickens also provided much of the family's meat supply. Sunday morning Frank would go down to the chicken houses and pick out a hen that he figured was beyond its prime egg laying days. A swift blow with the ax and the head was tossed into the henhouse yard where it was immediately attacked by the other hens. After a minute or two the running and flapping of the headless body was over and it was off to the house to do the plucking.

No matter how it was accomplished, chicken plucking was a messy, but necessary, job. Grandpa Frank would usually simply start pulling feathers. If Grandma or Leta was to do it, they would make sure there was a lot of hot water available and soak the bird in a hot pail for a few minutes followed by a cold dunk. They claimed that the hot water made the feathers a lot easier to pull out. The wings had a lot of feathers, but didn't supply much meat so those were usually clipped off using poultry shears. Next, the largest feathers were pulled from the rear toward the head, or where the head used to be. It was important to pull only a few feathers at a time. If large handfuls were grasped, instead of the feathers coming loose, the skin would tear. After the largest feathers were gone the smaller ones were pulled and saved in a cloth sack for use in making pillows. Very little of anything was wasted on the farm. Once the chicken-plucker tired of pulling small feathers, the nearly featherless bird was taken outside. There several sheets of newspaper were rolled up and one end lit with a match making a torch. The flames were played over the bird to singe off the remaining feathers. Finally, the bird was gutted and prepared for cooking. Several family members considered the giblets the best part of the chicken so those were never wasted. Leta always claimed that the gizzard and neck had the best tasting meat. In those days, Sunday night's chicken didn't arrive all neatly shrink wrapped from the grocery store. Even at the age of four or five, we clearly understood where our food really came from, and that other creatures routinely gave their lives so that we could live.

From time to time a fox would be seen in the area and it usually didn't take too long before it started causing problems around the chickens. After spending a few days checking out the chicken houses and fences and finding no way inside, the fox would usually start excavating his own entrance underneath the wire. Frank would check the fences every day and when he found evidence of digging he would plug the hole with rocks. That seldom discouraged the fox which simply started another hole at a new location.

Each chicken house had an attached outdoor chicken yard enclosed by a four-foot tall chicken wire fence. The hens usually spent most of the day in the yard before retiring to their nesting boxes inside for the night and to lay their eggs. Each hen had its own nesting box and would lay eggs nowhere else. That made it easy to keep track of which hens were good layers and which were slacking off. One trick that Bertha swore by to fool a hen into increasing its production was to deposit one or two porcelain eggs into the nest and leave them there for a few days. Maybe this improved the attitude of a bird that was discouraged from doing all the hard work just to have her eggs stolen every day!

The usual solution to a fox problem was Tex. While Howard was stationed in Texas during WWII, he somehow acquired a mid-sized white and black dog. Later when Howard was assigned elsewhere and couldn't take the dog along, he packed Tex up and shipped him north by train. Tex soon became everyone's best friend around the farm. Everyone's except the foxes', that is. Tex was often the first to know if a fox was in the vicinity and he felt it was his responsibility to guard the chickens from this intruder. He would often spend the night sleeping down by the chicken houses of his own accord, daring the fox to show up.

One time, in spite of Frank's and Tex's best efforts, an especially crafty fox was being very successful at stealing chickens. Somehow, it would grab a chicken two or three times a week even if Tex was close by. Finally, Frank decided it was time for a new strategy in order to outwit this critter that was taking a large toll on the chickens. Having full faith that Tex would not harm the chickens, he decided that the dog should spend the night directly inside the chicken house that was the one usually raided. Just before he turned in for the night, he made Tex a bed of hay and locked the chicken house door.

Sometime after midnight Frank and Bertha were wakened by a loud racket coming from the direction of the hen houses. Chickens were squawking and flapping and Tex was barking. Grabbing a lantern, Frank headed down to find out what was going on. By the time he reached the area, everything was quiet, but most of the chickens were nervously walking around in their yard instead of roosting in the hen house. Frank called to Tex several times, but there was no response.

After sunup, Frank inspected the chicken area once again. He found a gap in the fence where two sections of chicken wire joined and there were several red hairs and a few white hairs snagged on the wire. Still there was no sign of Tex anywhere. Frank searched the farm and called to Tex all day, but the dog did not appear. That night at supper he told Bertha, "I think the fox got into the hen yard and Tex took off after it. He must have chased it into the woods where they fought. I'm afraid Tex may have got the worst of it."

There was still no sign of Tex the next morning, nor the next. On the good side, there were no more missing chickens or new fox signs in the area. Frank and Bertha made up their minds that their beloved Tex was gone. "He gave his life defending the chickens," Frank said. "It was his duty and he fulfilled it."

The next morning while Frank was doing the milking, Tex came slowly limping into the barn on three legs. One ear was badly torn and his white fur was caked with dried blood. "Thank God you're back. We had given you up for dead," Frank told him. The rest of the milking would have to wait. Frank gently picked up the trembling dog and carried it up to the house where his wounds were carefully cleaned and bandaged. After several days of Bertha's good cooking, and Leta's considerable nursing skills, Tex began to show signs of returning to being his old self. A few weeks later he was back on patrol around the chicken coops. There were no more chickens lost to a fox for a long time afterward.

Behind the house and slightly up the hill was the ice house. It was strategically located so that it was constantly in the shade of the huge maple trees during the warm months of the year. Although many Leyden residences had electrically powered refrigerators by the 1950s, the farm had not yet been electrified. Instead, the only source of refrigeration in the house was provided by the melting of ice in an old-fashioned, tin lined, oak icebox just as it had been for many years. For decades, blocks of natural ice had been sawn by hand from the farm pond during the coldest days of winter. These blocks were hauled to the ice house where they were stacked in a big pile and covered with a foot or more of sawdust as the first layer of insulation. Next, the sawdust was covered with a couple of feet of loose straw or hay. Finally, a few old blankets or empty grain sacks were piled on top. If enough ice was harvested, and enough sawdust and hay applied, usable ice could still be found all through the summer. The ice house must have been a wonderful place to hang out on those hot, humid, New England summer days!

By the 1950s, the ice house had been out of use for quite some time. Instead, ice was provided by an ice truck that followed a delivery route from the ice plant in Greenfield. "The Iceman Cometh" (apologies to Eugene O'Neill) once a week and using large ice tongs would place a solid block of ice (about one cubic foot, weighing nearly 60 pounds) into the upper compartment of the icebox. As the ice slowly melted, cold water would flow downward and collect in a pan that sat on the floor below the icebox. The pan needed to be emptied at least daily to avoid a minor flood in the kitchen. In especially hot weather there was a good chance that the ice might completely melt before the ice man returned. In that case, a second block of ice would be temporarily stored in the root cellar, heaped over with a pile of straw or hay which in turn was covered with a couple of wool blankets.

The center section of the icebox was where food was stored to be kept cool. Cold air cascaded downward from the ice into the food storage area. The icebox only had a capacity of about three cubic feet of storage. Compare that to the refrigerator in today's typical kitchen which has 20 to 25 cubic feet of capacity. Only small quantities of foods that absolutely had to be kept cool were stored in the icebox. Even butter, which is always refrigerated today, was often kept on a cool pantry shelf instead of in the icebox.

Sometime in the mid-50s or so, ice deliveries stopped. There were no longer enough iceboxes in town to make an ice delivery route practical. The need for refrigeration became the driving force for the farmhouse to finally be wired for electricity.

Up a slight rise east of the ice house and toward the main barn was the sugar house with an attached shop/tool shed. In the very early spring, that sugar house was used to make maple syrup from the huge maple trees that lined the long driveway and grew in the wood lot up in the pasture. About half the sweet maple production was stored as syrup and the other half was processed further to create granular maple sugar. The granulated product was used in many recipes in place of store-bought cane or beet sugar. During WWII when sugar was rationed by the government, some of the granulated maple sugar produced on the farm was taken to Greenfield and bartered for needed supplies.

Near the ice house was a small smokehouse for curing hams and smoking other meats. Since icebox space was severely limited, smoking meat was one of the best means of meat preservation. Frank would butcher a couple of hogs every fall and much of the meat would be smoked. Generally the smoked meat was left hanging in the smokehouse until needed. With the arrival of electricity, the smokehouse was abandoned in favor of a freezer. Bertha always claimed, however, that using smoked meat in her recipes gave them a better flavor than meat from "that dad-burned freezer."

Underneath the house, and accessed by an outside door, was the root cellar. It was probably dug out from under the house after the house was built. The floor and walls were simply moist dirt and rocks. Of course, the walls of the cellar were lined with shelves containing all the Ball and Mason jars full of home canned beans, beets, applesauce, corn, etc. There were even canned potatoes and meat.

This was where the winter's supply of squash, turnips, potatoes, etc. was kept. It was also home to a wonderful assortment of spiders and insects. Several bushels of apples were stored here each fall, but they would seldom last all winter without spoiling. Apple pies baked in the late winter were usually made from apples that had been sliced thin and dried in the sun months before. In one corner of the root cellar were the masonry crocks for sauerkraut. Each fall, the last of the summer's cabbages were shredded and heavily salted down. The sauerkraut-to-be was packed into the crocks with a weighted wooden lid sitting directly on top of the cabbage. Sometimes as the sauerkraut aged, a fuzzy mold would grow on the top layer. This was simply skimmed off and discarded exposing layers of first class 'kraut below.

Somewhat hidden off to the side of the house and a little behind was the latest location of the outhouse. There was no half-moon carved on the door like in the cartoons, but it was a two-holer. The exact location changed every few weeks at least during the warm months when digging was easy. A new hole would be dug, the outhouse moved over it and the old hole filled in. It had mostly fallen into disuse by the time I was old enough to understand what its purpose was.

The reason that outhouse usage fell off was the installation of a new-fangled flush toilet on the second floor of the house. The oak water box sat high on the wall above the stool. A pull of the porcelain knob at the end of a brass chain caused water to rush into the bowl and the contents to mysteriously disappear to places unknown. Bertha however was never one to take to needless modern contraptions and continued to use the outhouse from time to time long after the rest of the family had given in to modernism.

The water supply for the house, including the modern flush toilet, began at a natural spring high on the hill behind the house. It was actually located in Zimmerman's cow pasture. That water spring was also the source of the small brook that flowed behind the house and eventually into Leyden Glen becoming part of the water supply for Greenfield. From the spring, a buried lead pipe went down the hill and ended at a large wooden barrel in the attic over the kitchen woodshed. Water flowed into the attic barrel continuously and overflowed to a drain that dumped outside near the brook. Water was fed by gravity from the barrel to the kitchen sink and to the toilet.

There was no such thing as running hot water in the house. Hot water was heated in a small cast iron tank attached to the left side of the firebox of the wood fired range in the kitchen. To use hot water, one lifted the lid off the tank and dipped some out assuming that the stove was fired up so that there would actually be hot water. When the hot water level got low, it was refilled with cold water using a pail from the sink. Water for Saturday night baths was heated in metal pails on the cook stove and carried up the back stairs to the tub in the bathroom. Hot water was always in short supply and was not to be wasted, a rule strictly enforced by Bertha.

As was typical of many old New England farmhouses, the house did not have any central heat. The kitchen was heated due to cooking on the wood fired kitchen range. The dining room had a small wood fired stove as did the parlor. Other rooms were unheated, including the bedrooms upstairs. Of course there was no insulation in the walls or attic so the house tended to be a bit cold and drafty much of the time during the winter.

After sundown, light was provided by kerosene lamps. I must have been about ten years old when Uncle Howard Wood, an electrician from Vermont, finally installed electricity in the farmhouse. Only the kitchen, dining room, and parlor had electric lights, with one bare bulb in the middle of the ceiling of each room. Each room also had one or two power outlets, most of which were seldom used because there were few appliances to plug into them.

Whenever the subject of electricity, or any other modern convenience, would come up around my grandmother, the conversation always took the same direction. "I've lived all my life without electricity and I don't see why I need it now," Bertha would repeat over and over to anyone who would listen, no matter how many times they had heard her say it before.

"But these are modern times. It's the 1950s. You've got to move into the modern age," someone would say.

"I don't want to be modern," she would say. "I like things just like they are." With that, she would suddenly find something important that needed her attention in another room or outside.

One time Jessie decided that she had heard enough of this and decided to press the issue. Jessie felt that the vacuum cleaner was the greatest invention ever made. Naturally, her mother would not hear of owning or using one. One day Jessie arrived at the farm and presented Bertha with a brand new vacuum cleaner. After Jessie demonstrated what it could do, Grandma stated that it was too noisy and hurt her ears. Besides, it couldn't do anything she couldn't do with a broom. For a long time she continued sweeping the floor with her broom. Eventually she agreed to allow Leta to use the vacuum, but she never used it herself. On cleaning days, Bertha would sweep dirt into piles which Leta would then vacuum up. "No sense wasting electricity by vacuuming the whole darn floor," Bertha would say.

There actually was one electrical device in the house before the arrival of household electric power. It was a large table model radio that was powered by a huge dry cell battery. The battery alone must have weighed ten pounds or more. Usage of the radio was very restricted because as the battery lost its charge the volume got weaker and weaker. "Turn that thing off. There's no need to listen to all that foolishness. Batteries are expensive," Bertha would say.

Nearly all the hours of every day were consumed by doing the 1001 things necessary on the farm to tend their animals and crops, make and mend clothes, repair fences and equipment, etc. Surplus time, if any, was used for resting up to prepare for the next day's tasks. On Saturday night however, if the battery was relatively fresh, and the weather conditions were right, it was time to sit around the radio and tune in WWVA from Wheeling, West Virginia. No other station would do. If WWVA couldn't be tuned in, the radio was shut off to save the battery and it was tried again the next Saturday. Why WWVA? I have no idea. I didn't realize it at the time, but looking back I now realize that WWVA was just one of several unexplained bits of southern connection attached to Bertha's history.

Much of the income from selling milk, butter, and eggs was used to purchase grain for Pat, the milk cows, and the chickens. Any left-over cash went for whatever few necessities were needed on the farm. For a few years in the 1950s, feed grain could be obtained in large sacks made of colorful patterned cotton cloth instead of burlap. Grain was needed for the animals anyway, so the colorful cloth bags were a source of free material. Bertha and Leta would often collect these bags and make shirts and dresses from them using an old Singer foot treadle sewing machine. They would proudly show off their new "feed bag dresses" at family functions.

Late spring and early summer was an especially busy time of year on the farm. In addition to the usual chores, planting needed to be done in May. That was followed by the start of haying in June. The bulk of the hay feed for Frank's horse and cows over the coming winter months was harvested from the meadow below the house. Frank rarely had to purchase a lot of hay because the valley meadow, that has now grown up to brush with several ponds, was an excellent hay producer.

Many years, there would be three full cuttings thanks to the meadow's very fertile soil and abundant moisture.

About a third of the meadow would be hayed at a time. Frank's horse, Pat, did much of the work. Frank would hitch Pat to the sickle bar mowing machine and the first day would be spent cutting the hay. After two or three days of drying, Pat would pull the dump rake to make piles. Finally, the faithful horse would pull the wagon through the meadow while the piles were picked up and loaded by hand using pitchforks. In order to greatly increase the size of the hay loads on the wagon, a big hayrack was installed on the bed effectively increasing the width and length of the wagon. The rack had short stakes around the sides to keep the hay load from slipping off.

Frank's hay was always stored loose, not baled. When hay was being put away, everyone in the nearby family who was old enough to walk was involved. Bertha always worked side by side in the hayfields with Frank, Leta, and often Uncle Howard or Uncle Rolland. Sometimes Henry would help using his pickup truck with a hayrack he had built to fit it.

My first "job" at the age of three or four was to ride on Pat's back holding onto the harness with both hands as he pulled the wagon. I wasn't there to provide Pat with any directions, he didn't need any. It was just a good, safe place to keep me out of trouble, and out of the way, so my mother could help load the hay. The horse would slowly walk between the piles stopping occasionally to wait for hay to be loaded. If instructions were needed, Frank would simply call out "Pat, gee" if the horse was to go to the right or "Pat, haw" if it was to turn left. If Pat was to startup from a stop or go faster, Frank would click his tongue two or three times. A stop required a simple, "Whoa."

My sister, Orilla, three years older than me, would often be assigned the job of stomping down the hay on the wagon. She would walk around on the loose hay packing it down so that more could be loaded. In order to minimize the number of trips back and forth to the barn, it was important to make each load as large as possible. The stomper on the wagon would also direct the loaders where each huge forkful of hay should be placed. Hay was alternately built up around the edges, then the center, then back to the edges again. That way each added forkful helped hold on the hay below it. The height of the load was determined mostly by the height to which the workers on the ground could lift the heavy forkfuls. Orilla's career as a hay stomper came to an abrupt end one day when a large snake slithered out of a forkful of hay that she was spreading high on the wagon. Although the load was quite tall, she jumped right off the wagon and ran out of the hayfield. I don't believe she was ever convinced to help with haying again.

At the barn, the hay was pitched from the wagon into the haymows (rhymes with cows) that took up most of the upper floor of the barn. Some of the crew would unload the wagon with hayforks while the rest of us would stomp around in the mows packing it in tightly. The horse and cattle stalls were below on the first floor and there was a large opening in the upper floor adjacent to the mows where loose hay could be thrown down to feed the animals. One time, when I was helping put hay away in the barn, I unintentionally gave everyone a good laugh. The hole in the floor had become totally covered over with a lot of loose hay and I forgot that it was there. Not paying attention, I was running from the rear of the barn toward the wagon and ran right over that pile of hay, or tried to. I must have looked like something out of a cartoon movie when, while still running, I suddenly dropped straight down out of sight through that hay to the lower floor. Luckily, there was also a lot of hay below the hole, so nothing was hurt except my pride.

Haying was hot, dry, itchy work. Often, while most of us were involved with delivering a load to the barn and mowing it away, Bertha would disappear into the house. She would reappear awhile later with a pitcher of her special oatmeal and ginger drink. I don't know what else was in it, but it sure tasted great and was the cure for a bad thirst before heading back to the meadow for another load.

It wasn't all work on the farm. Sometimes family parties were held there including many birthday and holiday parties. Grandma didn't care where Thanksgiving was held, but she always insisted that the family Christmas was to be held at the farm. Once or twice a summer a family picnic might be held. Sometimes it was in the wood lot high on the hill behind the farmhouse to increase the chance of a breeze on a hot humid day. Pat would be hitched to the wagon and hauled everyone to the top along with all the picnic supplies. Sometimes the picnic would involve fern picking. There was a certain type of fern that grew wild in a few locations on the farm. I don't remember what its name was, but florists would buy burlap bags full of them for use in flower arrangements.

A few years, in the fall, we had a big family clambake. Uncles Howard and Rolland were always in charge. It was held on level ground below the farmhouse on both sides of the brook. A big hole would be dug and large rocks placed in the bottom. A huge fire was built in the hole on top of the rocks and kept burning for at least 24 hours. The idea was to get the rocks and ground around the hole very hot so that the residual heat would do the cooking once the fire was smothered. On the morning of the clambake, the fire was allowed to burn down to coals and then the clams, unhusked corn, and other goodies were placed in the hole. Immediately, several bushels of seaweed were placed on top and then about six inches of fresh dirt on top of the seaweed. Where they got all that seaweed, 100 miles from the ocean, I have no idea. After some period of time known only to Howard and Rollie, the pit was opened and the feasting began!

In 1953, Frank died. He had suffered a stroke one day while walking down to the barn to do the milking. He was unable to return to the house and could only call feebly for help which nobody heard. Leta discovered him lying by the barn door when she went to investigate what was taking him so long to do the milking. He was totally paralyzed on one side and partly on the other. The parlor was converted into a special room for him complete with an adjustable hospital bed. The bed was oriented near a window which gave him a view of the barn and his cows in the lower pasture. After several months of being confined to the bed he died. Henry, Alvin, Howard, and Rolland did all they could to keep the farm going, but it proved to be too demanding in addition to their regular jobs and families.

No longer able to operate the farm by themselves, even with help, Bertha and Leta moved to Northfield. Leta had bought a small house there and they moved away from Leyden for good. Not long after, Henry sold the farm, much to my disappointment. It became a speech therapy center and its farming days were over.

Chapter 9

BAD FENCES MAKE BAD NEIGHBORS

Some towns had an official appointed position of Fence Inspector. It was the duty of the Fence Inspector to arbitrate disputes about whether or not someone's fence encroached upon a neighbor's property. Of course, most fences had been in place for decades or even a century or more, so most disputes had been settled long ago. In many cases the location of a fence represented the practical, agreed, property line, whether it aligned perfectly with the official surveyor's pins or not (if they existed or could be found.) Thus, there usually wasn't a lot for the fence inspector to do, but from time to time he was called upon to help settle some significant neighbor disputes that might go well beyond his official duties.

I recall Henry telling an interesting story at the supper table one night, about an incident that started with a fence dispute. The disagreement wasn't over the fence location, but rather its inability to contain the livestock that it was intended to confine. I'm not sure if the location of the story was in Leyden, or in another small town nearby. Nor do I recall any of the real names involved, so I'll just call the main characters Orville and Bart. The following really happened, or at least Henry swore that it did.

Orville had come to town a few years before. He had moved his family into a rather rundown old property and spent a lot of time fixing it up until it became one of the nicest places in town. Each spring, he planted a very large vegetable garden that provided produce for his family all summer. His big root cellar was filled each fall with all sorts of squash, potatoes, carrots, etc. to be used in the coming months. His wife did a lot of canning and after they had electricity, she did a lot of freezing.

Bart lived next door to Orville on a small farm that had been handed down to him through several generations. Bart's property was the exact opposite of Orville's. His house looked as if it had never seen a coat of paint, the roof was missing numerous shingles, and broken windows had been "repaired" with whatever was available at the moment. The yard was mostly brush and weeds that were never mowed. Out behind the house was an old chicken coop housing a few hens that usually ran loose through the gaping holes in the chicken wire. Connected to the coop was a small tumble down shack and a board fence corral that normally housed nothing except ants and spiders. One spring day, Bart decided to put the shack and corral to use, so he bought two baby pigs that he intended to raise through the summer and slaughter in the fall to provide the winter's hams and bacon.

Have you ever smelled the odor of a never-cleaned chicken coop? How about the odor of a never-cleaned pigpen? Now imagine both odors side by side. Oh, did I mention that the pigpen abutted Orville's vegetable garden?

It didn't take the baby pigs long to discover there was a much better menu next door in Orville's garden than that which Bart provided in their slop trough. Of course Bart's rotted, broken down, board fence didn't even slow them down. Some mornings Orville awoke to find two pigs munching on his best veggies. At first he would run into the garden and chase the pigs back through the fence and then block off their latest opening with a bit of wood, chicken wire, or whatever was handy. As the pigs and their appetites grew, Orville had had enough. He stomped next door to confront Bart. After a few minutes of heated discussion, Bart agreed to reinforce his fence and contain his critters.

A few days later the pigs were back in Orville's garden

once again. Another confrontation with Bart resulted in more promises followed by more flimsy fence patches. The next day Orville had pigs in his garden once again. Orville called the Fence Inspector and complained about Bart's fence being inadequate to contain his pigs. The Fence Inspector wasn't at all sure if he had the authority to do anything about it, but he agreed to talk with Bart who promised to build a new fence. However, Bart kept putting off the start of the fence project and his pigs kept dining at the Orville Buffet next door.

In danger of losing his entire food crop, Orville decided that he needed to build his own fence. He would build it strong enough to keep out the ever growing oinkers next door that were getting fat at his expense. A few days later Orville had his entire garden enclosed with wire calf mesh stapled to solid wood posts. He asked Bart to split the cost of the materials with him since it was Bart's pigs that created the need for the fence. Bart agreed to the cost split, but said he was a little short of cash at the moment and would pay up the first chance he got.

A few weeks went by with no pigs (actually beginning to be good size hogs by now) in Orville's garden. Those weeks also passed without any cash arriving for Bart's half of the fence expenses. Meanwhile, the quality and quantity of the slop that Bart was supplying wasn't getting any better. Hogs are rather smart animals in spite of their reputation and their slovenly habits. Knowing that there was a larger and much better tasting repast next door, the hogs set about trying to defeat Orville's new fence. Brute force and chewing didn't work; the fence was too well built. The answer was digging. Orville returned from work one day to find two well-fed hogs sleeping in the sun smack dab in the middle of his garden. Several of his crops were a total loss. Furious, he ran out to chase them back through the hole they had dug under his fence, but they would not move. He yelled, he pushed, he cursed, but they didn't move. Finally, when he prodded one with his toe, it bit him on the leg.

Orville had reached his breaking point. He was not a violent man, but this was too much for him to take. The only weapon

Orville possessed was an old single shot, Trapdoor Springfield .45-70 over his fireplace. The rifle had passed down through his family from some ancestor's Indian fighting days out west. Somewhere he had some ancient shells for the gun and down to the basement he went in search of them. A few minutes later he entered his garden with the Springfield and a pocket full of thumb-sized shells. Orville chambered a round and took aim at the closest pig that was sprawled in his cantaloupe patch. KABOOM! White smoke from the black powder round filled the air. At the loud noise, the second hog jumped up and faced Orville as if to charge him. KABOOM! Two dead hogs were lying in Orville's vegetables.

Hearing the shots, Bart came running to see what was going on. "What have you done?" he screamed. "You've shot my pigs! You've no right to do that! That's murder! Those hogs were my winter meat supply! I'll get you for that," he screamed.

Grabbing a loose fence board, Bart started toward Orville.

"I've got more shells," cautioned Orville without actually chambering one.

Bart reconsidered. Wisely, he dropped the board, turned, and stomped back inside his house cursing Orville all the way.

Orville's wife was panicked. She knew help was needed, but didn't know who to call. In many small towns such as Leyden, there was very little crime and thus no need for a regular police force. One of the selectmen was usually designated as the acting chief of police to handle the few police issues that came up during the year. In desperation she called the Town Clerk and told him that she was afraid that Orville and Bart were going to come to blows. Soon, someone with some unspecified official capacity arrived to check out the situation and found two dead hogs in the garden. Orville was sitting on his front steps with his head in his hands, and Bart was hiding inside his house. Orville told of the events leading up to the shooting of the hogs and how he just couldn't take it anymore. The official went next door to hear Bart's version and found him quite shaken by what had just transpired.

The town had no applicable ordinances and town officials had very little formal training in law enforcement. Their usual approach was to attempt to broker a settlement between the offender and the injured party rather than make an arrest or pass judgment. An arrest meant having to deal with a lot of unfamiliar paperwork, and assigning guilt could make an enemy of a former friend. In this case it wasn't clear to the official exactly who the injured party was. Orville was clearly defending his damaged property, yet it was Bart's hogs that had been shot.

Finally an agreement was reached in which Orville would pay to have the hogs butchered and Bart would give Orville some of the meat in payment for his lost vegetables.

From then on Bart kept only chickens.

Chapter 10

THE SAGE OF GORE HOLLOW

There has always been a certain attraction to small back-woods New England towns by people who want to get away from the mainstream, be left more or less alone, and just live a peaceful life in the hills close to nature. This was likely a factor in the decisions of many of the earliest settlers who chose to scrape out an existence among the rocks, trees, and hillsides of what became Leyden instead of farming the flat, fertile meadows of the Connecticut River Valley.

Throughout the 1950s, and probably for many years before, Leyden was home to several individuals who chose to live a quiet, solitary lifestyle removed from many of the constraints of society. Many people might have described them as hermits, or near hermits, but I don't remember ever hearing them referred to as such. Nevertheless, for lack of a more descriptive term, I will refer to them here as hermits. In those days, I think that most folks were a bit more tolerant of a divergent lifestyle than many are in today's cookie-cutter world of sameness. The Leyden hermits didn't live in caves like in the cartoons, and they didn't always live totally alone, nor avoid all contact with others. The general opinion of the community was that they were people who wanted to just be left alone and for the most part the citizenry respected and granted that wish. Leyden was a good place to get away from everything and everyone and live your life as you wanted without a lot of hassles.

There may have been several Leyden residents in the 1950s, that fit this description, but I can specifically remember three or four such individuals that immediately come to mind. The first lived about a half mile down the road from the Y where Greenfield Road and Brattleboro Road intersected. His name was Leon Severance. Leon lived completely alone in a very old, rundown house close to the road. I have no idea how old the house was, but its condition spoke loudly that it had seen its share of winters.

I once heard a story that back in the mid-1800s, the house was a station on the Underground Railroad used to smuggle slaves north to freedom in Canada. I have no idea if there was any truth to the story or not, but the house certainly looked like it could easily have been 100 years old or more. And Leyden was just the sort of out of the way place that was needed for this illicit activity. Maybe there was some kind of a carry-over from those "keep out of sight" days because Leon never seemed to go anywhere and was rarely seen outside the house by passersby. On the rare occasions when Leon was observed outside, he was often feeding his chickens which ran loose between the house and a small barn or shed. Sometimes he could be seen tending his vegetable garden behind the house. If somebody waved to him, he seldom waved back and often acted as if he didn't even see the person. It appeared as if he had no known relatives, at least none that any of the town's people knew of, although Severance was not an uncommon surname in the area.

George Howes was Leon's lifeline for a number of years. George lived in the Center where he operated the Howes family's small store from after WWII into the early 1950s. Another of George's activities was to operate the Leyden Stage. Since George had to frequently go to Greenfield to resupply his store, he decided that it would make sense to also provide a pickup and delivery service. A big part of the Stage's operation was to run errands and make deliveries for folks who didn't get out much or didn't have adequate transportation. The Stage even made regular runs delivering milk to the dairy for some of the small farmers in town. George made deliveries of food to Leon Severance about once a week. I don't believe he was ever allowed inside the house and George never talked too much about what he knew about Leon.

When Leon died, one or two of the selectmen and some county officials checked his house and inventoried the contents. They may have been the first to enter the house in many years. I can't imagine that too much of value was found and I don't know what became of Leon's belongings. Apparently, the inventory takers didn't talk too much about what they found. However, it may be that they found something quite unexpected in the attic. I was quite young when Leon died and was never told anything about what it was that they found. A few whispered comments and a word here and there told me that there was a story to be listened to if only somebody would tell it to me.

Finally, one day long after Leon died, I asked Jessie, "So, Mom, tell me what they found in that old guy's attic."

Jessie always had a talent for deftly steering a conversation in another direction when it approached a topic she wanted to avoid. "Hush up and run over to the garden and get me two big onions. I'm trying to cook supper and I'm all out of onions," she said.

When I returned with the onions I pressed the question again. Realizing that I wasn't going to give up easily, she sat me down in one of the kitchen chairs and looked at me with that stern "don't mess with the school teacher" look on her face.

"When you are older maybe your father will tell you what they found in that attic, but I never will," she told me in the stern tone of voice reserved for conveying the message that the conversation was over and was not to be reopened. Time passed and I forgot about Leon Severance, so I never did find out what his secret was in that old attic. If a reader of the book knows, I wish they would contact me.

The second "hermit" that I remember was John Howes. I presume he was related to the other Howes families in town, but he didn't seem to have a lot of contact with most of them. He lived in a large old rundown house just up the East Hill (Frizzell Hill) Road from where it intersected the Brattleboro

Road. The house had no phone, no electricity, and very likely no plumbing.

Like Leon Severance, John Howes lived totally alone and was not often seen. He was thin and of rather small stature with a very long gray beard that reached nearly to his belt buckle. His only method of transportation was "shank's mare" as Jessie called it. Every so often we would see him walking up the road past Zimmerman's toward our house. He always carried an empty burlap sack. His destination was usually George Howes' store where he would obtain a few supplies. Orilla and I would watch closely for him as he headed home with his now filled burlap sack slung over his shoulder. Orilla and I were sure he was really Santa Claus, but why was he so thin? In the winter to add to our confusion, he didn't drive a sleigh or even wear a red suit.

In spite of his love of solitude, and somewhat scary appearance, John liked to talk and tell stories to people he would meet along the way. Many of his stories had to do with his experiences fighting in the army. He claimed to have been a member of Teddy Roosevelt's Rough Riders in the Spanish American War. He also had stories about being gassed in the trenches in WWI. I have no idea how much, if any, of it was true. I suspect he just liked to tell stories, true or not. He seemed to especially like to talk with children, or maybe it was just that children would listen to him while many adults would not. We kids always liked to see him coming up the hill because he would always give us a few coins to purchase an ice cream cone at George's store. While giving out the coins he would always say in a sing-song voice "I scream, you scream. We all scream for ice cream."

Whenever she spotted us with him, Jessie would call us inside to tend to some real or imagined errand. She never allowed us to walk to the store with him. After he was headed home well past Zimmerman's barn we were then allowed to go get our cones.

Dottie Howes, George's wife, once told me that one time John Howes was doing something at his house and somehow broke a leg so badly that he could not walk. With no other means of transportation, and no phone, John started crawling. Going cross-country through the fields and pastures was a shorter route than following the roads so that's what he did. It probably made for easier crawling as well. The straight line distance from John's house to George's store was over half a mile. However, it was steeply uphill and he had to cross a couple of stone walls and several barbed wire fences along the way. Eventually, he reached the Center, crawled across the Greenfield Road, and made it to the store where he was loaded into a car and driven to the hospital in Greenfield.

After John died, the dilapidated house was purchased by Doug Barton. A tremendous amount of remodeling was required to make the place suitable for a family. June (Barton) Damond once told me that although she was quite young when they bought the house, one thing she remembered when first walking through it was that the only evidence of any toilet facilities was a hole in the kitchen floor.

Another unique individual I remember was Bert Whitney. I believe that Bert lived in Leyden all his life. Somewhere along the way he picked up the title "The Sage of Gore Hollow." I presume that "gore" refers to the Colrain Gore as described in Arms' book. The gore apparently was a piece of unclaimed land that sat between the Fall Town Township (Bernardston and eastern Leyden), and Boston Township #2 (Colrain) in the mid-1700s. Residents of the gore did not live in any township. Arms claims that nearly all of West Leyden was part of the gore.

Bert lived way back in the West Leyden hills down a road that wasn't much more than a pair of wheel tracks. It was still an official road, but I don't believe the town did any maintenance on it. If they did, there was little evidence. The only other thing I remember being on that road was the high power rifle range that belonged to the Leyden Rifle Club. The range had once been a rather nice facility, but it had pretty much fallen into disuse except for one weekend a year in the summer when the National Guard held their rifle qualifications there. In my later teen years I would often drive out to the range for some shooting practice. I always had the place to myself. The road passed very close to Bert's front door and frequently he would be sitting outside in a chair by the door as if he was expecting somebody to come by, although the average time between visitors must have been very long indeed. Sometimes I would stop and chat with him for a while, and listen to his stories.

Unlike Leon and John, I remember Bert having a vehicle of some sort. I think it was a beat up old truck. He would appear in the Center from time to time on his way to or from Greenfield and would stop at the shop to buy some gas or kerosene. I think Bert did a little farming because I remember the first time I ever met Bert was when I rode to his place with Henry to shoe Bert's workhorse. What I remember of Bert's house was that Leon's and John's looked like mansions in comparison to his. Although he lived more "off the beaten track" than Leon or John, Bert wasn't quite as socially secluded as they were. I remember him attending Old Home Day celebrations and even an occasional church or Town Hall event. He claimed to have participated in some mining operations in West Leyden during his younger years. The mines were located not far from his house and were rumored to have produced small quantities of metal ores including copper. It was said that some gold ore was uncovered also, but it is likely that it was actually iron pyrites or "fool's gold." But, since gold and copper are often found together, who knows?

In the winter time, Bert's only source of heat, other than his cook stove, was one or two kerosene-fired space heaters for which he purchased fuel at Henry's shop. The kerosene was taken home in a pair of rusty WWII Jerry cans. His heaters were the portable type that had no outside vent and discharged kerosene fumes and carbon monoxide into the room while consuming the room's oxygen. Over the years numerous people have been killed or suffered brain damage from the carbon monoxide given off by that type of heater. Even then they were known to be dangerous. They have been banned for many years now for good reason. Apparently Bert's old house was drafty enough that the fumes never reached the deadly level.

Bert's adult daughter Clara lived with him and from time

to time she would make her way to the church on Sunday. She would often ride along with Bert when he went somewhere and whenever he stopped at the shop, she would walk over to our house and ask Jessie for newspapers, magazines, or other readable items. She never cared how old the reading materials were, "No matter how old it is, I've never seen it before, so it's new to me," she would say.

One other individual deserving mention was Henry Farnum. He lived in an old house in the woods on Alexander Road, northwest of Beaver Meadow. His sisters, Lucy and May, lived with him. He did a little farming and sold firewood to nearby residents. In much the same manner as Leon, John, and Bert, Henry and his sisters lived without modern conveniences. In the late 1950s, the Farnum residence was one of the few remaining homes in Leyden still without electricity.

Some residents weren't quite as reclusive as the above examples, but they still resented being bothered by anyone no matter how good the cause. Sometimes we would learn the hard way just how much they resisted contact with others.

A common method of making money for non-profit organizations in those pre-curbside-recycling days was to have a paper drive or bottle collection. Glass bottles were not recycled in the 1950s; they were reused. Emptied bottles were returned to the bottling plant where the soda company or dairy would simply clean them and use them time and again. I wonder why they don't still do that today? Glass Coca-Cola bottles had the bottle's year of manufacture cast into the glass on the bottom. It wasn't unusual to be drinking a Coke from a bottle made 20 or 30 years earlier. Sometimes we would decide who was going to pay for the Cokes by the bottle dates. The kid with the newest bottle had to pay. Other times, as we sat around sipping our Cokes, we would speculate about where our bottles had been and wondered if anybody famous had ever drunk from them.

Small soda bottles carried a 2-cent refund, quart size was worth a nickel, and glass gallon milk jugs were worth a quarter. A truck load of bottles could result in some serious change for a church youth group or ball club. Paper collections weren't quite as profitable as bottles, but they were easier to deal with. Many people cashed in their bottles themselves, but you could usually talk them into donating paper to a fund raiser.

I remember one time that some group I belonged to was having a paper drive to raise funds for some cause or other. One of the parents owned a big dump truck and he was driving us around town in it after dark stopping at houses with lights on to request donations of old newspapers and/or magazines. We preferred magazines because their paper netted us more money per 100 pounds.

Several of us were riding in the back of the dump truck on top of the paper pile when the driver stopped in front of a house in West Leyden that had just one faint light showing at a window. I didn't know much about the owner except the rumors were that he was one of the more eccentric people in town. He had a reputation of becoming very angry for little reason. I would have preferred to have passed that house by, but the driver had stopped, so we decided to give it a try. Several of us piled off of the truck, ran up to the door and knocked.

"What the Hell do you want?" came a shout from inside.

One member of our group was in the middle of explaining who we were, and why we were there, through the closed door, when it was suddenly yanked open. A face with a long tobacco stained beard, and breath that could do a skunk proud, was suddenly thrust nearly nose to nose with our spokesman. The man let out a loud whistle followed by "Get em!"

Expecting to be attacked by dogs we turned and started to run back toward the dump truck when from around both ends of the house came about a dozen large white geese in full "honk." They easily caught up with us and began biting us with their long bills and slapping us with outstretched wings. We piled into the truck and I swear that dump truck burned rubber leaving the scene!

Chapter 11

THE CENTER

Week in, week out, from morn till night,
You can hear his bellows blow;
You can hear him swing his heavy sledge,
With measured beat and slow,
Like a sexton ringing the village bell,
When the evening sun is low.
Longfellow

The mountains, hills, or ridges (depending on your personal point of reference) that form Leyden run north-south from the Vermont line on the north to the Greenfield town line on the south. Geologists tell us that these were originally formed by buckling of the earth under pressure of plate tectonics (of course we didn't know that in the 1950s.) The glaciers of later ice ages ground off some of the high spots and scooped out the valleys (we did know about the glaciers, however.) Lateral moraines along the sides of the glaciers deposited huge boulders in sometimes odd locations. The result of all this geological shenanigans was the formation of three primary ridges in what would become Leyden. Much of the eastern ridge became known as East Hill, along with a few other names, and is the highest and steepest of the three. The western ridge became home to the loosely defined community of West Leyden. That ridge sloped away to the Green River which formed the boundary with Colrain to the west. Leyden Center, or the New Center, was established atop the center ridge and formed the heart of the town. If there was a Village of Leyden, that would be the Center.

Leyden Center was the place where all the town buildings were located except for the outlying schools. The original center was located on the eastern slope of the West Leyden ridge. Originally, the Old Center on the Old County Road, had one or more churches, houses and other buildings clustered around the Carpenter Tavern which still exists. I don't remember ever hearing any story as to why the center was moved, but around 1840 it was relocated. In the 1950s, all that remained of the Old Center was the tavern and one house where the Davis family lived.

Anyone driving into Leyden Center from Greenfield would approach from the south. The first house on the south edge of the Center belonged to Darwin Hine and family. It was very unique and was located on the east side of the road just before the hill leveled out. Darwin was a very talented individual with a wide range of skills. I remember the gorgeous coffee tables he used to make by hand from thick cross-sectional slabs cut from the stumps of large trees.

Darwin built the foundation for his house and roofed it over with what would normally be the first floor. Then they moved in. Living in the basement turned out to be not very bad, so it was many years before the upstairs was completed. He had the coolest house in the summer and an easy one to heat in the winter. His son Glen and I were very good friends although Glen was a few years younger than me. One day while playing at his house I fell out of an apple tree and knocked myself unconscious. When I awoke, I was inside, lying on a large table, with Glen's mother trying to wake me up. It was at least two or three days before I felt normal again.

Soon after graduating from high school, Glen entered the military and ended up with his name engraved on "The Wall," the Vietnam memorial in Washington. Of the over 58,000 Americans who lost their lives in that conflict, I believe Glen was the only one from Leyden. I never understood the reason for that war and why it was necessary for all those young Americans to die there. It, like Korea in the early 1950s, certainly set the pattern for a seemingly unending series of "no win," politically motivated, wars our country has engaged in ever since.

A bit farther north on the east side was George Howes' barn. By the 1950s, it was used only for storage. My grandfather's horse drawn wagon was pretty much worn out and George had a good one sitting in his barn. It had been there for a number of years. One day Grandpa, George, and Henry opened up the barn to check out the wagon. I went along because I had always been curious as to what was inside. After inspecting the wagon, a deal was struck and Henry towed the wagon to his shop where he converted it from a single pole, two horse hitch, to a double pole single horse setup.

Continuing northward, next came a series of houses on the left which were built quite close together. They sort of defined "downtown Leyden" although the east side of the road was a large cornfield. I always thought it was odd that those houses were so close together when all the other houses in town were well separated. They looked as if they had been lifted off a street in downtown Greenfield and dropped down in Leyden. The southernmost house, belonging to the Beaudoin family, was where Henry and Jessie first lived after they were married in 1929. The middle house, Newcomb's, had a large barn behind it, as I suppose they all did at one time. I once was told that the barn had been used to manufacture some sort of tools. Inside could still be found several examples of a large clamping device used to hold a handsaw while setting and sharpening it. None looked as if they had ever been used, so I assume the story was correct and that they had been manufactured in that barn, but never sold.

The last building in the row was the Howes home and general store. George's store was quite small, but many basic necessities such as soap, sugar, and flour could be obtained there. The chief necessity that I remember was ice cream. A few times a month after supper, Henry would give Orilla and me a few coins and send us to the store to buy dessert.

We would return with either a pint or a quart of ice cream, whichever the week's budget would permit. Henry loved ice cream and never saw any reason for the existence of any flavor other than vanilla. The only topping he ever used was a goodly slug of pure maple syrup. Soon after 1950, George closed what had been his family's store for many years. That made ice cream a much more infrequent treat at our house.

Originally there had been a fourth house in the row. The church parsonage used to sit at the north end close to the store. However, at some point in the past, church leaders decided they no longer could afford a resident minister for the tiny congregation, so the parsonage sat empty for a while. From then on, a shared minister would drive in from Bernardston to hold Sunday services. Bill and Doris Glabach, and family, rented the parsonage and lived there until one night in 1948 or 1949 when it caught fire and was totally destroyed. Later, George Howes bought the parsonage lot from the church, filled in the hole, and built an addition onto the house where he and his wife, Dottie, lived.

Not long ago, Dottie told me a story about how on one early spring day, Sonny Dobias arrived at the Newcomb house next to George and Dottie's with a spreader full of manure to apply to their neighbor's garden plot. The spreader was pulled by a team of large work horses. When Sonny was done with the spreading, he left the team and spreader parked in the driveway and went into the house to collect his payment. While he was inside the house, something spooked his horses and they took off running with the empty manure spreader bouncing along behind them. Instead of running down the road toward home as horses often will do, for some reason they started galloping in a circle around George and Dottie's house. Dottie happened to be outside at the time as were Harriet Hine and her kids, who were visiting.

As the horses charged around the northwest corner of the house, Dottie and Harriet pushed the kids tight up against the house to keep them safe. Opposite the north side was a large tree that had been taken down, but not yet cut up. The horses swung a little wide and the flying manure spreader caught the tree and hurled it toward the terrified women and kids. Luckily there was only one casualty. Dottie received a very badly broken leg, but Harriet and her kids were safe. Down the hill at the Zimmerman farm, Marion heard the commotion and realized something bad was happening. She immediately drove up to see what she could do to help and arranged for medical attention. Dottie spent the next eight weeks teaching school on crutches.

The parsonage site abutted the south side of Henry's vegetable garden, which is now the new Town Common. Across the road, between Zimmerman's cornfield and Henry's apple orchard was the Robertson Memorial Library built in 1913. I remember being told that it was a Carnegie Library. A Scottish immigrant, Andrew Carnegie, the steel giant, funded the construction of over 2500 libraries between about 1880 and 1929. His emphasis was on towns that did not have a library and could not otherwise afford one. It is claimed that very few needy towns were refused a construction grant when one was requested. Leyden may hold the record for having the smallest Carnegie Library in the world. Certainly it was, and is, one of the smallest free-standing public libraries anywhere. Once I learned to read, I was a regular visitor when the library was open on Saturday mornings. The librarian, Edith Howes, would help me select books, but many of the volumes were very old and I often had difficulty finding any that were of interest to me. The monthly visit of the Franklin County Book Mobile had much more modern offerings.

Next, on the left was Henry's shop, across the road from his apple orchard. Unless the weather was cold or stormy, the large doors on the south and east sides were usually wide open permitting everyone in the center to hear the ringing of the anvil as Henry worked. Continuing on, just past two huge ancient sugar maples on the right, was Henry and Jessie's house. Someone once told me that the house had been built in 1858. I have no idea if that is correct or not, but remodeling in the early 1950s, produced large quantities of old-fashioned cut nails that were the dominant type of nail used in the mid-1800s. What I do know is that there were a number of pioneer-style features. For example, the floor in the kitchen (which I suspect was the oldest part of the house) was not supported by sawn lumber. Instead, the joists were small diameter tree trunks or branches that had been flattened on the top side with an ax. When the upstairs was enlarged, much of the original roof was removed to add a dormer. A long, square, hand-hewn ridgepole was found which ran the length of the house. When that beam was removed and sold to a museum, it paid for much of the cost of the renovation.

Across the road was the original Town Common, a small, triangular piece of leftover land where three roads met. Most old New England towns had a common in the center of the village. These were sort of the original public parks. In most towns, the common served several purposes. As the name suggests, it was land that was shared by everyone in town.

The old Town Common and the church, in winter.

On Saturdays in the 18th century, in many towns the common was the mustering place for the local militia. If it was of sufficient size, during the week anyone was allowed to graze their sheep or cattle there. It must have been rather unpleasant doing marching drills on Saturday mornings after sheep and cows had inhabited the common all week. Leyden's common was so small that only a militia man or two would fit on it, and a single sheep would starve in short order. The common contained less than 300 square feet of grass, a granite boulder with a bronze plaque listing the names of all the Leyden participants in WWI, and a flagpole. The pole was about 25 feet high and was topped by a brass ball which, so I was told, was cast from expended shells picked up on a WWI battlefield. Because the common was just across the street from our house, our family assumed responsibility for mowing the grass, planting a few flowers in the spring, and flying the town flag on holidays. Orilla and I were assigned the task of running the US flag up that pole soon after sunrise. As tradition and respect required in those days, we made sure that the flag was taken down and properly folded shortly after sunset.

The ravages of time and weather had taken their toll on the flagpole and although it was still quite strong, it was in dire need of a paint job and a new rope. One summer day, when I was about 13 or 14, I decided to paint the pole. Henry had some aluminum paint left over from a recent project in the shop, so I grabbed it and a brush and headed for the common. The biggest problem was how was I going to get to the top of the pole? I returned to the shop and poked through some old pieces of harness and belting. I soon had a crude climbing rig assembled out of three belts. Critical junctions were reinforced with rivets using the brake lining machine in the garage. The first, and widest, belt was securely fastened around my waist. The other two belts were looped through the first one and fastened loosely around the flagpole. To climb, I wrapped my legs around the pole and leaned back to tighten one of the belts. The loose belt was then lifted upward and my weight shifted to that belt. Gradually, I made it to the top only to realize that my paint was still on the ground! So I polished the brass ball and returned to the ground for my paint. Once finished, the pole looked brand new and numerous residents complimented me on a job well done.

A short way to the north past the common was the Gerry residence on the left. Jessie bought the place one year when it was sold for taxes. Henry had approved of her buying it, but had made it very clear that it was her deal. He had enough things to worry about and was not going to have anything to do with a rental property. The Gerrys rented from her for many years before she eventually sold it to them. There used to be a small building to the south of the house that apparently had been a small store and post office. In the 1950s, you could still make out the very faint words "Post Office" painted on the front. Arms' map shows the name Vining as being the original residents at that location, and he lists Vinings as Leyden postmasters from 1861 - 1864, and 1866 - 1878, so I assume the house and small building dated from about that time or earlier.

Directly in front of the Gerry house, the Zimmerman Hill Road (not called that in the 1950s) turned sharply to the right and steeply down the hill. The Guilford Road (maps call it Greenfield Road today) continued straight ahead. In the center of that triangular intersection stood a gigantic American Elm tree which must have been several hundred years old. Like so many other elms, it eventually fell victim to the Dutch Elm disease.

Just north of the intersection on the right and across from the Gerry house was the site of the old cheese factory. It was built around 1870, and produced cheese from dairy products supplied by some of the local farmers. It wasn't a very profitable venture, however, and within a few years it went out of business. By the 1950s, there wasn't any of the building remaining other than some of the foundation. Poking around, one could find pieces of rusty equipment that I presume were original to the factory. You had to be careful though because there was a lot of broken glass due to the site having been used to discard numerous unwanted items over the years. Just a short distance down the hill, on the south side of the road, was the location of the original blacksmith shop that burned in the early 1920s.

Back at the common, if you turned westward up the hill, you were on the West Leyden Road. Very soon at the top of the hill you would come to a very small red brick building on the left with a solid iron door locked with a padlock. Some folks thought it was the town's original (only) jail. Actually, it was the town vault where all the official town records were kept. I don't know when the vault building was constructed. One story was that it was built as a fireproof location for records soon after the old Town Hall burned in 1929. Examination of the building would suggest it was considerably older than that. Henry always believed that it was on his land and that was fine with him. Before he moved away in the late 1980s, he donated or sold that tiny piece of land to the town. However, I recently came across a deed dated 1917 for land conveyed to Ed Howes for the piece of land where the new blacksmith shop was located. That deed refers to another deed dated 1887 containing the wording "except that part of said tract which Hart E. Mowry conveyed to the Inhabitants of the Town of Leyden for a location for the Town Vault." That seems to suggest that the land where the vault sat may have belonged to the town long before Henry was born.

Opposite the vault was the site of the old Town Hall (which burned in 1929) with the only church in town next door. The church was one of the oldest buildings in town, built in 1841. Across the road from the church, and just west of the blacksmith shop, was the new Town Hall which was built in 1932. Sitting south of the Town Hall was the fire station, built about 1958, and south of that was the shed where the road equipment was kept.

Going west just past the church, the single house on the left belonged to my Uncle Bill and Aunt Doris Glabach. When the parsonage where they had been living burned, Bill first built the adjacent garage. The family (Bill, Doris, and children Billy, April, and Mary) lived in it while building the house. The "Little House" as they called it, consisted of a single room partitioned by furniture and hanging blankets. A cook stove was the only source of heat, and bathroom facilities were in a privy out back. "Oh the beauty of being poor white trash and not knowing it," cousin Bill recently told me.

Down the hill, a bit on the left, was the old hearse house. It sat at the entrance to Judson Ewer's driveway. In the 1950s, the town used the building for general storage of items such as snow fencing. Originally it housed the town's horse drawn hearse which was long gone by the 1950s. According to Arms' book, in 1801 the town had voted to acquire a hearse to transport the deceased to the new town cemeteries that had been established. Previously, burials had taken place in private burial grounds, often on the property of the deceased's family. Sometime in the 1920s, with motorized vehicles all the rage, the horse drawn hearse was no longer used. With no longer any need for the hearse, and the town in need of storage space, the hearse was given to Arthur Howes, the road superintendent. It was broken up and rotted away. Henry used to talk about what a mistake it was for the town to get rid of that hearse. He said that it was very ornate with curved glass sides and was always in excellent condition. By the mid-1950s, it would have been a valuable antique.

Although there was no official definition of the boundaries of Leyden Center, it was more or less agreed that it ended somewhere just west of the Center School. The school was a half-mile or so down the hill past the hearse house just before the road started up the ridge that marked the start of West Leyden, which had no official boundaries either. The school sat more or less at the unofficial boundary between the Old Center which was located up the hill in the area around the Carpenter Tavern, and the New Center.

Chapter 12

TOWN HALL TALES

The local government of small New England towns, such as Leyden, in the 1950s, was the closest thing to a pure democracy this country has ever seen. There were no political parties vying for the opportunity to impose their self-serving agendas on the populace. The people voted directly on nearly everything of major importance, and many decisions were made at town meetings that were open to one and all to participate.

Many official positions were unpaid or received only token compensation. The *1958 Leyden Annual Report* lists 14 town officers. Those 14 were paid a total of $1630, for an average annual salary of just over $116 each. Obviously nobody ran for a public office in order to get rich! And, once out of office, there were no high paid lobbyist jobs, fat book deals, or cushy speaking engagements waiting. There were also a number of minor positions that really didn't amount to much such as fence inspector, inspector of barns and animals, inspector of slaughtering, tree warden, librarian, Town Hall janitor, etc. Many of the holders of these positions did so mainly out of a desire to help others and the town.

A copy of the annual report was provided to each Leyden family (or tax payer) and contained a wealth of information as to exactly how the town officers had spent the tax money they collected. Every dollar spent was accounted for. I even found my name in the 1958 edition showing that I was paid $22.00 as part of the gypsy moth control program.

Courtesy of Richard DiMatteo

The new Leyden Town Hall.

Once a year, the annual Town Meeting was held at the Town Hall. It was always held after the annual report had been sent out containing the selectmen's recommendations for expenditures for the coming year and listing other business to be conducted. Every adult resident of the town was encouraged to attend and participate in the discussions. A goodly percentage did exactly that. These were real town meetings, not the glorified political rallies with prepared questions and answers that get passed off as town meetings during campaigns these days. Real binding decisions were made about important issues and how tax money was to be spent. Residents were also welcome to bring up topics that were not on the posted agenda and the elected officials actually listened. Decisions were made by the people who would pay the taxes that created the funds that paid the bills. What a concept! What ever happened to the America our founders created? If that America still exists anywhere, I'd bet on it being alive and well in Leyden.

The town meetings were conducted by the town moderator. The moderator's job was simply to officiate the meeting, make sure proper procedures were followed, and order was maintained. In the 1950s, I remember George Howes or Edric Cook being moderator most years. After the business meeting ended, voting was done by secret ballot for selectmen and other major town offices.

Some years there would also be a special town meeting in addition to the annual meeting. A special meeting might be called by the selectmen to resolve an issue that couldn't wait for the regular meeting or might take too much time to be conducted along with the town's regular business. A special meeting might be called to appropriate money to buy necessary equipment or transfer money from the general fund to some other worthy purpose.

Most of the day-to-day business of the town was supervised by the committee of three elected selectmen. Each held a three year term with one of the terms expiring every year. Custom generally dictated that the senior member of the board was the chairman. They supervised the rest of the town employees, oversaw distribution of funds, and basically represented the town in nearly all aspects. Some of the leading citizens held office for many years.

The job of constable was rather unique. Anyone familiar with British law might think that the office of Leyden Town Constable was a law enforcement position, but it really wasn't, at least not in the sense of public safety. It was more of a civil process server position. The constable would serve summonses, subpoenas, eviction notices, and warrants. In Leyden the primary function seemed to be to post the selectmen's warrants, especially to publicize the Town Meeting and its agenda. I don't know if it is still on the books, but Massachusetts law used to identify one duty of a constable as follows: "Shall take due notice of and prosecute all violations of law respecting observance of the Lord's Day, profane swearing, or gambling."

For many years Spencer Howes was the Leyden constable. He was also the sealer of weights and measures and as such had to annually verify the accuracy of commercial measuring devices such as the gas pumps at Barton's and the Leyden Garage. One day, when I was assisting him in doing this, I asked him about the duties of the Town Constable. I was particularly interested in any law enforcement responsibilities he might have. He told me that as far as he was concerned he didn't really have any enforcement authority at all. In response to my question about whether he had a gun, he said that he had a rusty old .32 somewhere, but he wasn't sure if it still worked or not. He added that even if it did, the ammunition he had for it was so old it probably wouldn't fire.

George Howes was the tax collector and Harold Campbell was the Town Treasurer in addition to being Town Clerk for many years. Most residents simply sent George a check for their taxes, but every year George had to do some in-person arm twisting to "get the blood out of a few turnips." One time after an especially difficult tax extracting session, George arrived at Harold's house to hand over the tax receipts. It was a cold day, and expecting to be inside for just a few minutes, he left his car running to keep it warm. Sitting on the front seat was a large box of fresh eggs that he had just purchased from a farmer. Exiting the house, George found that his car had rolled down the driveway, crossed the road and done a nose dive into the ditch. Little damage was done to the car and Harold soon had it back on the road thanks to his John Deere tractor. The inside was a different story. For weeks thereafter, no matter where they went or what the weather was, George and Dottie drove with all the windows open to slightly relieve the odor of rotten eggs!

Almost every year, Henry was asked by town residents if he would run for selectman, but he always turned it down even though he was always very involved with the affairs of the town. He said he was honored to be asked, but that he didn't possess the necessary people skills for the job. He was a cut-to-the-chase kind of guy, not a wheeler-dealer or administrator. Privately he would admit that there were really two other reasons he didn't want to be a selectman. First, he got a lot of gas and equipment repair business from the town and that he felt it would be a conflict of interest for him to be a selectman. Second, he felt it was important for concerned citizens to keep a watchful eye from outside the official town government. "We can't expect the selectmen to always do everything and always do it right," he would say. "A citizen has a greater responsibility than to just pay taxes."

The official office of the selectmen was in a small room on the first floor of the Town Hall just off the dining room. It had its own wood stove for heat. The furniture consisted of a large table and several uncomfortable wooden chairs obviously designed to keep meetings short. One wall of the room was totally taken up by a very large wood cabinet. The front of the cabinet consisted of two large doors fastened by a hasp and padlock. I was always curious about what was in that cabinet and asked Henry what he knew about it. He responded that, although he had been the Town Hall janitor for many years, he had never seen that cabinet opened. He presumed that the selectmen had the key to it, but he had no idea why it was locked or what was in it.

What was in that cabinet? What was so valuable or secretive that it needed to always be locked away? Moreover, why didn't Henry, who knew just about everything about the town, know what was inside? Or, was it a secret and he wasn't telling? As youthful curiosity will often insist, one day I just had to have an answer. I could have simply asked one of the selectmen, but that was too simple. And, if it was really a secret, they might not tell me anyway. I needed to see for myself. I had noticed that the hasp was not properly installed and had the screws exposed to the outside. Making sure that nobody was around, I went to the shop and found a screwdriver of the correct size. Armed with my trusty screwdriver, I proceeded to remove the screws from the hasp, leaving the padlock still locked in place. Slowly opening the large doors I discovered a huge two pan balance and accompanying weights and accessories. Everything seemed to be made of brass. A large lever in the front lifted the balance arm off the rests so that objects could be weighed.

Overall it greatly resembled a gigantic 2-pan laboratory balance or something you would see at the assay office in a western movie. I never found out the purpose of the balance, or why Leyden had it. Until writing this I have never told anyone that I had broken into the cabinet and knew what was inside. I assume it was used somehow by the sealer of weights and measures and may have been standard equipment for all New England towns.

The first floor of the Town Hall also contained the kitchen and dining room which were the facilities for all of the church suppers. The dining tables were nothing fancy, simply built from construction lumber. One end of the kitchen contained the largest wood burning stove I have ever seen. It looked like the huge stoves you see in some old hospital photos from the Civil War, and maybe it was. Most of the cooking and baking was done on that cast iron, fire belching behemoth, no matter what the season. To the right was a small propane fired gas stove that was added sometime in the 1950s. The gas stove was hailed as a big improvement since it kept the kitchen much cooler than the wood stove during the summer months and could be fired up much faster. I never trusted that gas stove because it seemed to me that ever since it was installed there was an odor of gas in the kitchen whether the gas stove was being used or not.

There was no running water in the building. Whenever a supper was to be held, one or more farmers would deliver 40-quart milk cans full of water. Water for dishwashing was heated on the huge wood stove and carried to the large sink for washing. Waste water from the sink simply dumped onto the ground outside and ran down the dirt road making the area around the kitchen door rather muddy. It must have been sometime in the 1960s when a well was drilled at a site Henry dowsed near the woodshed.

Since there was no running water in the Town Hall, there were no flush toilets either. There was a women's restroom just off the dining room and a men's that was accessed from outdoors on the west side of the building. Both contained smelly chemical toilets that amounted to a toilet seat above a large bucket containing a strong disinfectant. The most disagreeable job at the Town Hall was cleaning those toilets. The bucket had a large handle like a pail. The full bucket was carried into the trees behind the building, dumped into a hole and covered over. The bucket was rinsed, replenished with disinfectant and reinstalled in the toilet. I always tried to arrange to be elsewhere when it was time to empty those buckets.

The main hall was on the second floor along with a coat closet and a ticket booth. The floor was made of narrow maple boards that would get sprinkled with a special wax for dances. For town meetings, Christmas parties, graduations, and other events requiring seating, rows of wood folding chairs would be set up facing the stage. There were some single chairs, but most units consisted of three chairs with fold-up seats attached to a single frame. From the time I was old enough to move those heavy chairs, one of my jobs was to set them up for meetings, or to take them down for dances. The worst thing was to have to carry them up or down the stairs since many times they were stored in the dining room.

One end of the main hall consisted of the stage with an entrance door at each end. The stage curtain was of the old-fashioned roll-up type. One had to be very careful raising the curtain or one end would roll up faster than the other, resulting in the whole thing binding to a stop when about half open. This would sometimes result in considerable laughter from the audience that had a view of only the feet and legs of the performers doing their thing behind the half-raised curtain.

In the early 1950s, the Town Hall was still the site of numerous entertainment activities by and for the residents of the town. There were frequent Saturday night square dances and performances by various local singing and acting groups were fairly common. The schools put on their music programs there every year and, of course, the eighth grade graduation ceremonies. Once or twice a year there would be a play, minstrel show, or vaudeville show put on by local residents. From time to time, an auction of unwanted, but still functional, items was held as a fund raiser. It was always fun to bid on the box lots, the contents of which were undisclosed. You could often win a box for a bid of a quarter or 50 cents and then take it outside and dump it out to see what treasures you had purchased. One time several of us guys each won a box lot. We took out whatever items we wanted, scrambled the remains back into the boxes and turned them back in to be auctioned off again. I remember a time that one of us bought the same junk twice except inside different boxes.

A different type of auction altogether was a box social. The girls and ladies would seal all the components of a meal for two into a cardboard box along with a slip of paper containing her name. Then the box was decorated in whatever fashion the cook wished. Nobody was supposed to know which fancy box contained food cooked by which girl or lady. At the event, the men in attendance would bid on the boxes. Once a bidder won a box, he was forbidden from bidding on any others. He then opened the box to find out who his dinner partner would be. I can remember attending only one box social. It seemed like a very risky event to me. What if I didn't like the food inside? What if I ended up having to have dinner one with the mother of one of my friends? After the early 1950s, as TV became more common, and access to more professional entertainment was easier, the entertainment use of the Town Hall declined significantly.

There was an old upright piano that saw frequent use for all sorts of events in the hall. Depending on what was going to go on, the proper location for the piano would be either on the stage or in a corner of the main hall floor. Now this was not your lightweight modern day electronic piano, but a full-fledged wooden upright with a heavy cast iron frame. There was no ramp or other device to facilitate moving the piano on or off the stage. Brute force was the only method available. Moving the piano between the stage and floor was no mean feat for two or three strong men.

Late one afternoon, Jessie suddenly realized that the event that was going to occur in the Town Hall that evening required the piano to be on the stage. Unfortunately it was on the main floor at the time and would need to be relocated, and soon. Henry was not back from shoeing. Bill was not available and neither was George Howes, George's brother, Cliff, nor anyone else she had called upon to do the task previously. In desperation, she walked over to the Gerry house and talked with Lee Gerry about her problem. Lee was not what you would call a muscular person. Rather, he was of the thin, wiry body type, but his strength was noted to be out of proportion to his size. He always claimed that a bit of "liquid reinforcement" made him a lot stronger.

Lee agreed to help move the piano if Jessie could come up with somebody to help him. As he began walking toward the Town Hall to look the situation over, Jessie told him she would send him some help as soon as she could locate someone. After several more phone calls, she had exhausted all the possibilities she could think of. Everyone she tried was either not home or had some excuse for avoiding wrestling with that heavy piano. She went up to the hall to give Lee the bad news and see if there was a way to rearrange the room leaving the piano where it was on the main hall floor. Like it or not, for that evening's event, the piano was just going to have to be off the stage.

When she arrived, she was astonished to find the piano sitting on the stage. Also sitting on the edge of the stage with his feet on the main floor was Lee Gerry partaking of some "reinforcement."

"Oh, wonderful!" Jessie exclaimed. "Who stopped by to help you?"

"Nobody," Lee replied

"Well, how in the world did you ever get that heavy piano up on the stage all by yourself?" she asked

"This was all the help I had right here," he said, raising his bottle of "reinforcement."

Now anyone who knew Jessie at all knew that she held a very strong negative opinion of adult beverages, especially while their consumption was underway. But this time she had met her match. Lee Gerry and his "reinforcement" had saved the day for her.

"Thank you, Lee," she said. "But I think you really ought to finish that outside."

Chapter 13

COUNTRY ROADS
MAY NOT TAKE ME HOME

If a typical Leyden resident in the 1950s, had been asked if there was anything he or she disliked about the town, it is likely that the emphatic response would have been, "The roads!" It was bad enough that many of the roads might be blocked by snowdrifts for days during the winter, and the same ones might be impassible during Mud Season. To add to the agony, during the warm months there were potholes, wheel ruts, wash boarding, and loose gravel to be navigated. Presumably to avoid litigation, many of the passable roads were posted: "Road Under Construction Travel at Your Own Risk." Some roads had those black on white signs posted in the exact same locations for several years with little, if any, evidence of any construction activity. Even the partially paved road up from the Greenfield line was subject to frost heaving, broken asphalt, expanding tree roots, and just plain roughness. To compound the agony, many stretches of road were so narrow in places that if two vehicles met, one would have to pull over and stop so the other could continue.

The reason for the condition of the roads was strictly monetary. The few households in town simply could not afford to pay the taxes it would require to maintain everything in good condition. Being one of the lowest population towns in the state didn't help either when the state handed out money. The 1958 Leyden Annual Report lists 25 named roads. Of these, six did not incur any maintenance expenses and were probably abandoned, but still on the books. Other than in, or near, the Center, few if any roads and intersections were supplied with identifying signs. If you lived there, you probably knew the name of your road, but others who had lived nearby all their lives might not know the official name of it. Many mailing addresses were simply "RFD Bernardston, Leyden, Mass." and it was expected that the mailman would know where you lived.

Most years the town's "road gang" consisted of only three men that constituted the only full time employees of the town. For quite a few years in the 1950s, Austin Dobias was the "road boss." Others on the crew, at least from time to time, included Earnest Brooks, Johnny Wells, and Sonny Dobias. Earnest was a descendant of one of Leyden's early pioneering families. The Brooks family went way back in the history of the town. They lived part way up East Hill on a branch road to the south that today is appropriately named Brooks Road. Earnest started out as a tractor driver and eventually became the road boss.

Short of manpower, always short of money, and lacking anything resembling proper equipment, the road gang had their hands full just doing essential repairs. In the early 1950s, the only road equipment the town owned was a Caterpillar D4 bulldozer tractor and a manually operated road grader that was pulled behind the Cat. Every spring after Mud Season, the worst of the unpaved roads were graded with that equipment to fill in pot holes, improve drainage, and reduce the wash boarding. One worker would slowly drive the bulldozer. At the rear of the grader, another worker, usually Earnest, would twirl large controls resembling ship's wheels raising and lowering the ends of the grader blade and changing its angle.

Going into the 1950s, the town did not own any trucks. The first truck obtained was a four-wheel-drive, gasoline powered, Ford dump truck. In addition to road repair work in the summer, that Ford truck took over a lot of the snowplowing duties from the D4 in the winter. If gravel was to be hauled, the town would hire local farmers and their trucks or contract with a sand and gravel company to do the hauling as well as supplying the material. For major road improvements, the town depended on money from the state when it was available. Along with state money came state controlled engineering, planning, and management of the projects with the town playing a minor role.

An ongoing project for many years was to pave the road from the Greenfield line to Leyden Center. Each year the pavement would be extended a little farther north. How much farther was determined by the available funds. In addition to just paving, the road was also widened where possible, and some curves tamed, as the work progressed. Every summer another segment would be paved and finally it reached the common opposite Henry and Jessie's house. Unfortunately, the chip-seal type of paving used was not a cure-all. It did reduce the dust, and for a few years provided a smoother driving surface, but soon cracks and potholes started appearing. One visitor to Henry's shop pointed out emphatically that, in his opinion, the Main Road was in better shape when it was just gravel.

With the paving stopped at the common, everyone in town was expressing their opinion as to which way the paving should continue the next summer. It seemed that everyone stopping at the shop that year had a firm opinion of where the paved road should go. Some felt the paving should continue northward to the Vermont border less than 2.5 miles away. Others believed it should go into Beaver Meadow and then on to Bernardston. Still others felt that the thing to do was to connect The Center to West Leyden via a paved road. Naturally, the part of town that a person lived in had a huge influence on their opinion.

Finally the decision was made that the paving should continue toward West Leyden with the ultimate goal of reaching the Colrain line at the Green River Bridge. Imagine: a paved road all the way from Greenfield through Leyden Center to Colrain. It was almost like the first transcontinental railway, but without a gold spike!

Chapter 14

MUD SEASON

Every winter, as the sun resumed its march northward and the days gradually lengthened, the snowstorms became smaller and less frequent, but more wet. Sometime in late February or March, the break point was reached when the winter's accumulated snow began melting faster than the spring storms could replace it. This was the harbinger of every school boy's dream: Mud Season!

In the early 1950s, nearly all of Leyden's roads were dirt or gravel. Even in the middle of summer, many roads were not well maintained due to the town's budget, equipment, and manpower limitations. Some of the narrowest roads consisted of little more than one set of wheel tracks with little or no width for passing even when the roads were dry. Add in the difficulty of huge water puddles and deep mud holes, and meeting an oncoming vehicle could turn into a major springtime adventure!

After seemingly unending weeks of winter, all the snowplowing had resulted in several feet of snow piled up along the roadsides. Untold tons of the white stuff waited to be melted in the fields and hills, which generally sloped downward toward the road, adding to the accumulation of water and mud in the roadways. Early in Mud Season, the dirt and gravel roads became saturated with water, but the mud and water would freeze solid overnight. This would help to make the roads passable in the morning until they melted, although the frozen mud ruts could destroy a car's alignment or roll a tire off a rim. Sometimes a car's wheels would drop down into a set of frozen ruts and the car would follow those ruts, just like a locomotive follows railroad tracks, regardless of which way the driver turned the steering wheel.

As the sun moved northward, and days grew longer, this arctic-like world gradually warmed. Water and ice began to melt and frozen mud turned into a thick brown soup. The melting started in the road itself because the sun heated the exposed rocks and dark dirt faster than it did the white snow on the roadsides. Often the water that melted in the road had nowhere to go because snow banks still blocked the drainage at the roadsides and culverts were still plugged with ice. So the water flowed into potholes and wheel ruts and sat there to be joined by even more water as more snow melted. As water accumulated in the road, puddles would often extend from bank to bank. To the inexperienced, or those with a low clearance vehicle, Mud Season presented numerous opportunities to get stuck right smack in the middle of the road and usually in a huge puddle or mud hole. Getting stuck presented an opportunity to get to know one or more fellow residents when you sloshed to the nearest farm to ask the farmer to pull your car out of the mud with his horse or tractor.

For us school kids, Mud Season was Leyden's version of Spring Break. We never knew exactly when it would occur from one year to the next, but the school calendar always allotted several days or even as much as a couple of weeks off for Mud Season. It wasn't that the teacher's wanted a vacation in Florida or Mexico. Rather, nobody could count on getting the teachers and kids to and from school through all the water and mud. So the town basically hunkered down and waited for the melting to subside and the roads to dry out, at least a little.

It was a busy time for the road gang. They went all over town draining huge puddles, filling potholes and washouts, opening up frozen culverts, and trying their best to respond to an unending list of requests for road repairs. Along the way they pulled numerous cars out of the mud receiving only a "Thank You" for their efforts.

I always enjoyed Mud Season. Not only because there was no school, but because I really enjoyed experiencing the transition from winter to spring. One of the most fun activities for me was playing in the puddles and small streams created by the melting snow. For days, our front yard would resemble the drainage system of the Mississippi River. I built dams, sailed boats, and created canals from one puddle to another. With this hands-on experience, I probably learned much more about hydrology and fluid flow than I did years later in engineering school.

Once the snow was mostly gone, everything started to rapidly green up. Spring bulbs popped up in people's yards and the farmers began getting out in their fields again. Cattle and horses that had been cooped up in barns all winter ran and chased each other, thoroughly enjoying their new freedom and the taste of the first green grass of the season. High on each dairy farmer's priority was to clean out the barn from all the manure and used bedding that had accumulated over the winter. Manure was loaded into a tractor-pulled spreader and used to fertilize the hay and cornfields so that there would be a good crop of cattle feed in the months ahead. Today I guess that would be called recycling.

Finally the day arrived when our mothers said we could stop wearing long underwear! Long johns were standard equipment for most of us from about Halloween until after Mud Season. There was no question that they kept us warmer, but they never seemed to fit just right and your legs felt sort of numb as you walked. One of the worst parts was that you had to be sure to give yourself plenty of lead time before heading toward the restroom, or outhouse (yes, there were still some outhouses in Leyden in the 1950s)! Each kid only had a couple sets and by mid-February they were getting rather thin. I was lucky to be allergic to wool, so I wore the cotton kind and didn't have to put up with the months long itching that many other kids had to deal with.

With the disappearance of long johns, normal bed sheets

139

made their annual reappearance. About the same time in the fall that Jessie gave the long johns edict, she started making up the beds with flannel sheets. As a rule, bedrooms were unheated, or nearly so. Admittedly, the flannel felt a lot warmer to slide into than the smooth sheets, but I never cared for the fuzzy feeling.

Mud Season was followed soon by another schoolboy's delight: Fishing Season! The Leyden boys always looked forward to April 1 as much as they did December 25. That was the opening day of fishing season. By early March, the talk at recess was usually about plans for where we were going to be headed on opening day. If it fell on a weekday, attendance at school would be sparse indeed. The teachers usually understood, so we didn't have to fake an illness. Most of the fishing streams in town were small, as were the fish in them, but we still had loads of fun trying to catch our limit of 12 trout a day.

Most of us didn't have a store-bought fishing pole, so in the days leading up to the start of the season, we would scour the woods looking for the perfect hardwood sapling to carve this year's first fishing pole. It had to be thin and whippy yet strong. We would use our pocketknives to trim off all the twigs and peel the bark. Sometimes we would drill a small hole through the pole near the tip and thread the line through it and back to the handle end. This gave the option of easily changing the length of line. Most of the time, however, we simply tied a length of string or fishing line to the smaller end and attached an Eagle Claw hook to the other end. Pinch on a split lead shot or two and you were done.

Much of the day before the season opened was spent in the garden, or in another moist soil area, digging for night crawlers and worms. Sometimes you could get a good can of worms with just a little digging and other times it seems you turned over enough dirt to plant a cornfield and still came up short. Sometimes a good batch of night crawlers could be caught by soaking a patch of dirt around sunset and then coming back after dark with a flashlight to pick up the wigglers that had come to the surface. The crawlers breathed air through their skin and when their tunnels became flooded they came to the surface to dry out a bit and get some air. At least that's the story we told each other.

One time a middle-aged fisherman, I'll call him Leroy, had an idea for how to improve the soaked dirt process and speedup the harvest of night crawlers and worms. His plan was to drive them to the surface by the application of electricity. I think he may have read about such a scheme in a fishing magazine and wanted to give it a try. Anyhow, one day Leroy let it be known that he was going to "plug in" his yard that evening. That was not to be missed!

After supper, we went to check on the activity at Leroy's. A small audience had gathered there to watch the show. First, Leroy thoroughly soaked a patch of ground with water to which he had added a small amount of salt. "The salt is there to make the water conduct electricity better," he explained to his new fan club.

While he waited for the water to penetrate the ground, he drove two metal rods into the earth a few feet apart in the wetted area. He then attached a wire from one end of an electrical cord to each rod and ran the other end into the house where he plugged it into a 115 volt outlet. He returned with a pail in hand expecting to harvest his crop. However, after several minutes of waiting, not one worm or crawler had appeared.

Leroy disappeared back into the house to discover that all he had accomplished was to blow a fuse. "I know how to fix that problem," he said. Leroy returned to the lawn and moved his metal rods a little farther apart while explaining to us that this would reduce the current flow. Then, just to insure that he didn't blow another fuse, he pulled a penny out of his pocket and inserted it behind the screw-in fuse saying, "Let's see you blow that!"

With current now flowing from the 115 volt source (thanks to the penny), a wait of several minutes still produced no crawlers or worms, and luckily no smoke or flames from the overloaded circuit. Onlookers offered all sorts of advice as to why no wigglers were appearing. A popular theory was that the electricity needed to be DC current not AC, and that Leroy should try a car battery. Several observers commented that a car battery would also be a lot safer. Others suggested that the voltage was too low and that a higher voltage might drive the worms out of their hiding places. Leroy agreed that higher voltage was worth a try and disappeared into the house again. He emerged after a few minutes looking more confident than ever. "This oughta do the trick," he said, "I've got it tied into the power for the electric water heater. Let's see what those buggers think of 240 volts!"

Sure enough, within a few minutes several good sized worms and crawlers were seen to be wiggling out of their muddy holes. Overjoyed, Leroy stepped into the wetted ground and set down his pail to commence the harvest. By the way, did I mention that the pail he was carrying was made of metal? Leroy grabbed the first couple of wigglers he saw and dropped them into the pail without incident. Spotting a large crawler just emerging from the ground, he leaned forward to pick it up with one hand while balancing himself with the other hand on the rim of the metal pail which was sitting on the wet ground. The 240 volts instantly fried the crawler so that it blew like a fuse possibly saving Leroy's life. I swear Leroy got off that wet ground onto dry earth without ever setting down another foot. We all shared a good laugh at Leroy's expense and agreed that the old shovel method was the best way to go.

My most frequent fishing stream was the one that flowed down off the hill behind the farmhouse where my grandparents lived. It crossed under the Brattleboro Road and then flowed across the hay field ending up in a large swampy area at the base of a wooded hill where it joined another stream. It wasn't very wide and in the hot days of summer, it would nearly dry up. But, in the spring it had a good flow and the population of brookies was usually pretty good even though it was quite a ways from any brook large enough for the Division of Wildlife to bother stocking. To be legal a trout had to be at least 6-inches long. No need to carry a ruler. I had measured from the tip of my middle finger of my left hand to a fold line on my wrist and found the distance to be exactly 6-inches. The rule was "If you catch it, you clean it," but Jessie was always very willing to add trout to the menu for that night's supper.

One spring I was invited to spend a few days with my Uncle Alvin Wood and Aunt Alwina. Alvin worked in the Standard Oil office in Pittsfield and they had a home directly on Cheshire Lake. Since most of my fishing experience so far had been on streams that I could just about step across, visions of fishing from a boat on a real lake and catching huge fish danced in my head. As a going away gift, Henry presented me with a genuine store-bought fishing pole and reel, the first I ever owned.

Shortly after I arrived Friday evening, Uncle Alvin took me out in his row boat to give the lake a try. We only caught a couple of small perch and a few bluegills, but at least they were different from the brook trout I was used to. Alvin showed me how to descale them, something that I had never had to do before with my trout. Saturday and Sunday's results were about the same. Uncle Alvin had to work on Monday, and since I was forbidden to use the boat alone, I was limited to fishing from shore all day.

In one area there was a pretty good sized patch of lily pads within an easy casting distance from shore and Alvin had told me stories about people catching big bass near lily pad areas. In my tackle box were several floating bass lures that I had never tried. The only thing I had ever used was a worm or night crawler so I decided to give a bass lure a try.

My first cast landed in the lily pads and when I reeled it in there was a good sized lily pad water skiing along behind. After a few more casts with similar results, I finally got the hang of making the lure land near the pads, not in them. It was cast out, reel in, cast out, reel in. Unlike worm fishing, the idea was to keep the bass lure moving so it resembled a swimming minnow.

"What happened?" I suddenly asked myself. Just as the lure hit the surface of the water something grabbed it and pulled the line very tight. My fishing pole bent nearly double and then popped out of the handle. At the same time, the line broke. I was left standing on the shore holding nothing but the handle of my new fishing pole. The rest of the outfit was skipping across the tops of the lily pads being towed along by whatever struck my lure.

That was my new fishing pole and I wasn't about to lose it. Uncle Alvin's rule about not touching the boat while he was gone was forgotten. I unchained it and rowed out into the lily pads to where I last saw my fishing pole. Naturally, as I was poking around in the pads with an oar, Alvin came home and not too gently reminded me of the rule about not touching the boat.

I had two more days at the lake and I was back to fishing with a stick and string. When my folks arrived to take me home, I was telling them my story about "the pole that got away" when Uncle Alvin presented me with a brand new pole, identical to the one I had lost.

For many Leyden residents, spring meant it was time to plant the vegetable garden. Nearly every house in town had some version of a garden. Some contained only a few tomato plants while others might be home to 20 to 30 different varieties of vegetables. Henry always planted a large garden located south of his shop between the dirt road from the Town Shed and the old parsonage lot. When he retired and moved away years later, the land where his garden had been for 50 years or more was purchased by the town to use as a Town Common. That seems like a good use for the land that Henry spent so much of his spare time working for much of his life.

Henry hated all the rocks in his garden and as a boy I spent countless hours throwing them out of his planting area into piles along the sides. The odd thing was that the next year just as many rocks would still need to be removed. Henry's theory was that chunks kept breaking off of the ledge rock below and winter's frosts worked them to the surface. There were so many rocks that as the years passed, the planting area shrunk in size, surrounded by a low rock border. One year Henry bought a garden tractor with a rotary tiller attachment from the Montgomery Ward store in Brattleboro. He planned on using it to "plow" his own garden, but after using it a few times he decided that the rotary action brought too many rocks to the surface. He later modified an old horse drawn cultivator to pull behind the garden tractor and that was quite successful.

While my Grandpa Wood was alive and living on Henry's farm, once or twice during the growing season when the weeds were going strong, Henry would borrow Frank's horse and cultivator to cultivate his garden. Henry's garden always had a bumper crop of weeds and the cultivator was dragged through the dirt between the rows digging out a lot of the weeds as it went. I was less than 10 years old and cultivating days were the high points of my spring. We would go down to the farm in Henry's truck where Frank's horse, Pat, would be harnessed up and the cultivator placed in the truck. Henry would drive back home to the garden leaving me to ride Pat from the farm the mile or so to the garden. After the cultivating was done, I rode Pat back to the barn, just like Roy Rogers.

Most years, Casper or Phil Zimmerman would plow and harrow the garden space for Henry in exchange for some equipment repairs or just because they knew he needed it done. They would often spread a load of manure too which has always been one of the secrets to a successful garden. Memorial Day was usually spent getting the seeds into the ground. That was a little later than many people planted, but the soil was warm enough by then for good germination. Some seeds, such as beans, would just rot in the ground if the dirt was too cold. Henry did not believe in fertilizing the entire garden, "No sense helping the weeds to grow," he would say. Instead, he would prepare each row extra deep and sprinkle in powdery "commercial" fertilizer. Then he would use the handle of his hoe to work the fertilizer into the soil, cover that over with other soil and proceed to plant his seeds. Most of the time, this method worked very well.

One year, Henry was very proud that he had all his seeds planted before the end of May. "We'll have some terrific early vegetables this year" he said. It was a family tradition that once the garden was planted, each evening after supper, we all would wander over to see what had popped up that day and make bets on what was going to make its appearance next. But that year, the rows showed no progress, day after day. Even the radishes, which were always the first to shove the rocks and pebbles aside to spread their leaves to the sun, were nowhere in sight. Henry's joy of days before was replaced with a growing concern. As we slowly walked back to the house one night, trying to convince ourselves that tomorrow many rows would surely sprout their green shoots, Henry was totally quiet. As we approached the huge maple trees at the edge of the driveway, he suddenly stopped. "Ray," he said, "get two empty tin cans and a little water and meet me in the shop."

A few minutes later I found Henry in the shop near the big drill press running the fine, gray, contents of a large unmarked paper sack through his fingers. Nearby was a second sack containing a similar appearing gray powder. "I bet I used the wrong bag," he said. "Put a little from this bag into one can, add some water, and stir it with a stick. Then do the same with the other bag."

"Why?" I asked. "What's the difference? They both look pretty much the same to me."

"That's what we are going to find out. Add just enough water to make up a thick paste in each can."

After I did as instructed, we set each can beside its bag, locked the shop and went home. "In the morning we'll take a look at what's in those cans," Henry said.

In the morning, I was up long before breakfast. I grabbed the shop key and ran over to check the cans. Henry was close behind me. Running up to one can, I found that it still contained a wet sludge with some of the material settled to the bottom and a thin layer of water on top. The second can contained a hard gray mass that I couldn't push a screwdriver blade into.

"What's the difference?" I asked

"Just like I suspected," Henry replied. "That bag contains cement. Maybe I used the wrong bag."

Chapter 15

CROSSING THE BOG

One summer, in my late teens, I worked as a member of the Leyden road gang. I drove my shiny black 1956, Ford Victoria back and forth to work every day. Since I had some surveying experience, I became the designated interface with the survey crew staking the changes to the right of way for the latest section of the improved road to West Leyden. As the representative of the state government, which was paying most of the bills, the state engineer had much of the say as to where the route would go and how it would be constructed. Simply widening an existing roadway wasn't a terribly challenging engineering job and wouldn't attract the attention of his higher-ups, leading to raises and promotions. However, the Leyden hills, ridges, and streams frequently overruled the engineer and pretty much determined where the road must go. In most cases, that was exactly where the existing road already ran, much to the engineer's disgust.

Just east of the Wiles farm was a unique piece of terrain. Arms' book calls it Peleg's Bog, but I never heard it called that, just "The Bog." Nearly everyone in town knew of it and had heard the stories told about its past. The existence of a bog requires a low spot with higher ground on all sides. There has to be a reliable source of water on at least one side, either from a small stream or a spring, and a narrow weir-like outlet opposite creating a very slow flow of water through the depression. Most bogs used to be lakes or ponds that over the eons filled in with sediment and layer upon layer of dead and decaying vegetation. Water oozes slowly through the thick bed of material creating a deep layer of viscous, quick-sand-like peat with a thin, firm, mat of live vegetation growing on top. To the uninformed, the surface of a bog often appears to be solid ground, but such is often not the case.

Over the years, numerous stories, some real and some hearsay, had been told and retold about the bog. Parents warned children in the area to never go near it because it was a strange and dangerous place. It was sort of Leyden's version of the English Moors, but minus *The Hound*. Due to the unusual environment, there were several types of vegetation that grew there and nowhere else in town. Local botanist, Judson Ewer, could sometimes be seen cautiously wandering the bog in search of rare and unusual botanical specimens. I recall hearing once about someone growing, or trying to grow, cranberries in the bog. It might have been a likely place to grow them if one was willing to accept the risk of walking around on the thin surface to tend and harvest the berries.

Everyone seemed to have their favorite story of misfortune that overcame someone who foolishly ventured into the bog. I remember a story Bert Whitney told once when he stopped by the shop for his usual five gallons of kerosene. It was during the time that the West Leyden Road improvements were in the planning stages, so the bog was a frequent topic of conversation around Henry's shop. Bert's story concerned an Indian girl who was sent into the bog by the tribe's medicine man to gather certain medicinal plants that only grew there. The girl never returned, but Bert claimed that sometimes on a cold night you could still hear her screams rising from the bog along with the mist. Of course Old Bert always had a story or two to fit any occasion.

Others claimed that many years ago, a farmer who tried to hay the bog, had lost his team of oxen to the quick-sand-like peat. The strange sounds sometimes heard emanating from the bog were said to be the final breaths of the oxen as the suffocating peat closed over them forever. A more recent story told of a farmer who nearly lost his life when his tractor got stuck in the bog and began quickly sinking. Presumably, the oxen and tractor are still down there somewhere waiting to be discovered by some archeological team in the distant future.

The original West Leyden Road headed downhill directly toward the bog, then turned sharply to the south before rounding the bog's edge. After a short distance it turned back to the west and up the opposite hill toward Wiles' farm. The road going up the western hill lined up nicely with that coming down the eastern rise, but there was a large loop around the bog in between. The pioneer road builders put in that half-circle to avoid having to deal with the tricky, often unstable, surface of the bog. No matter how practical this detour was, it did not set well with the state engineer. Unimpressed by the stories, and heedless of warnings from longtime residents, he insisted that the improved road must go directly across the bog, not around it. He felt that all the stories about strange happenings in the bog, and others, were nothing but myths and old wives' tales. As far as he was concerned, the improved road was to go straight across the bog. He was in charge, and since this was years before the invention of the environmental impact statement, little time was lost getting the okay to proceed.

When our survey crew reached the bog, we sighted a center line straight ahead. Ever watchful of where we stepped, we planted our stakes in a perfectly straight line. The engineer's plan was simple. It called for hauling in gravel to raise the level of the route across the bog closer to that of the hills on either side, just as would be done for any ordinary low spot. The first step was to install a large culvert for drainage. Otherwise, the added fill would act as a dam across the narrow shallow stream that flowed through the center. To many people's surprise, the culvert was installed without incident.

Soon the dump trucks started arriving with their loads of fill hauled all the way from a gravel bank in Northfield. After each truck had backed up to the bog and dumped its gravel, a bulldozer would level and compact it. Load after load, day after day, as gravel was dumped, the dumping point moved farther out into the bog. As surveyors, one of our jobs was to measure the progress of the fill and calculate the amount of gravel used each day. It was a simple computation using the daily change in elevation for a number of fixed points. In theory it worked well as long as the fill stayed put.

At the end of each day our survey crew would arrive and we would measure the height and length of the filled roadbed. The height was then compared to the previous day's height to compute the amount of fill hauled in that day. It didn't take long for us to realize that the roadbed was not rising anywhere near as rapidly as it should for all the gravel that was being dumped day after day. After a few days, we could no longer ignore the growing discrepancy between the number of truckloads of gravel being dumped and the very slow change in elevation of the roadbed. We pointed this out to the state engineer who simply accused us of bad calculations. "What do you guys think is happening?" he asked. "Is somebody sneaking in here at midnight and stealing gravel?"

The next day, out of curiosity, the survey crew chief decided that we should measure the elevation of the fill not only at the end of the day, but also the following morning before the day's dumping began. Just as he suspected, our measurements showed that the entire mass of gravel fill was sinking considerably overnight. It wasn't just dropping in a few spots or an inch or two. The entire project was over a foot lower in the morning than it had been at the end of work the day before. The dumping operation built up the roadbed elevation during the day, and the weight of the gravel caused it to slowly drop at night as the wet peat below oozed away due to the pressure created by the added weight of gravel. No soundings were ever taken, so nobody had any idea how many feet of wet peat lay below the intended roadbed.

We continued the twice a day measurements for a few days. Everything came to a head one morning when our elevation readings showed that in spite of numerous truckloads of gravel being dumped the day before, the elevation at the start of work that day was actually lower than it had been at the start of work the previous morning. Gravel being dumped and leveled all day long had actually resulted in a lowering of the roadbed! The survey crew chief again went to the state engineer with the results and was told once again that we obviously had made a mistake.

When the same thing happened again the next day, the data could no longer be denied by even the most optimistic state official. The final convincing point happened that day while we were eating our lunch. Somebody pointed out to us, and the engineer, that low hills had appeared close to both sides of the fill area. "These hills were not there when we started the job," he stated. "The entire surface of the bog was perfectly flat before we started dumping gravel, now it has hills. You know what else? The culvert we installed has nearly disappeared." He pointed out the very significant rises on both sides of the fill area that were several feet higher than the roadbed. They almost looked like large motionless ocean waves. Everyone agreed and wondered why they hadn't noticed the new hills and missing culvert before.

Even the state engineer had to finally admit that in spite of dumping load after load of gravel, day after day, instead of the roadway rising, the surface of the bog on either side had elevated considerably. Apparently the weight of all that gravel had pushed the wet peat to the sides and upward against the thick membrane of vegetation roots. It was rather like filling a plastic bag with dough, and then pushing down on it in the center.

It was time for a new game plan. The gravel hauling was stopped and the focus shifted to eliminating the peat problem. For the soupy peat to flow it had to contain a lot of water. If the water was removed, the peat would stabilize and stay put, thus supporting the weight of the gravel above it. At least that was the theory. Obviously the answer was to simply drain the bog. The simple solution of going around the bog instead of across it was still not a consideration.

The first drainage attempt was to enlarge the small opening on the south side of the bog to increase the outflow of water. Although the opening was enlarged several times, the water flow hardly increased at all because wet peat would flow in and plug the hole a few minutes after it was cleared. Water flows very slowly through peat.

The second attempt involved using a backhoe to dig a drainage ditch all the way from the roadway fill area to the south end of the bog. After two or three days, this idea was abandoned due to having to get the backhoe unstuck, and its operator rescued, numerous times. Eventually, the backhoe operator refused to work in the bog anymore.

For the third attempt, a crane with a clamshell bucket was brought in to dig a ditch from the outlet at the south end north to the fill area. This had at least a theoretical advantage over the backhoe. The crane could be positioned on firm ground, and the boom used to throw the bucket out into the bog and then pull it back. The operator would haul in a load of material, dump it, and repeat over and over until he had a ditch. The idea behind the ditch, no matter how it was dug, was that the water would seep into it from the sides and then flow out the enlarged opening at the end. The flowing water would keep the ditch and outlet open. The crane operator was the next to understand the wisdom of the pioneers in building the road around the bog, not through it. He would work all day digging a ditch, only to find the next morning that it had totally filled back in with wet peat. Only a dark stripe of peat with no overlying vegetation marked the location of the previous day's digging.

Still firmly convinced that a ditch was the answer to all his problems, the state engineer decided that the problem with the clamshell was that it didn't remove material rapidly enough. His newest theory was that if the ditch could be created quickly enough, the resulting high flow rate of water would keep it flushed open. So how do you create a complete ditch all at once?

That job fell to a dynamiter. The town had previously used a dynamiter from time to time, but always to blast ledge rock in order to straighten a curve in the road or lower a hill a few feet. His name may have been Maurice Thompson, but we all called him Boomer. He was characterized by one or two missing fingers on one hand, the result of a blasting cap accident. "An accepted hazard of the business," he called it. Since there wasn't much else going on due to the interrupted fill work, several of us were drafted as helpers for Boomer.

In those days, dynamite was little more than sawdust saturated with nitroglycerine and packed into a cardboard tube. It was quite percussion sensitive, meaning that if one stick went off, any others nearby would also detonate without benefit of blasting caps. Sometimes it could also be rather temperamental. Signals from a 2-way radio in the vicinity had been known to accidentally set it off at times. Yet, sometimes an intended blast didn't go off as planned.

Boomer explained to us that his plan was to imbed a stick of dynamite every three to four feet in a line across the bog from the south edge of the fill area to the outlet. That was what he needed us to help with. Once the charges were in place, we were to take cover and he would make the final hookup with a blasting cap. As we helped him gather up his supplies, Boomer explained that when the first stick would be set off, the next stick in the line would go off when the blast wave hit it. Stick after stick would explode as the shock wave moved down the line. This would blast a wide, deep, ditch across the bog with what we would perceive as one big blast. That was the theory. Boomer was so optimistic we didn't bother to point out to him that so far the score was bog 4, theories 0. As we walked out onto the bog, he told us it should be a sight to behold.

Off we went out onto the bog with everyone else watching from a safe distance behind a truck or large tree, just to be sure. I don't know if those watching were more interested in seeing what was going to happen with the big sack of dynamite, or if they were expecting some of us to be swallowed up by the bog. Either way, they were so focused on the danger from the dynamite and the bog that they hadn't given any thought to a rescue plan for any of us in case we needed one. I didn't spend much time worrying about the peat. My job was to carry the sticks of dynamite in a large plastic bag over my shoulder and that was enough for me to worry about. The first man in line used a long rod to poke a deep hole in the soft surface wherever Boomer indicated. The depth was initially about three feet with a gradual increase in depth as we moved south toward the drainage opening. Boomer would then hold up one or two fingers of his good hand indicating the number of dynamite sticks he wanted me to give him. He dropped these into the hole and gently tamped them down. The last man in our team carried a large bucket of dry sand which was used to refill each hole up to the top.

Once we reached the last hole, Boomer sent the rest of us up the hill to safety along with the leftover dynamite. He charged the last hole with two sticks. Then he whittled a small hole in the end of a third stick, gently inserted a blasting cap, and attached it to a long spool of electrical wire. This stick was gently lowered into the hole on top of the other two and, finally, he filled the hole with sand. Boomer then walked slowly backward toward where we were waiting near the Wiles' house, unrolling the wire as he went. Instructions were given to stop all traffic on the road. Each of us ducked behind a vehicle or a large tree, but made sure we had a good view of whatever was going to happen. Boomer took one last look around, up and down the road, and settled down behind the plunger.

"FIRE IN THE HOLE! 1, 2, 3!" he yelled. With that he pushed down rapidly on the plunger.

Silence. Nothing happened. Nobody moved nor said a word. Even the birds had stopped singing as if they too had expected something momentous to occur.

After a minute or so, Boomer raised the plunger and once again yelled "FIRE IN THE HOLE! 1, 2, 3!" and gave it another push, seemingly faster and harder than before. Once again nothing happened. "Something's wrong," he said. "I need to go down there."

We were all given stern instructions to stay exactly where we were and under no circumstances were any of us to follow him or even think about getting close to where the plunger was sitting. Down the hill he went. As he walked away, we all whispered to each other how there was no way we would go down there with all that dynamite set to blow. Somebody commented that he wasn't sure if he was witnessing the bravest act he had ever seen or the most foolhardy.

When he reached the point where his wire disappeared underground, Boomer punched a new hole about two feet from the previous end hole and dropped in two more sticks of dynamite. In the top stick he set another blasting cap, hooked it up to the wire and walked back to us.

"This time she's going to really blow," he said. After taking another look around, once more he yelled "FIRE IN THE HOLE! 1, 2, 3!" and pushed the plunger.

Blow it did! Mud, water, and tons of thousands of years-old wet peat flew at least 150 feet upward in a thick brown curtain all the way from the fill area to the outlet. For a moment it seemed to hang motionless in the air before it rained back down. Straight down; down into the ditch that had existed for only seconds. Someone pointed out the curious slow moving waves, like ripples in a pond, moving outward through the bog from the blast line. The only other evidence of the blast, besides an echoing rumble like distant thunder in the hills, was a brown strip of peat running the length of the bog. There was no ditch, not even a depression. The blast had thrown the saturated peat straight up and it had come straight back down. There was little if any lateral movement. "I've blown hundreds of ditches, but never saw that happen before," Boomer said.

By this time summer was coming to an end. It had been worked on all summer, but the road still hadn't crossed the bog. But I was done. It was time for me to focus on going back to school. The next summer I was busy helping to survey the route for 191, so I never saw how the bog problem was finally solved, but somehow it was. I assume that, eventually, the weight of all the gravel caused it to reach the solid bottom that had to exist somewhere under all the peat. Today the road crosses the remains of the bog in a straight line just as the state engineer envisioned. However, that had to be the most expensive half mile of new road ever constructed in Leyden.

Chapter 16

READIN RITIN 'N RULERS

And children coming home from school
Look in at the open door;
They love to see the flaming forge,
And hear the bellows roar,
And catch the burning sparks that fly
Like chaff from a threshing-floor.
                              Longfellow

There were three active one-room schoolhouses in town when I entered the first grade in 1948 at the age of six. There was no pre-school, no kindergarten, and nothing beyond the eighth grade in Leyden. Each one-room school had a single teacher who taught students in grades one through eight. Orilla and I attended the Center School which was located nearly a mile west of our house at the foot of the ridge that defines the start of West Leyden. The other schools still in use in the late 1940s, and early 1950s, were the South School, and the Beaver Meadow School. Years earlier, a fourth school on East Hill had been closed. Henry and several of his brothers and sisters began and ended their formal education in the East Hill School. Later, Jessie taught there for a few years. At one time there had been a fifth school in West Leyden and Arms claims that at one time there were six.

Each one-room school consisted of a single classroom, a hallway with coat hooks, and an attached woodshed to store fuel for the wood stove. Each school had electricity, but no running water. Toilet facilities were of the pit type. Playground and PE equipment consisted of whatever we brought from home or found to amuse ourselves in the great outdoors. The number of students in each grade at each school usually numbered from one to five. In some years, a school might not have any students enrolled in one or more grades, making for an "easy year" for the teacher.

Our teacher at the Center School was Pearl E. Rhodes who began teaching there in 1946, I believe. She and her brother lived in West Leyden on a farm with their parents. We called her "Pearly," but ONLY if we were certain that she was out of earshot. Miss Rhodes was a strict, but fair disciplinarian. In addition to a verbal dressing down in front of the whole school, a student getting on her wrong side risked being assigned the least desirable task on the weekly jobs list.

On my first day of school I had a big advantage in that my sister Orilla was a fourth grade "upper classman." She showed me the route to walk to school and introduced me all around once we arrived. The first grade consisted of only two students: Peter Snow from West Leyden, and me. I had never met Pete before we started school, but we were immediately best of friends.

A few weeks after school started, I was invited to spend a Saturday at Pete's house. The Snows owned a farm in West Leyden and Pete showed me all around. After a while, Pete asked if I would like to ride his bike. Naturally I said "Yes," so Pete hauled it out of the barn. I was six years old and had seen very few two wheeler bikes, and had never ridden one. I couldn't admit that to my new best friend, so I pushed it up the driveway to the dirt road, meanwhile looking it over and trying to figure out how in the world I was going to ride the thing. The road sloped downhill past the farm, so I pointed the bike downhill, got on, and started pedaling. Much to my surprise, it didn't fall over. The faster it went the easier and more fun it was. Suddenly I heard someone yell, "Slow down.

Put on the brakes!" I didn't know anything about any brakes, so I just kept pedaling. As I approached the steepest part of the hill, suddenly Pete's father, Al, came running up beside me huffing and puffing. He grabbed the handlebars, stopped the bike, and likely saved me from a major crash.

Courtesy of Leyden Historical Commission

All eight grades at the Leyden Center School in February, 1949.

Standing left to right: Pearl Rhodes (teacher), Mary Snow 7, Irene Barton 7, Norman Barton 8, Gerald Kennedy 6. 1st Row (along wall) left to right: Barry Wiles 6, Wendel Barton 3, Ray Glabach 1, Ruth Snow 5. 2nd Row left to right: Peter Snow 1, Juanita Gerry 3, Ray Flagg 4, Orilla Glabach 4. 3rd Row left to right: Gregory Wiles 5, Leland Gerry 4, June Barton 5, Phil Zimmerman 8. 4th Row left to right: June Wilder 6, Eddie Snow 6, Bobby Beaudoin 8, Gordon Barton 8

Pete had several enviable talents. As far as I was concerned, his best talent, and one I greatly envied, was his ability to wiggle his ears. I had never before known anyone who could do that, and had no idea that it was possible. I first became aware of Pete's ear wiggling ability one day when everyone in the school was listening to Miss Rhodes explain the details about some upcoming project. Pete was sitting just in front of me and appeared to be riveted upon what the teacher was saying. At one point the teacher said to pay very close attention. Just then Pete's ears started wiggling. I was amazed and burst out laughing, much to the displeasure of Miss Rhodes. I was marched to the front of the room and told to explain what I thought was so funny.

"Pete wiggled his ears!" I exclaimed.

"Is that true, Peter Snow?" she asked.

"Who me? I can't wiggle my ears," he replied.

I think Miss Rhodes knew about Peter's ear talents all along. I was let off without any punishment, but Pete's desk was relocated to the front row where she could keep a closer eye on him.

Any student who lived within about a mile of the school was expected to walk to school and back home every day. Beyond that distance a bus was generally provided. The bus usually consisted of a parent with a "SCHOOL BUS" sign attached to the back of a station wagon or large car. The school had no running water, so the bus also delivered a blue and white masonry water "cooler" containing the day's water supply of about five gallons. Water was rationed out during the day in cone shaped paper cups. Sometimes, if the water didn't arrive, or if it ran out, two students would be assigned to walk the half mile to Judson Ewer's house to get a new supply.

There were no teacher's aides. Most days the only help the teacher received was from the students themselves. One day a week, or maybe every other week, a special teacher would arrive to teach music for an hour. Extra music time was allocated if we were preparing to put on a program at the Town Hall. Once a month, Mr. Rinehart, a special teacher for handwriting instruction, would make his visit. He would travel from school to school and instruct all of us in cursive handwriting. He had gorgeous handwriting which none of us boys could come close to duplicating. "He's trying to make us all write like girls," Pete would say.

Following the monthly writing instruction session, each student was required to place on their desk three examples of their class work that had been written in cursive during the previous month. Mr. Rinehart would then go from desk to desk and stamp a 1, 2, or 3 in red ink on each page. I always dreaded this because I had terrible handwriting and usually collected a full set of threes. Whenever Mr. Rinehart stamped a three, he would slam it down loudly so that everyone knew the kid's paper had been busted. The worst part was the little lecture that came afterward in which I was told that I wasn't trying hard enough. I was made to believe that I had the worst handwriting in the school, maybe the worst he had ever seen. Perhaps I did and it's only gotten worse with age. I understand that some schools no longer require cursive writing.

Twice a year the traveling school nurse came to perform a rudimentary physical on each student. She used a stethoscope to listen to us breath, took our pulse, looked in our ears and checked our scalps for lice. It wasn't unusual for lice to be found in the hair of one or two students. They were given written instructions to be taken home to the parents describing how to treat the condition. One very effective method was to wash the hair with kerosene! I always dreaded the nurse's eye exams. The eye chart resembled rows of a symbol much like a capital E except the fingers could point left, right, up, or down. Nearly all my responses were a guess as to which way it pointed because all the symbols looked alike to me. No matter which way the fingers pointed, to me it was a blur. I used to try to memorize the responses of the kid ahead of me in order to get a better score. Finally, in the fourth grade I was fitted with my first pair of eye glasses. It was worth being teased with the nickname "Professor" by the other kids in order to see a much clearer world.

Every student was expected to participate in some way in the operation of the school. It was an important part of the learning process in those days. Reading and writing were important, but it was just as important to learn how to be a reliable, helpful member of the community. Various jobs rotated among the students on a weekly basis. Those in the lower grades had simple tasks, such as straightening the books on the shelves, putting the encyclopedias in alphabetical order, or cleaning the blackboard erasers at the end of each day. The task I disliked the most was eraser cleaning. The school had black, natural stone, slate blackboards which were written on with white chalk, creating a lot of dust. Felt erasers the size of a small brick would build up quite a load of chalk by the end of the day. The assigned student's job was to take all the erasers outside and clap them against each other dislodging the white chalk dust into the air. My first day of eraser duty resulted in my returning to the classroom looking like a white ghost, much to the amusement of all. Nobody had bothered to tell me to stand with my back to the breeze when clapping them. I figured out later that it was sort of an initiation rite welcoming the new guy to the school.

Every Friday, at the end of the day, another assigned student had to wash the blackboards to remove the layer of built up chalk and ready them for the next week. The last of the day's drinking water supply was poured into a bucket and the boards wetted down with a sponge followed by drying with a rag.

The older the student, the more demanding, and potentially dangerous, the job assignments would be. During the winter months, the 7th and 8th grade boys were responsible for the fire. The classroom was heated by a large wood burning stove at the rear of the room and it required frequent attention. One boy was assigned the task of keeping the wood box near the stove supplied with split wood. This meant going into the wood shed and splitting large chunks with an ax, carrying the split wood into the classroom and stacking it near the stove. The second task, assigned to a different boy, was responsibility for the fire itself. Whichever boy was assigned the fire task for the week was expected to be one of the first students, preferably the first student, to arrive in the morning. He would set the fire with crumpled paper and kindling and have a warm fire burning by the time most of the students arrived. It was also his responsibility to add wood to the fire as necessary during the day. On cold winter mornings, we would all gather in a circle around the stove and get well warmed up before beginning our lessons.

Can you imagine giving that kind of responsibility to 12 and 13 year old boys today? The teacher would be hauled into court. Headlines would read "Child Abuse in Leyden Schools", "Ax and Matches Found in School." I don't remember anybody expressing any feelings of being abused or being taken advantage of. We simply knew we were expected to help out at school just like we did at home. I don't remember anybody ever getting hurt performing their assigned tasks. Most of us felt proud of our jobs and gladly accepted responsibility for them.

So, how did one teacher, with very minimal adult help, manage to teach all eight grades at once? In some of today's schools it often takes a teacher, a teacher's aide or two, special education teachers, a media specialist, and a counselor or two. Have you ever heard the expression "If you really want to learn something, teach it to someone else?"

In the one-room school houses, there were actually plenty of helpers: the students in the upper grades. The older students spent considerable time helping the younger ones to learn and, in the process, increased their own knowledge of the subject. I think I learned more about reading from eighth grader, Irene Barton, than I did from Miss Rhodes. For the system to work, there were rules that had to be followed. The teacher's word was law and there was no appeal. If a teacher doled out punishment to a student, his parents could be expected to support the teacher instead of demanding that she be fired. We students didn't just learn "book learning." We also learned personal responsibility, character, how to help others, citizenship, and respect for authority.

Recess was always the most fun part of the day. Unless there was a downpour or a howling blizzard, we were expected to go outside for recess three times a day. The teacher had certainly earned a few minutes break from us. Morning and afternoon recess was 10 minutes and lunch recess was 20 minutes, including eating time. Most days we played baseball on the side hill behind the school. The pitcher threw the ball underhand and the batter stood in front of a section of old stone wall which served as a backstop. Our bases were flat rocks, and if we were lucky, someone would have brought a real bat from home, otherwise, we'd hunt for a decent substitute in the woods. We all learned quickly how to hit to the right side of the diamond as that was the steepest downhill and if the fielder missed the ball, it was a home run for sure. Miss Rhodes, standing outside the door ringing the handheld school bell, signaled the end to the game for now and time to get back to work. The game would resume at the next recess, or the next day, exactly where it left off. Somehow the bell from the Center School found its way into Henry's shop after the school was closed. It is in my possession today.

When I entered the fourth grade, it was the first year of the new consolidated elementary school now known as the Pearl E. Rhodes Elementary School. Arms' book refers to it as the Center School, but it was never called that. The three one-room schools were closed for good and all the students in town went to the new school. It boasted two classrooms with only four classes per room. In addition, there was a cafeteria, oil-fired central heat, and bathrooms with real flush toilets. The staff consisted of two teachers (Miss Rhodes was one), and a cook. The cook was my aunt, Leta Wood, Jessie's sister. In the one-room schools, lunch had consisted of whatever you brought from home, plus or minus whatever you could trade for from somebody else's lunch pail. It was a brand new experience to grab a tray and get in line to be served whatever the hot food of the day was. Leta was a wonderful cook and it was amazing what she could do with the WWII government surplus foods that made up most of her supplies. Of course every Friday it was fish sticks.

At the new school, I almost immediately met Shirley Johnson, whom I thought was pretty cute. She was a third grader and had spent grades one and two at the South School which was located fairly close to her parents' farm. Through the rest of our elementary school years we were frequent partners in various school activities. As we grew older, she was my favorite dance partner at the Town Hall square dances, but

I guess I was very shy and things never progressed any further than that.

From grades four through eight there were five of us in my class at the new school: Peter Snow, Willie Herron, Marilyn Croutworst, Carol Siren, and me. Marilyn was the smartest of the bunch and if I managed to get a better grade than she did on a test, I felt I was doing pretty darn well.

Although there was a new school building in a whole new location, the rules about transportation stayed the same. My cousin, Billy Glabach, lived just west of the church and we walked to and from the new school together nearly every day. There was quite a bit of elevation difference between the location of the new consolidated school and where we lived in Leyden Center. We had no problem walking downhill to school in the mornings, but the long walk uphill in the afternoon wasn't a lot of fun, especially on a hot day.

One day, as we were being slowly passed by a heavily loaded dump truck, we got a bright idea about how to make the uphill grind a lot easier, and a lot more fun, although a tad dangerous. Due to road construction somewhere beyond the Center, big dump trucks were frequently hauling gravel up the hill. The steep hill required the driver to shift down to a very low gear not far past the school. When we heard a truck coming, Billy and I would hide in the trees just below Herbert Orr's house where the hill was the steepest. As the truck slowly passed our hiding spot, we would dart out just behind it and grab onto the tailgate with both hands. We didn't try to climb on because we figured the driver would see us in his mirrors or we might not be able to get off in time when the truck reached the top of the hill and sped up. Instead, we stayed on our feet at the rear holding onto the tailgate. The truck would pull us up the hill as we took very long jumping steps. As the truck approached the top of the hill and began to increase speed, we had to remember to let go soon enough, otherwise, we would fall flat and have some skinned knees and elbows to explain when we arrived home, as Billy discovered one day.

Every recess at the new school meant that the boys, and a few of the girls, would be playing baseball, just like at the old schools. It was great to actually have enough players to fully outfit two teams. At the old Center school, one or two of the members of the team that was at bat often had to play defense for the other team while waiting for their turn at the plate. It was a major improvement to be playing on a more or less flat field, but it was still pretty rough. Ground balls were still very unpredictable, so the infield played quite deep. In the winter, baseball was usually replaced by other activities such as sliding down the hill behind the school. One cold winter day some of us got bored with ordinary sliding. It really wasn't much of a hill and we were used to a lot more adventure, such as sliding behind George Howes' barn. Behind the school was a small playground equipped with several swings and a tall metal slide. Somebody suggested that we try sliding down the slide on our feet. After a few attempts it became obvious that the rubber soled boots most of us were wearing just were not going to slide down that metal very well.

As was often the case, Peter Snow had an inspiration. He came up with a pail from somewhere and filled it with water at the hose bib on the back of the school. He then climbed up the slide ladder and proceeded to slowly pour the water down the surface of the cold metal slide. The water quickly froze solid and after a few buckets, Pete had a good coating of ice all the way down. Naturally Pete was the first to give it a try and made a good run on his feet, but squatting down. After a few others followed Pete's lead, it was my turn. Everyone else had squatted to do their run, so I decided to be the first to slide all the way down standing straight up. Everything went according to plan until I was about half way down. Suddenly my left boot hit a section of the slide that didn't have any ice coating. That foot suddenly stopped, the right one kept going, and I pitched headfirst off the left side. I threw out my left hand to break my fall and broke my wrist instead. Of course everyone testified to the teacher that I broke it falling off my sled on the hill.

Leyden schools carried a student only through the eighth grade. There was no in town provision for education beyond that grade. State law said a student had to attend school until at least 16 years of age, but they could get permission to leave school at a younger age if they were needed to help run the family farm or if they had secured some other full-time employment. As a long-time member of the school board, Jessie was the one that had to be convinced that it was in a teenager's best interests to not continue his education.

After the eighth grade, most students went on to ninth grade in Greenfield High School or later to Pioneer Valley Regional School which opened around 1957. To celebrate the completion of the 8th grade, in June every year there was an elaborate graduation ceremony at the Town Hall complete with diplomas, speeches by officials, speeches by the graduates, and much applause. The graduating girls wore their best dresses and boy graduates wore a suit coat and tie for the first time in their lives. When our class graduated, each of us had to make a speech about what we planned to do with our lives. Pete and Willie each talked about becoming farmers following in their father's footsteps. I think Carol was going to be a nurse, and Marilyn wanted to be a teacher. Henry had made it clear to me that there was no way I was going into the blacksmith business, so when it came to my turn, I said that I wanted to be a nuclear physicist and search for the elusive positive electron. I had no idea what that meant, but I had recently read it somewhere and thought it sounded impressive. Besides, Pete and Willie had already played the farmer thing to the hilt. Many in the audience looked at each other and asked, "What the hell is wrong with this kid?"

I never became a physicist, although I studied a lot of physics en route to becoming a chemical engineer. I know Willie went on to manage his father's farm. At some point, Pete became a grocer in Greenfield, eventually managing the Stop & Shop, I believe. According to the 50th reunion "yearbook" of the class of 1960 at PVRS, Marilyn held a variety of occupations including therapist, writer, insurance agent, and herbalist. I have no idea what Carol became. We never did have a reunion of the five of us to talk about old times and swap lies about how great we had become.

Leyden's eighth grade graduation, June, 1956. Left to right: Pearl Rhodes, teacher; Pete Snow; Marilyn Croutworst; Willie Herron; Carol Siren; Ray Glabach; unidentified woman; F. Sumner Turner, superintendent of schools.

After the 8th grade I spent a year in purgatory, otherwise known as the Greenfield Junior High. I was in the college prep curriculum and got thrown into a section made up of all the students that were expected to be troublemakers. I didn't have anything in common with anyone else, I had no friends, I disliked all my teachers, and I was miserable. I guess the staff at Greenfield simply assumed that being a hick from Leyden was enough to label anyone a problem.

When the towns of Northfield, Bernardston, and Gill opened the Pioneer Valley Regional School (for grades seven through twelve), Leyden contracted with PVRS to provide post eighth grade education. It was a huge improvement over Greenfield. School was fun again. Most of the students were from small towns and farms and we all had a lot in common. After the first year, education in Leyden ended at the sixth grade with the students in the seventh and eighth grades attending PVRS as well. The number of Leyden students was increasing. The 1958 Leyden Annual Report shows that on December 22 of that year, there were 21 students in grades one through three with teacher Helen Smith. Another 29 were in grades four through six with teacher Pearl Rhodes. Another 29 students were attending PVRS with 17 of those in grades seven and eight.

Several of the original teachers at PVRS had a major impact on me personally. Miss Lawley was the main math teacher and she really knew her stuff. In addition to being an excellent math teacher, she was a strict disciplinarian. She certainly would not fit in today's schools, but I am very glad that she taught me high school math. A student was expected to speak only when addressed. No gum chewing or note passing was permitted, and even a hint of looking at another student's paper during a test would bring her ever present ruler down hard on the desk followed by an F on the test and a trip to the principal's office.

The physics teacher, Mr. Dryer(?) had a major impact on my future. Although confined to a wheelchair, he was also the school's first track and field coach. I was the team's javelin thrower and he called me "Spear-Chucker." I got the job due to some pretty good throws in phys-ed class, none of which I was able to duplicate once I was an official track team member. It seemed that the more I practiced, the shorter my throws became. But, Mr. Dryer wouldn't let me give up and kept encouraging me in a humorous manner. As the last months of my senior year approached, I had decided to study liberal arts in college mostly because I didn't know what else to do. When Mr. Dryer found out about that, he approached me in the physics lab one day.

"I never thought you would take the easy way out," he said.

"What do you mean?" I asked.

"I heard you are going to major in liberal arts. I thought you were going to be a scientist or engineer."

"I was," I said, "but I have a lot of other interests that I want to explore."

"There will be plenty of time to explore those later. But,

if you don't get a strong base in the sciences first, you never will."

"What about you," I asked. "What did you study to become a teacher?"

"I didn't intend to be a teacher. I studied chemical engineering. But in this wheelchair, I couldn't get around well enough, so after graduating from college, I took this job."

In the fall of 1960, I entered the University of Massachusetts majoring in chemical engineering.

Chapter 17

THE CELLAR SAVERS

The first Leyden Town Hall in the new center was located immediately to the east of the Methodist Church. It caught fire and burned in July of 1929 and was rebuilt in a new location in 1932. There was no way of extinguishing the flames once they got going. "It wasn't a total loss," one longtime resident once told me, "We managed to save the cellar!"

In the 1950s, the remains of that cellar, charred pieces of wood, broken glass, and occasional bits of metal were still very much in evidence on the site. Sumac and small maple and ash trees were making a valiant attempt to reclaim the site for nature. Boyhood curiosity prompted me to interrogate my father and Uncle Bill about what had happened there on that fateful night years before I was born,

They claimed that the fire had started in the kitchen of the building while a canning demonstration was being prepared for some young girls.

Supposedly, the girls stepped out of the building for a few minutes and while they were gone a wind came up which blew some window curtains too close to their stove. The curtains caught fire, and shortly after that the building was in flames. Leyden did not have anything resembling a fire department, no firefighting equipment, and of course no municipal water system.

When the fire was discovered, town residents living nearby

saw the flames and heard the commotion. Word went out to many of the nearby farms and farmers for whatever help they may have been able to provide. Soon a fair sized crowd had gathered, but there was little that anyone could do without water and equipment. Several farmers had responded with whatever water carrying equipment they had. Most of the farms were dairy farms and milk was stored in 40-quart metal cans that had a tight fitting push-on metal lid, the kind commonly found in antique shops and flea markets today. Several farm trucks appeared on the scene loaded with milk cans full of water, and a couple of wagons arrived with sap gathering tanks full of water. But, there was no way to hose it onto the burning building. The fire was so hot that it was impossible to get close enough to form an old-fashioned bucket brigade.

The east wall of the church became so hot that it hurt to touch it and the paint blistered (this was many years before the east wing was added to the church to the detriment of its old-time New England architecture.) Blankets and burlap grain sacks were wetted with water and slapped against the church wall in a feeble attempt to cool it.

The hero of the evening was a farmer who arrived towing his spray rig behind his tractor. Some say it was Ray Robertson. The farmer owned a large apple orchard thus possessing a good spray rig. It was soon obvious that the Town Hall was beyond saving and would be a complete loss. Increasingly, there was a great fear that the adjacent church might also catch fire and it was getting too hot for the men to use the ineffective wet sack approach any longer. The spray rig was set up and used to wet the east wall of the church as best it could. Men dumped water from the milk cans into the sprayer's tank so that a fairly constant mist of water was directed toward the church. Much of the water mist evaporated from the intense heat before hitting the structure, but enough got through so that it, along with the fireproof natural slate roof, saved the church from being a second disaster.

The ashes had hardly cooled before the leaders of the ever resilient Leyden community began making plans to replace the Town Hall. Much more than a place for the selectmen to meet and to hold the annual town meeting, along with the church, it had been the social heart of the town. It was where the church suppers took place, Saturday night square dances were held, and wedding receptions were held. Key to the planning was to build the new structure well away from the church or any other building to guard against the possibility of a future multi-building disaster. That is why the new Town Hall was erected across the street and well away from the church or any other building. This may or may not have been about the same time that Henry agreed to have the town vault constructed on one corner of his property. It was made of fireproof brick with a steel door to protect all the town records.

Sometime, not long after the original Leyden Town Hall burned to the ground, Henry Glabach was appointed the first Leyden Fire Warden, a position he held along with a later appointment as Fire Chief for 48 years. At first it was largely a meaningless position because there was no fire department, no firefighting equipment, no firemen, and the town budget did not provide money in order to obtain any. Henry worked out an agreement with the Greenfield Fire Department that they could be called upon for assistance in major fires. But, due to the travel time and their crew's unfamiliarity with Leyden, by the time a fire truck from there arrived it was usually way too late to be of any real help. From his very first year Henry worked tirelessly to improve both the town's firefighting equipment and the training of volunteers who would use it. When he finally retired from the position, the town had first class firefighting equipment, a fire station, and a well-trained core group of volunteer firefighters.

Fire was a very real hazard to be considered and often, if a building fire got started, it was a total loss. Not only was the Fire Department very rudimentary for many years, sufficient water supplies for fighting a major fire were few and far between. Usually the only water available for fighting a fire had to be hauled to the fire from some distance.

Fortunately, most buildings, even in the Center, were far enough apart that if one caught fire, the danger of losing much of the town was minimal. An exception could have been the parsonage fire in 1948 or 1949. That could have easily resulted in a major disaster for the town. The parsonage sat at the north end of a row of four close houses, along with some barns and outbuildings, south of the blacksmith shop. My uncle, Wilhelm (Bill) Glabach, wife Doris, and kids Billy, April, and Mary rented the parsonage from the church. It had not housed a minister for quite some time.

They were all asleep upstairs when the fire started one night. Cousin Bill recently shared with me his memories of that event which took place when he was five or six years old. He said that his mother woke up and thought he had gone to sleep leaving his light on. When she got up and went to turn it off, she discovered the fire. The family escaped down the center stairs and found refuge at the Beaudoin house at the end of the row of houses. Nearby neighbors came to help, but there was little they could do other than run in and out of the burning building salvaging whatever they could. Bill remembers that his mother had done laundry that day and one thing that was saved was the clean laundry. Odd, the things one remembers after 60 years. By the time fire trucks arrived from Greenfield there was little they could do except wet down Howes' store next door.

The church and the town buildings had no water system at all even though a half-dozen or so houses in and near the Center shared a common water supply from a good spring in West Leyden. Sometime in the 1880s, a water line had been run from the very reliable Brandy Brook Spring in West Leyden to several houses in the Center area. A simple gravity/siphon system, it went into the basement of the Miner house and was distributed to the others from there. However, that supply line was small and of course there were no fire hydrants. During the 1950s, Uncle Bill Glabach did most of the maintenance on the system to keep water flowing.

All other houses and farms in the town depended on their own private spring, well, or surface water for their needs much as they still do today. Even near to a pond or stream, water quantities were often quite limited. During the dry summer season, it was not unusual for ponds to turn into mud holes and streams that were free flowing in the spring to turn into a trickle. Some years some wells and springs would run totally dry, requiring residents to haul water for their stock and domestic needs from a more dependable source, often outside of town.

Whenever there was a significant fire event, calls would go out to Greenfield, Bernardston, or other nearby towns for help. In the early days, obtaining outside help was sometimes an iffy thing. If fire danger was high in the whole county, sending a truck and crew to Leyden would reduce the protection level elsewhere. Besides, by the time a fire truck had traveled to the fire location from Greenfield, Bernardston, or Colrain, usually about all that could be done was to prevent the fire from spreading to any nearby structures.

As Fire Warden, there was little that Henry could do to protect the town from the ravages of fire because of a lack of effective firefighting equipment. When there was a fire, he would head for it with a few Civil Defense supplied fire extinguishers to help out as best he could. His sole official responsibility seemed to be to issue burning permits. According to Massachusetts law, if a farmer wished to burn a brush pile he was supposed to first obtain a permit from the local Fire Warden. If the weather was not terribly dry and the farmer promised to have enough help on hand, a permit would generally be issued. This was years before the concern for the potential air pollution began to outweigh the concern for the actual fire danger. I imagine that today the primary concern would be for the amount of "greenhouse gas" the fire would produce even though the process of natural decay would produce the same amount or more of global warming gas.

After several years of persistent lobbying by Henry and several other influential members of the community, the selectmen finally managed to find a meager amount of money to allocate to firefighting equipment. The budget was very tight, so most of the equipment was second or third hand. In fact, much of it was never built as firefighting equipment in the first place. All the money went for buying equipment. The labor for putting everything together to build a fire truck was donated by Henry, his brother Bill, and a few others. It was assembled in Henry's shop.

A small, green, used International flatbed truck (about a 1934 or 1936 model I think) was purchased and someone donated an old 250 gallon steel oil tank which became the water tank for the fire truck. The water tank and most of the rear portion of the truck were painted fire truck red, but the front stayed the original green. Next, a new small portable fire pump was purchased and mounted on the rear of the truck in such a way that it could draw water from the tank, from a pond or stream near the truck, or it could be quickly removed and carried by two men to a water supply. A large reel of rubber hose was mounted on top of the truck and several 50-foot lengths of canvas 1 1/2-inch fire hose were rolled up and stored on one side.

On the rear of the truck were two soda acid fire extinguishers. These were common fire extinguishers for use in schools and public buildings in those days, but they were not the best thing to be carried on a bouncing fire truck. A soda acid extinguisher was a copper cylinder with a screw-on bronze cap. A short rubber hose and nozzle was attached very near the top. The cylinder contained about 2 1/2 gallons of water in which a pound of baking soda was dissolved. The underside of the screw-on cover had a wire basket supporting a glass bottle filled with about a half pint of sulfuric acid. On top of the bottle was a loose fitting glass stopper. To use the extinguisher, it was quickly inverted, causing the acid to run out of the bottle into the baking soda solution. Everyone who has ever played with vinegar and baking soda knows what happened next.

The acid reacted with the baking soda creating huge volumes of carbon dioxide gas. The gas pressure rapidly increased forcing the water out the rubber hose and nozzle. Once activated, it didn't stop until all the water had been pushed out or the soda & acid mixture was depleted. It was a one-shot deal requiring a recharge kit to put it back in action once it had been used. The problem with having them on the fire truck was that the bumps and jolts of the moving truck would often cause some of the acid to slosh out of the glass bottle thus diluting the effect if the unit was later inverted to fight a fire.

I remember one time, before the town bought the Mack fire truck, there was a fire somewhere in West Leyden and I rode along with Henry in the International to the scene of the blaze. While Henry and a few others were busy putting the water pump on the truck into action, I grabbed one of the soda & acid extinguishers, flipped it over and expected to start putting out the fire. Instead of a solid stream of high pressure water, I only got a wimpy stream that didn't project more than five feet. I quickly grabbed another extinguisher and had similar results. As I was giving up in frustration, I think it was Jerry Kennedy whom I heard yelling, "Hey, Ray! Did you think you could piss the fire out?"

One side of the truck carried four Civil Defense hand pumped fire extinguishers and the other carried four Indian Tanks. Indian Tanks were designed for fighting grass fires and were often the most useful items on the truck. Each consisted of a metal tank that was worn on a firefighter's back like a backpack holding about five gallons of water. A hose from the tank led to a trombone-like, hand operated, pump that sprayed the water. They could be quickly adjusted for either a spray or a solid stream. The tanks were easily filled from the main tank on the truck or from any convenient stream or pond. They were very effective at putting out grass fires, but were almost useless against building fires because they didn't pump enough water.

The International did not have a 2-way radio; in those pre-Mutual Aid days there wouldn't have been anybody to talk to on the radio if it had existed. Nor did the truck carry any protective gear for the firefighters. A fireman fought the fire wearing whatever he arrived on the scene with, most likely whatever he happened to be wearing when he got the fire call or heard the truck go by. If he had to go inside a burning building, he held his breath and squinted through the smoke.

At the left rear corner of the truck was a 5-gallon GI gas can painted red. It contained the gas & oil fuel mixture for the portable pump's 2-cycle engine. The story went that a very inexperienced firefighter once grabbed that can and poured the contents into an empty Civil Defense extinguisher thinking that the can contained water. Luckily someone stopped him just before the well-intended fireman would have begun to spray gasoline onto the flames!

During most of the year, the fire truck's home was one of the two bays in the Town Shed which belonged to the Road Department. There was a small wood stove in the shed that normally kept the temperature above freezing. In especially cold winter weather, the fire truck was relocated to Henry's blacksmith shop where the stove was larger and more frequently tended. As winter weather approached, along with chimney fire season, a set of tire chains was always installed to improve the chances that the truck could make it through snow and ice to where it was needed.

There tended to be three main fire seasons every year. The first ran from mid-March into May after the winter's snows were gone and before the rains and greens of spring reduced grass and forest fire danger. This fire season was primarily grass and forest fires. Farmers who had been cooped up all winter were anxious to get outside and prepare for planting. Fields full of dry weeds would mysteriously catch fire and occasionally a legally obtained permit would get out of control. Growers of wild blueberries would intentionally burn their blueberry pastures to increase the yield of fruit. On a warm, windless, day in April Henry would say, "Better get ready. Somebody will be burning today."

The second fire season was mid-to-late summer and coincided with the completion of haying. This was the season of barn fires. I saw more than one farmer's barn lost to spontaneous combustion caused by storing wet or improperly dried hay. These days it is fashionable for some "experts" to say it can't happen, but I have seen it first hand and have fought several barn fires started by wet hay. If you want to get some idea of what spontaneous combustion is, sometime when you mow your lawn, rake all the green grass clippings into a pile, the bigger the better. After a few days, thrust your hand deep into the center of the pile.

Leyden farmers were usually very careful to not put hay into their barns unless it was totally dry. But once the hay was cut and lying in the field, the farmer was at the mercy of nature. He knew he should wait until it was completely dry to put it in the barn, but June weather in Leyden was often uncooperative. Letting the hay lie too long on the ground in wet weather could result in a worthless crop that horses and cows would refuse to eat. So, sometimes a farmer would take a chance. A small amount of wet hay buried under other layers of insulating dry hay would sometimes start to compost just as your lawn clippings do. As the hay began to decompose, it gave off heat. The heat could sometimes build up until the auto ignition temperature of the surrounding dry hay was reached. Casper Zimmerman had a thermometer with a long stem that he would stab deep into stored hay to monitor what was going on. I recall helping the Zimmerman's take down a pile of hay bales one fall after Casper's thermometer had shown a reading that was a little into the danger zone. In the center of the pile were a couple of charred bales. A fire had started in the middle of the pile, but luckily it had gone out, probably from lack of oxygen. A few months later, the Zimmermans installed a huge electric fan in the back of the barn and stacked hay bales in such a fashion that the fan circulated drying air among them.

The third fire season began in the late fall or early winter as residents were beginning to make more use of their wood burning stoves and furnaces. It was chimney fire season. In most years, chimney fires were the most common reason for the fire truck to be called out. In those days, the majority of homes in Leyden were heated by wood. Some had central heat from a wood fired furnace in the basement. Others had several wood stoves throughout the house. Nobody seriously attempted to heat their home using open fireplaces. They consumed far too much wood for the amount of heat obtained. It was common, however, for older houses with fireplaces to have them converted to use a cast iron stove or fireplace insert that fed into an original chimney.

Chimney fires were common in the late fall or early winter, at the start of the heating season. Firewood that had been cut in the spring or summer was sometimes still a little green. The creosote given off by burning less than thoroughly dry wood in a stove or furnace would condense and cling to the chimney walls. The creosote deposits were flammable and if they were not removed by annual cleaning, which was rarely done, they could ignite. A fire burning in a chimney could easily pass into the wood of the house because many of the old chimneys were made only of one layer of brick with no clay liner. Many of those brick chimneys had had no maintenance since they were built, maybe a hundred years before, and missing mortar or loose bricks could be a path to destruction for the house. To compound the problem, a lot of chimneys passed upward through the house instead of being attached to the outside. It was not uncommon for the stove pipes from more than one wood burning device to share a common chimney...something not allowed by today's building codes.

Henry and the other volunteer firefighters hated chimney fires. Not only was there high risk of losing an entire house, but they often occurred at night, could be dangerous to fight, and of course it was always very cold weather. If the location was a long way from the Center, the fire truck's water lines and fire extinguishers might freeze en route to where they were needed. I recall hearing stories of how sometimes it was necessary to thaw the lines and extinguishers with a blowtorch so that the fire could be fought. Unfortunately, there was often little that could be done for the chimney fire itself except standby in case the fire spread to the wood of the house. Sometimes it was necessary to take an ax and chop holes through the house walls in order to inspect the sides of the chimney or get to a suspected fire location.

One tool that sometimes was often quite effective for extinguishing a chimney fire was a dry chemical product called Imp. It came wrapped in a paper cube about four inches on a side. One or two of these cubes would be placed in the stove that fed into the chimney. The Imp was ignited and allowed to burn. As it burned, the Imp gave off a chemical smoke that would smother the fire in the chimney. Water was usually never used on a chimney fire unless there was great danger that the entire house might be lost.

A very memorable chimney fire occurred one day at the old Carpenter Stage Coach Inn on County Road. It was located in what was known as the Old Center and was one of the oldest existing buildings in town. It was generally known as the Charlie Bolton house, but Charlie had moved away by the time this fire happened. Henry was out of town shoeing horses, and several rather inexperienced firefighters responded with the fire truck. It was an especially hot fire and when they arrived they could see flames shooting out the top of the chimney. Fortunately the fire had not progressed to the house itself. A ladder was quickly propped against the house and one firefighter climbed onto the high roof, pulling behind him a charged water hose from the fire truck. He crawled cautiously up to the chimney, put the fog nozzle into the top opening and quickly turned on the water.

That's when he learned lesson #1 from Chimney Firefighting 101: "Never spray water down a burning chimney." When the spray of water hit the fire and hot bricks, it instantly turned to a huge quantity of steam. The hot, expanding steam immediately changed direction and exploded out the top of the chimney like a cannon shot. The explosion launched many bricks and one very startled fireman off the roof still clutching the writhing fire hose as if it was an enraged python with a bareback rider. Luckily he got off with minor injuries. The good news was that all that steam did put out the fire.

Whenever a fire occurred, Henry, as Fire Warden/Chief (or more likely his wife, Jessie), would get a call that the fire truck was needed. If he was out of town, Jessie would locate someone else with knowledge of the truck to get it on its way. Next she frantically placed call after call to residents notifying them of the need for firefighters. She always kept a phone list that indicated what times of day each potential firefighter was likely to be home and available. As the fire truck proceeded to the fire, the sight and sound were unmistakable even though the old International truck lacked flashing lights and siren. Usually, by the time the truck reached the fire several helpers were already there and others were following close behind the truck. The old International didn't have a lot of power, its load was heavy, and Leyden hills were steep. Often, by the time the truck arrived on site, the original fire source was beyond saving and the focus was on keeping the fire from spreading to adjacent structures.

The International was the only fire truck the town had until 1957 and by then it was getting pretty tired. Loaded down with 250 gallons of water and firefighting equipment, it barely had sufficient power to climb some of the town's steep hills. Realizing that newer and better equipment was needed, Henry and several others again lobbied for money to buy a real fire truck, build a fire station, and train a core group of firefighters. Some incentive was provided after investigation revealed that most residents would receive a reduction of their fire insurance rates if those three conditions were met. One of the insurance requirements was that to obtain the reduced rates, the new fire truck would have to carry a minimum of 1000 feet of 2 1/2-inch fire hose. The fact that there was not a single hydrant in town to attach all that hose to did not matter. Once the hose existed, everybody got the discount.

A special Town Meeting was called and limited money was approved. A concrete block fire house was built between the Town Hall and the Town Shed and a used Mack fire pumper, in good condition, was located in Connecticut. The truck was driven to Leyden for testing by personnel from the Greenfield Fire Department who announced that the truck was in excellent condition. The "new" fire truck had numerous advantages over the old International. It carried more water, had a larger pump that was driven by the truck's engine, and had two booster hose reels that were always hooked up and ready for use. Another advantage was that, in the winter, the hot engine coolant could be routed around the fire pump and water piping to keep them from freezing; however, the personnel driving the truck could freeze since it was open cab with no roof.

The Mack, Leyden's first real fire truck. Note the open cab.

During the summer of 1958 or 1959 Deputy Chief Tetreault of the Greenfield Fire Department put on a well-attended training course for the members of Leyden's very first official Volunteer Fire Department. Everyone learned how to operate the "new" Mack fire truck, wear protective gear, and put out various types of fires. Deputy Tetreault was very impressed with our truck when, while parked on the Green River Bridge, it drafted water all the way up from the river below. "There are few trucks in my department that could do that," he said. In between training sessions, the fledgling fire department worked with a number of land owners to partially dam streams and provide fire truck access to existing ponds, but these were often miles apart.

A new skill for everyone was learning how to use the 2-way radio in the truck to call the Mutual Aid Center or converse with personnel in fire trucks from other towns. For years, Leyden had depended heavily on fire equipment from Bernardston, Colrain, or Greenfield whenever there was a fire of any magnitude. A Mutual Aid organization had been created in which fire equipment was dispatched wherever it was needed from a central command center in the Greenfield Fire Department.

I was a teenager and was overjoyed by the prospect of the weekly firefighting training sessions that I was permitted to attend. That same summer I had won a seat in the chemistry section of the Summer Science Program given at Thayer Academy in Braintree. Jessie wasn't too pleased when I turned it down to attend firefighter training in Leyden instead. Henry didn't say a word, but I think he was secretly pleased to have his son taking the training right beside him. To this day I am glad that I did.

Sometimes there was no adult available to get the fire truck on the road when a call came in. This was an opportunity for high adventure for Cousin Billy and me. We were country boys and had been driving farm trucks and tractors since we were 12 years old. With or without a driver's license, we could drive the Mack fire truck as well as anybody, and did on several occasions. We knew how to get it pumping water once we arrived too. Once or twice we might have been just a touch short on common sense however.

One time, there was a call for a barn fire at Jimmy Britten's farm toward the south end of East Hill. His was not the typical Leyden subsistence farm, but was more of a full-sized hobby farm. He was a very successful architect in Greenfield. His farm was noted for its fine herd of Jersey cattle and big raspberry patches. Leyden residents could pick all the raspberries they wanted for a very nominal fee, rather like picking blueberries at Donnie Herron's.

When the call came in, Henry was out of town, as was Uncle Bill. Jessie took the call, but it was going to take some phone calls to round up a gang of firefighters. As soon as we understood what was going on, Cousin Billy and I started for the firehouse on a dead run. We jumped into the Mack fire truck and off we went with me driving and Billy manning the siren and clanging the bell. We attracted the attention of every potential firefighter along the way and accumulated a pretty good following.

To get to the Britton farm, we had to go up Frizzell Hill

Road to the top of East Hill and then go south. It seemed to take forever for the truck to get to the top of the hill. It had a lot more power than the International, but the truck itself was much heavier. Add in the weight of all that 2 1/2 inch hose and other firefighting gear, and top it off with a ton and a half of water and the Mack's engine had quite a load to deal with. What made the hill climb so bad was that a few years earlier the state highway engineer decided to take out the switchbacks on the steepest section. The new road went straight up with a steep grade instead of switchbacks weaving back and forth to create lesser slopes. The switchbacks had dated from before Model T days and "had no place in a modern roadway." I had to crunch the truck into its lowest gear in order to crawl up that long steep stretch. It was more than a little embarrassing that while struggling up that hill with the siren blaring and bell clanging, Phil Zimmerman and another driver actually passed us!

When we finally made it to the top, a plume of very dark smoke identified our destination. One of us immediately got on the radio and called the Mutual Aid Center. We had recently had training in truck to truck water relays and thought that this would be a good time to put it into practice. In a water relay, the first truck pulls water from a source such as a pond or river. A second truck attaches one end of 1000 feet of hose to the discharge side of the first truck's pump, drives up the road until it runs out of hose and attaches the second end to the intake side of its own pump. Additional trucks repeat this process until, finally, the last truck reaches the fire and is fed with a continuous, high volume, supply of water just as if from a fire hydrant. With that in mind we called for five additional trucks. Of course the downside of the plan was the time it would take for all the trucks to arrive from other towns and get the relay set up.

When we arrived at the farm, the barn was fully engulfed with flames shooting through the roof and out the sides. Some men were getting the last of the cattle out as we pulled up between the barn and a stone wall. Men started rolling out the booster hoses from the reels. Someone pointed out that the barn was a total loss and the 350 gallons of water on our truck "wasn't going to make a damn bit of difference." The house was near the barn and a better use of our water would be to cool the house to keep it from bursting into flames. However, I had driven past the house, the hoses were already out and cars had blocked the road behind. Phil Zimmerman jumped in and drove the truck around the barn and through the field behind it to approach the house. It was then we noticed that somebody had arrived with the old International and it was busy pumping water onto the house and the Mack had yet to pump one drop.

Another embarrassing incident for Billy and me was during one of the annual blueberry fires. As usual, it happened on a warm April or May day. A farmer was taking advantage of the warm dry weather to burn over some blueberry patches. Some wind came up, as it often does with a fire, and whipped up the flames which soon became too much for the farmer and his helpers to control. After the fire departed the blueberry patch, it headed for the pine woods. Once again, Billy and I were off to the rescue in the Mack. When we arrived, it was obvious where the fire was going, so we decided to head it off at the pass, so to speak. We drove the fire truck off the dirt road, across a field and started cross country up a hill. Upon reaching the crest, we were met by a raging inferno coming up the other side. Just below us, entire juniper and pine trees were bursting into flames as if doused with lighter fluid. The flames were quickly leaping closer and closer from tree to tree, often without touching the ground in between. Until you have actually seen how fast a fire can move uphill through dry grass and pines, it is difficult to believe. And, you don't want to be on top of that hill!

Our first instinct was to unreel the booster hoses and make a stand right there. Fortunately, our second instinct made a lot more sense and we decided to head back down the way we had just come. I don't know what Billy was thinking, but for some reason I don't remember being scared of the fire. I just kept thinking of how mad Henry was going to be if we burned up the new fire truck!

After nearly high centering the truck on a large rock, I finally got it turned around. If anyone saw us coming back down the hill, it must have been a comical sight. Picture a fire truck bouncing down the hill with flames licking at its tail. Had it been a few decades later, it probably could have been a prize winning video on *America's Funniest*. There was a small pond at the foot of the hill near the road and that seemed like a better place to make our stand. The flames wouldn't be moving as fast coming downhill and there would be a lot more water available. By the time we got near the pond, Henry was arriving in his pickup truck. He told us that several Mutual Aid trucks would be arriving soon. Taking over the driving, he dropped Billy and me off by the pond along with the portable pump which was always carried on the rear of the Mack. Henry instructed us that our job for the rest of the day was to use the portable pump to fill the water tanks on fire trucks that would be coming down off the hill for a refill. We set up the pump at the edge of the water, laid out 100 feet of 1 1/2-inch hose and wet down the nearby grass and brush to create a safe area. As he drove away, Henry's last instruction to us was that if the fire got close we were to abandon the pump and get ourselves out to the center of the pond.

Whatever the fire, wherever it was, or whoever needed help, there were always lots of Leyden residents who gladly dropped what they were doing to lend a hand. There was no pay, and none was expected. You helped your neighbor because it was the right thing to do and you never knew when you might be the next to need some assistance.

Chapter 18

THE PARTY LINE

Three of the most influential events that made the largest contributions to the dramatic changes in the American way of life during the twentieth century were: (1) the development of the reliable, inexpensive automobile; (2) the routine availability of cheap electric power, and (3) the telephone. All three were introduced to the sparsely settled New England hill towns such as Leyden later than they were in the more populated flatland areas. During much of the year, road conditions were not favorable to travel by early automobiles. Repair facilities, it they existed, were far apart. Telephone and electric companies were not inclined to go to the expense of installing poles and wires along miles and miles of long country roads in order to sign up only a few paying customers.

Nevertheless, Arms says that just before the turn of the century, the first telephones arrived in Leyden. That seems like quite a feat considering that phone service between New York and Boston didn't exist until 1894. By the 1950s, most homes in Leyden had telephone service. There were, however, some exceptions. A few houses didn't have phone service because the telephone company still hadn't seen fit to run lines down some long backwoods roads. Other residents, such as Frank and Bertha Wood living on Henry's farm, didn't see the need to pay a monthly phone bill when they had lived all their lives without "that contraption." The Gerry family, living next door to Henry and Jessie, did not have phone service until the late 1950s, or early 1960s. It wasn't that they were anti-telephone. They always used the phone in our house for both making and receiving calls. When they would get a call on our phone, one of us would walk over to their house and notify the requested party. It was not at all uncommon for the teenage daughter, Juanita, to be sitting in our living room talking on our phone with a boyfriend! For a few years, we sort of did a trade-off since they had one of the first TVs in town. Orilla and I spent some Saturday nights at their house watching TV broadcasts from Springfield or Holyoke. We seldom cared what programs were on; it was the uniqueness of the experience that intrigued us. We even enjoyed the commercials.

To most residents, phone service simply was not looked at as the essential utility that it is today. It was more of a convenience than a necessity. That was a good thing because service was not especially reliable in the hills back then. The phone wires were strung along the roads on poles and in some areas they were simply attached to convenient roadside trees. Falling tree branches sometimes broke the line and a heavy snowstorm or rain could short out the system. Sometimes the phones would be down for several days at a time, especially if the outage was widespread. The phone company always gave first priority to getting the much more populated areas outside of Leyden back up and running.

Prior to WWII, the party line was the most common type of phone service in the US. However, some large cities had eliminated party lines as early as the 1920s or 1930s. In the New England hill towns and other rural areas of the country, party lines existed well into the 1960s and 1970s. I would bet that party lines still exist in some areas of the USA even today.

A party line was essentially a single phone line that was shared by multiple residences. Henry and Jessie's house was initially on an 8-party line. That meant that any one of eight phone subscribers could use the line and if one person was using it, everyone else had to wait until that person was done with it. When there was an incoming call, the way you knew that a call was for your house was by the unique series of rings assigned to your phone. Jessie's house phone ring was two short rings followed by one long. Every house on the line heard each other's rings, so if you wanted to eavesdrop or even participate in the conversation, all you had to do was pick up the receiver.

Generally, everyone on the party line was cooperative and took a share-and-share-alike attitude. However, a few "line hogs" were sometimes a problem. The phone company recommended that calls on party lines be held to a maximum of five minutes out of consideration for others. But, sometimes phone conversations would go on for an hour or more. If the line was in use, and you wanted to use it, you would pick up the receiver, hear voices, and set it back down. The phone users would hear the clicks and hopefully understand that someone else wanted to use the line. In case of an emergency, it was not only permissible to interrupt the users and ask them to get off the line, I believe it was the law.

Jessie would sometimes get very frustrated when she needed to use the phone and some line hog had it tied up for well past what she considered to be an acceptable amount of time. On one occasion after she had been doing the pickup and set down routine for over an hour, she decided to tell the line hog exactly what she thought of her. After listening to the conversation for a couple of minutes, she interrupted, "Gertrude, this is Jessie. Nobody is interested in hearing about how your new cake recipe turned out. You've had the line tied up for an hour and it is time you let somebody else use it." It was probably quite some time before Gertrude and Jessie were on speaking terms again.

Sometime, probably in the mid to late 1950s, a lot of the eight-party lines were replaced with four-party. The system was the same, except there were only four subscribers to share a line instead of eight. Henry's shop was one of the four, as was the house, so there were only two other users on our line which greatly improved our service.

Being on a shared party line had one big advantage: The shop phone could be answered from the house; it simply had a different ring. That was often the case because if Henry was out of town, or working on something he couldn't immediately stop, Jessie would pick up at the house. Often she could take a message or schedule a shoeing appointment without bothering Henry. If the caller needed to talk with him, she would step out the door and holler as loudly as possible, "HENNNRY. ANNSWEEER THEEE PHOOONE!" It was said that many a meeting in the Town Hall was interrupted by chuckles resulting from hearing Jessie's vocalizations.

Just as with phone service, it was not at all unusual for a house or farm to still not be supplied with electric service in the early 1950s. To get electric power, the electric company needed to run a line past each house and, just as with phone service, if there were few houses on a long road, it would not be very cost effective. Also, as with phones, there were more than a few residents who saw no need for electric service, or could not afford it.

Arms' book states that the first electric service arrived in Leyden in 1932. That seems a bit late, given that some houses that were constructed before that date have the appearance of having had electric wiring installed when built. Nobody disputed the fact that electric lights were a tremendous improvement over kerosene lamps. Many existing homes had wiring installed as soon as the electric company provided power in their vicinity. Even in the late 1950s, my Uncle Howard Wood, who was an electrician living in Vermont, was still doing a lot of electrical conversions of old houses in rural areas.

Some of the first residential electric power systems were not the AC system we use today, but were DC, or direct current supplied by a bank of batteries. In our house and the shop in the 1950s, there were still vestiges of that earlier DC system, although, it was no longer in use. The wires were of a heavy gauge and were surface mounted using large porcelain insulators. I know that there used to be a bank of lead-acid batteries that supplied the electricity for the lights in the house. The early electrical distribution system was fairly unreliable for the same reasons that the phone system often went out. With a battery powered DC system in your house, the electric company's power, when available, was used to recharge the batteries. If the power company's lines went down, you still had electricity from your batteries, at least for a while. As electrical distribution became more reliable, in-house DC systems went out of favor. It is interesting that today DC systems are being given a second look due to the emerging field of solar electricity.

These days, every time there is a bad storm or some other type of emergency, the news media fall all over themselves to exaggerate how many hundreds or thousands of people are without power, always quoting the largest possible number anyone might believe. Electrical line workers are often brought in from hundreds of miles away from the outage area in an attempt to restore power to the suffering citizens. In the New England hill country of the 1950s, an electrical power outage was a nuisance, but was far from a life threatening event. Many people had lived most of their lives without electricity at all, and if it was not available for a few days, it was no big deal. Realizing that electric power couldn't always be depended upon, many people were sure to have a means of heating their homes, cooking their food, and obtaining water independent of the power grid. A day or two without power was an inconvenience, but not an emergency.

Chapter 19

SUMMER WAS TOO SHORT

Summer was the shortest season of the year, if you were a schoolboy in the 1950s. School got out about the middle of June and started again in September, shortly after Labor Day. The days in between rushed by like leaves blown in the wind. It was the time of lazy days, and not having to worry about getting a school project completed, or studying for a weekly spelling test. If you were having a good summer, you didn't even know what day of the week it was!

Memorial Day was the unofficial start of summer, even if there was about two more weeks of school still to go. Of course those two weeks didn't amount to much, since the teacher was just as anxious as we were to get it over with. Memorial Day was always a big event in Leyden, bigger than July 4th. It was the day for honoring everyone, living and dead, who had served in the US military, no matter how long ago. It was also the time for visiting the graves of all family members and friends. WWII was not long over, and patriotic fever still ran high. Everyone knew exactly why the USA fought in that war and they were proud of what our service men and women accomplished. It was not like all the wars since, that were not fought to win.

For much the same reasons, October 11 was celebrated in the fall. Originally called Armistice Day, (Army Stick Day as Grandpa Frank called it) it was to celebrate the signing of the armistice to end WWI on the 11th hour of the 11th day of the 11th month. I guess it wasn't an official federal or state holiday because we were in school unless the 11th fell on a weekend. In school, we were always required to have a minute of silence at that exact time. With the passage of time, that holiday has morphed into Veteran's day and has increasingly been demoted to that third tier of holidays that are celebrated mainly by the Post Office.

A major part of the Memorial Day celebration was always held at one of the town cemeteries, most often the South Cemetery, which was the only one that was well maintained in those days. The grass was always well trimmed, families placed flowers on the graves of loved ones, and the town placed small US flags on the graves of all who had been in the service no matter how long ago, even from before the USA became the USA. Veterans who still had their uniforms, and could still fit into them, would gather up the road from the cemetery and march in as a unit trying to stay in step and look very military. As the years passed, and waistlines grew, many uniforms became little more than a hat. Jessie would often be the one to arrange for the loan of rifles and blank ammunition from an American Legion or VFW post. A local official or two would say a few words and a minister would say a prayer. This was followed by a 21-gun salute fired by the veterans before they marched back out. Kids would scramble to collect the spent shell casings of the blanks that had been fired.

As we grew older, our summers meant more and more responsibilities, and we had less and less free time. From the age of about ten on, most days I was expected to tend the gas pumps at the shop. I quickly learned not only how to pump gasoline, but to how to check oil levels, inflate tires, and a host of other car related things. I became really good at knowing where the gas fill-pipe was located on most cars. Unlike today, when the pipe is just about always an ugly round door in the side of a rear fender, manufacturers used to be quite clever as to where they hid the thing. On many cars you had to tip down the rear license plate holder. On others it was necessary to flip up one of the tail lights. It was always very embarrassing to have to ask the driver where it was located.

Being around the shop, when Henry was away shoeing, provided me numerous opportunities to do things that I'm sure he never expected me to do at a young age. I remember one time when I was tending the shop, a farmer came in with a piece of iron that needed to be straightened. It was off of some tractor implement that had caught on a large rock and become twisted to the point of not being useable. Of course I had played around with the forge many times, but I had never used it to actually repair something before. I figured it wouldn't hurt to give it a try, so I told the farmer I'd get right on it and he could wait if he wished.

The forge fire was out, but I had seen Henry start it many times, so I soon had it roaring. The metal piece was too long to heat all at once which was good because there would be a cool end to hang onto. After several heatings, hammerings, and coolings the farmer agreed that it was much straighter than before and would probably now fit back on his machine. Afterward I wondered if he said that just to get it away from me before I totally ruined the piece.

Some years, the summer would be very dry, yet somehow Henry's garden would always produce a surplus of produce. There was no provision for applying irrigation water to the garden soil, so usually the only moisture received was from rain. Sometimes when it hadn't rained for quite a while, Jessie would collect the gray water from the kitchen and carry it to Henry's garden in a large pail. There, it was ladled out to nourish the youngest and most needy seedlings. Once the plants became well established, Henry would permit some weeds to grow among them. Common knowledge said that was a mistake because the weeds stole water and nutrients from the vegetables. However, Henry always said that the weeds provided some shade from the hot sun which helped to keep his plants from wilting. In August and September customers stopping at the shop for gas could usually count on being offered free fresh garden vegetables.

We pretty much ate out of the garden from about the end

of June until October. Whatever was ready for harvest was what we ate. Corn was always my favorite and it was not at all unusual for me to eat five or six ears at supper. Henry always planted two or three different varieties of corn with different maturities, giving us a plentiful supply from late July well into September.

With the coming of warm summer days, the annual fear of polio returned. The disease often didn't kill outright, but left its victims partially, to nearly totally, paralyzed. The most terrifying aspect was that there seemed to be little known about how it was spread. It appeared to hit children more than adults, and it was clear that it affected urban areas more than rural. It was generally believed to be quite contagious, so many people avoided crowds and gatherings during the hot months. This gave a small bit of comfort to residents of sparsely settled Leyden. Many parents did not take their children to Greenfield shopping, and I remember not being allowed to go to the county fair one year. One result of the horrifying ailment was demonstrated in dramatic fashion by a touring exhibit of a live polio victim sentenced to spend the rest of his life in an iron lung. The summer of 1952 saw the peak of the polio epidemic, and in 1955, Dr. Jonas Salk's vaccine became available. Inoculation of school age children, and others, was begun immediately and the effect was dramatic. Thankfully, today the disease is just about eradicated from the earth.

Summer was a season of hard work for Leyden farmers. Soon after the spring plowing and planting was over, it was time to start planning for the haying season. Most farmers grew and harvested on their own land, most of the hay that would be needed to feed their stock through the coming winter. The main crop was cut in early June. If it was a good growing year, one or two additional crops would be harvested also. After several years of being mowed, the strength of the grass began to weaken and sometimes farmers would plow the hay fields and reseed them. Since Leyden soil tended to be rather acidic, it was common practice to apply some lime at the time of reseeding. Large loads of lime would be hauled in from Lee, MA.

Haying consisted of several steps. First, the hay was mowed by a sickle bar mower. Some of the older mowers designed to be pulled by horses were still in use, but most were being pulled by a small tractor or WWII surplus Jeep. It was a rather comical sight to see a tractor or Jeep being driven around in a field towing a mower with a second person riding on the mower. The more affluent farmers had a mower which attached directly to the tractor. It cut a six to eight foot wide swath with each pass and required only one person to operate it.

After mowing, the hay needed to dry in the sun. This was a critical time weather-wise. Several warm sunny days were required for proper drying. If it rained, the drying had to start all over again. If the hay was wetted too much, it might become unusable as cow and horse feed. If it was not sufficiently dry when baled or stored in the barn, hay could grow mold and also be unusable as feed. Sometimes a farmer would try to speed up drying by moving the hay around with a tractor-pulled rake or tedder to get it up off the ground and permit better air circulation. That also would help minimize the formation of mold.

Once it was dry, the farmer would rake the hay into rows using a side delivery rake. Small farms would use an older dump style rake pulled behind whatever was handy, even a horse. By the 1950s, most hay was bailed, although some farms still put away loose hay. Balers were pricey machines and often two or three farmers would go in together on the purchase of one. Or, a farmer might buy his own and then rent out baling time to other farmers. The bailer was towed along each row, pulled loose hay in, tightly packed it into rectangular bales, and tied it tightly with two pieces of heavy twine. Then the bales dropped to the ground as the machine moved down the row. Today's widely used machines that automatically load bales onto a following wagon had not yet come into common use, or maybe hadn't been invented. Human muscle power was the only "machine" used to load bales onto a truck or wagon.

About the worst nightmare a farmer could imagine was to

get his hay baled, and then have it rained on before he had it picked up and stored in the barn. One time I helped a farmer cut the twine and spread out the hay to redry an entire field full of wet bales. After it had dried again, it was rebaled and this time it made it into the barn without getting wet. The Zimmerman's had a hayfield just below our house and they even cut hay in our apple orchard which adjoined their field. One day, as they were baling, it became obvious that a big thunderstorm was approaching. Several hundred bales were already on the ground. Casper continued baling while Phil and a few other family members worked frantically loading bales onto their truck, rushing to the barn to unload, and charging back for load after load.

Meanwhile, at the blacksmith shop, Henry and Bill had just completed building a truck body on a customer's new truck. The truck's owner, and his son, were there waiting for it to be ready. As the sky became more and more threatening, everyone at the shop became aware of the Zimmerman's frantic efforts. The tailgate and sideboards were quickly stripped off of the newly completed cattle truck body and everyone set out across the field with the new truck to start picking up bales. Fortunately the storm held off until all but about a dozen bales were in the barn before Mother Nature cut loose with a gully washer.

When I had reached the age of 12 or 13 years, I spent many summer days working for farmers in their hay fields. My job was often to drive the truck or tractor slowly through the field while men loaded bales. Once we had a load, I would drive to the barn, but one of the men always backed the load in. I often protested that it didn't look all that hard to back a truck into the barn using the mirrors and I should be given a chance. Tiring of hearing my constant requests, one day I was finally allowed to back a load in. The result was the destruction of the truck's right side mirror as it crunched the side of the barn door opening. To this day I have difficulty backing a vehicle using the mirrors.

As I got a little bigger I graduated to the loader's job. The loader rode on the back of the truck or trailer and positioned each bale as the men walking alongside tossed them up. As the height of the load increased, the men could not throw the bales to the top and I would have to catch them with a hay hook. I was only knocked unconscious once when, instead of me pulling it up, an extra heavy bale pulled me off the load headfirst onto the ground.

Several of the kids who lived on farms, raised one or more animals as a 4-H project. Usually, they would start with a young calf or pig in the spring and pamper the animal all summer long preparing it for showing at the Franklin County Fair at the end of the summer. If the animal did well there, it might be shown again at the Eastern States Exposition in Springfield, providing another wonderful excuse to miss several more days of school.

By late August, the sun was rising noticeably later, and setting noticeably sooner. If you ventured out of doors in the evening, often a light jacket was needed. Most years there would be a killer frost before September was done. That frost did in the tomato plants as well as the cucumbers, squash and peppers, but enhanced the flavor of the turnips and parsnips. Another big plus was the elimination of all the pesky mosquitoes until next May. The end of the fair season pretty much marked the time at which there would be a big drop off in the amount of work around the farms. The crops were in, and most of the preparations for winter were well underway. There was less need for kids to help. Soon after Labor Day it was time to buckle down for the start of a new school year.

Chapter 20

BASEBALL WAS KING

Organized, or semi-organized, competitive sports for adults still played a big role in many New England towns in the 1950s. Participation in physical sports was common in those days, before "sports" came to mean beer and snacks in an easy chair, while watching others play on TV. In Leyden, very few homes had a television, radio reception was often iffy, and the nearest movie theaters were in Greenfield, over 10 miles away. In the winter, some men played informal hockey on various ponds around town. For a few years, there was an organized men's basketball team that played in the Town Hall. Screens of half-inch hardware cloth covered the windows to avoid breakage and basketball hoops were installed on the east and west walls. The width of the room fell quite a few feet short of the length of an official basketball court, but the players didn't seem to mind. Visiting teams from other towns got a good chuckle out of Leyden's short court.

In the 1950s, many small New England towns still had local adult baseball teams. Players were young men anywhere from their mid-teens to their mid-thirties or more. The men's baseball team played their home games on the town field behind what is now the Pearl E. Rhodes Elementary School. Games sometimes drew a small crowd of relatives and fans to sit on the hillside and watch. It was a great way of relaxing and socializing following a hard week of farming or working in a Greenfield or Turner's Falls factory. There were regular game schedules with teams traveling to neighboring towns to take on the locals. Games were held on Friday nights or Saturday mornings with the losing team often providing the beer afterward.

Emulating the adults, we school kids played baseball at every recess, sometimes even if there was snow on the ground. During the summer months, there was often an impromptu game as long as we could come up with enough players. Most of us were Red Sox fans, and Ted Williams was our hero in spite of the BoSox' very predictable drop in the standings toward the end of season after season. In those days major sports figures tended to be good role models, rather than the overpaid, whining, spoiled brats that so many are today.

I inherited my interest in baseball, especially the Red Sox, from Henry. It seems that from the time I could walk, he was forever taking me outside to toss a ball for me to catch. Jessie would complain that a baseball was too hard, and I could get hurt, but he insisted that I had to learn to handle the real thing. "Rubber balls are for sissies," he would say.

The first baseball glove I had was one of his hand-me-downs from his playing days. It greatly resembled the gloves you see in the photos of baseball players from the very early 1900s. It was nearly flat with almost no pocket, very little padding, and the fingers were not strung together. The only way to catch a ball with that glove was with the palm of your hand. If it was a batted, or hard-thrown ball, it hurt a lot. After several catches, my hand began to swell up creating its own padding. As I got older and started playing ball with friends, I took a lot of ribbing about my old-fashioned glove. Every week I begged Jessie for a new, modern glove, but the answer was always the same, it wasn't in the budget. Finally, for my birthday, a new glove arrived embossed with the name "Williams," but who in the world was "Dick?" Regardless of the name, the new glove was a huge improvement. My hand hurt less and I finally had at least an even chance of scooping up grounders.

The World Series was always looked forward to with great excitement even though year after year, we Red Sox fans had given up hope long before September; not much different than today. Much of the interest in major league baseball in the late summer centered around which National League team was going to meet the Yankees in the World Series; something else that doesn't seem to have changed much. In those days, before TV advertisers imposed all the rules, World Series games were played in the afternoon. If the Series was on, it seemed as if everyone had an ear tuned to a radio, no matter what they were doing. One year, when the Series went down to the final game, the oldest boys in school convinced Miss Rhodes to allow them to bring a battery-operated radio to school and have the game on quietly while we were in class.

As time marched on, the focus moved from local adult sports to kid's sports, coached and regulated by adults. Most adults were becoming content to watch the pros play on TV rather than participating themselves, a trend that is still very much in evidence today in much of the US. By the late 1950s, most towns had begun to form official Little League baseball teams in which kids were suited up like little Mickey Mantles, had first class equipment, and had adult coaches who made every decision.

Junior (Wayne) Fisher, Peter Snow, Willie Herron, Billy Glabach, Wayne Chapin and I decided that we wanted to have a team to play against teams from other towns. We officially called it the Leyden Boy's Ball Club. We had several major problems to overcome. First, we didn't have a coach, but we figured we knew the rules, and who was the best player in each position, so we didn't need one. At times we needed a bit of adult help, so we prevailed on Junior Fisher's dad, Wayne Fisher, Sr. to fill that position. Second, where were we going to find enough kids in town to field a full team? There just were not enough boys in town to come up with nine bodies of roughly the same age, let alone nine good ball players plus a few bench warmers. Somehow a few younger and older players found their way onto the field. One was Junior's younger brother, Bobby Fisher. He was several years younger than most of us, but that kid could really play ball. A few times a ringer or two, such as Rodney Pillard, had to be imported from "just over the line" in Bernardston or Colrain in order to fill out a roster. Our team had some of the shortest and tallest players around! We rarely had any extras, so if somebody was hurt, we were in trouble. Our depth chart was nonexistent. Junior Fisher was the only player on our team who had a prayer of throwing strikes. On game days, it was Junior on the mound for nine innings every time.

Our third problem was money, or more correctly, equipment. We didn't have any. We had no hope of ever having real uniforms like other teams, but at least matching hats would be nice. Also, we needed a few things like a supply of baseballs, catcher's equipment, a couple of bats that weren't all nicked up from batting stones, a real home plate, and bases to take the place of the boards and flat rocks we had always used.

I remember one of our early games, against a team from Guilford, when the game had a significant delay because of a shortage of baseballs. As the home team, it was our duty to supply the baseballs for the game. Among several of us we managed to come up with two decent balls although one had to be improved a bit with some white paint. Usually two balls would suffice since they were seldom hit far enough to get lost in the woods, or brook, that bordered our field.

Somewhere around the third or fourth inning, I came to bat and hit a magnificent foul ball just outside the third base line and well back into the trees. We had a spare ball, so nobody spent a lot of time poking around in the trees and brush looking for the one I had hit. I then managed a small hit and outran the throw to first, bringing up Rodney. On about the second pitch, Rodney launched what may have been the longest baseball hit ever made at that field. It may have still been in the air, white paint and all, when it crossed the stream! After Rodney followed me across home plate, the game was stopped for lack of a ball. Finally the Guilford coach conceded that we could use one of their practice balls and the game resumed.

As happened so often in my boyhood, Jessie came up with an idea as to how our team might make some money to buy equipment. She didn't hand out any cash, or set us up to solicit donations. Instead, she suggested a way that the team could perhaps earn the money we needed.

The Saturday night Town Hall square dances, that used to be common, had pretty much gone away except for a few special dates such as Old Home Day. Jessie suggested that our team sponsor a few dances and see what happened.

"What about a band and a caller?" I asked. "Those will be pretty expensive and if we don't get a good crowd we could end up losing money instead of making any."

"Leave that to me," she said.

In those days, I was taking guitar lessons from Mr. Mason (?) at Gibson's Music Store in Greenfield. Jessie knew that he played in a small band. The next time we went to Greenfield for my lesson, she asked him about helping with our problem. They came to an arrangement that his band would be paid $30 a night. However, if the proceeds did not come to that, they would split the take with the boys.

Next, we needed a caller for the square dances. Jessie had that figured out also. A call to Uncle Ted in Dummerston (Henry's brother) resulted in his offer to do the calling for free. We were in business. The dances were held on alternate Saturday nights for about three months. At first, they were well attended, but gradually attendance dropped and we stopped having them, but not before we had made enough money to cover all our team's expenses for the year.

One way our team controlled expenses was to have our dirty, used, dark, scuffed up baseballs recovered. In those days all the baseballs used in the major leagues had their horsehide covers stitched on by hand. Maybe they still do. One day we learned about a woman in Guilford who covered balls for the big leagues. Somehow, we found out that she sometimes had new covers that had been rejected for some reason. When we had several balls that were badly in need of new covers, we would get them up to her and they would be returned looking brand new for a very nominal charge.

Eventually, a group of adults decided that Leyden needed to have an official Little League team, complete with uniforms, new equipment, and boys in the proper age bracket. The Little

League rules excluded most of us on the Boy's Club because we were a bit too old. I have no idea where they came up with enough kids of the right ages to field a full team. I suspect they imported some just as we had. From our point of view, the only good thing about the new team was that the ball field was mowed more often. I remember one game in which I was playing left field and the opposing team had two home runs because I couldn't find the ball in the tall grass!

The new Little League team pretty much took over the ball field and rebuilt it according to the Little League specifications, making it difficult for any other group to play that needed a full sized diamond, but we still tried. They leveled the old pitching mound and built a new one several feet closer to home plate. For a couple of games we tried pitching from the flat dirt where the mound used to be, but that caused all sorts of problems. Not only did it not "feel right," there now was a low hill between the pitcher and the batter. When a ground ball collided with that hill, there was no way to predict where it was going next. I remember one game when I was playing second base and a hot grounder was hit that would normally have come directly to me, just to the first base side of second base. Instead, it struck that hill and angled sharply to the right going foul. Needless to say, the visiting team was not impressed with our field.

To solve our problem with the relocated pitcher's mound, we decided to install a second home plate, at the correct distance from the new mound, for real baseball. That in turn required us to locate new positions for our first, second, and third bases as well. One of the problems with this arrangement was that the catcher was now much closer to the backstop and was likely to slam himself into it while trying to catch a ball that popped up behind him. After a couple of attempts at games with this setup, we decided that it wasn't going to work. Little League, with its adult leadership, had won. We closed out the bank account that held the remaining money from our dances and donated the proceeds to the 4-H club.

It wasn't a sport, but the town did have a couple of very active 4-H clubs in the 1950s. One was called the Leyden

Loggers. Head, Heart, Hands, and Health were the four Hs. Other than limited church youth groups that formed from time to time, 4-H was often the only organized kids group. There had been a Boy Scout troop at one time, long before I was old enough to join. I don't think there ever was a Girl Scout or Campfire Girls, but I could be wrong. When I reached the age of 11, Jessie wanted me to join a Scout troop in Greenfield, but I really didn't want to get into a group of strangers. And, I didn't see any need to learn about the outdoors from a handbook, I was living it. Henry pointed out that it would mean an extra trip to Greenfield every week, so the idea sort of died on the vine.

Orilla was in 4-H for a few years and learned a lot about cooking and sewing. I was a member for a while, but it didn't seem to be my thing. I've never been that much of joiner. There was a wide variety of project areas covered by 4-H, most of which centered on some aspect of farming, especially rearing of livestock. Boys and girls who took their 4-H large animals, usually a cow or a pig, to the county fair in September, were absent from school for a week and many slept in the hay near their animals. These kids were the envy of all the rest of us that did not get to do that.

I never raised a large animal over the course of a whole year. I did talk Henry into converting the space under the garage at the house into a stall. One year, we boarded a milk cow over the summer. It was my job to stake the cow out in the orchard on a long dog-chain during the day and get it back into the stall in the evening. Henry and Uncle Bill tried their best to teach me how to milk the thing, but I never developed the knack, so they had to do it.

The next winter, we boarded a riding horse in the stable and I rode it quite often playing cowboy. That horse did not like the feel of the saddle cinch being tight, so it would inflate its chest when being saddled. Once saddled, it would breathe normally and the saddle would be too loose. Once, as I was riding up the hill past Zimmerman's house, the saddle started to tip to the left side and me with it. I managed to get my feet onto the ground before the saddle turned totally upside down. Instead of trying to fix it, I just led the horse home. I wish I had a photo of me leading that horse with the saddle strapped under its belly.

Chapter 21

THE CHURCH'S

JUICY BURGER SECRET

He goes on Sunday to the church,
And sits among his boys;
He hears the parson pray and preach,
He hears his daughter's voice,
Singing in the village choir,
And it makes his heart rejoice.
Longfellow

As he walked up the steps in front of the church, Bill Glabach noticed two cars pulling into the shared parking lot between the church and Town Hall. He couldn't see the faces of the vehicle's occupants, but he didn't need to. He knew every car in town and who owned it. These two were the first to arrive for the service every Sunday. He thought that the car's occupants liked to sit in the quiet of the church before others arrived. After a quick wave of his hand, he unlocked the door and entered the church foyer. He noted the familiar somewhat musty odor of the more than a century old building. He liked that smell. It was the smell of history, and of something solid that had endured for many years. Turning to the right, he climbed the steep circular stairs to the Sunday School room and glanced at his watch. He was right on time. Taking a firm two handed grip on the thick rope that hung down through a hole in the ceiling, he lifted both his feet off the floor causing the heavy bell in the belfry above to move just a few inches in one direction. Releasing his hold, the rope moved upward a little through the hole as the bell swung back the other way. After three or four repetitions of this cycle, he was rewarded by the first muffled "clunk" as the clapper struck one side of the bell. One more strong pull on the rope and the rhythmic "clang, clang, clang" rang out over the Leyden hills announcing to everyone that they needed to hurry if they were going to arrive in time for the start of the weekly service.

The Methodist Church was one of the oldest buildings in Leyden. It was constructed in 1841 as a joint effort between the two active religious groups in town, the Methodists and Universalists. It was originally known as the New Meeting House and served double duty as the location for town meetings and other functions until the Town Hall was built next door in about 1883. One of the stories I heard about the church when growing up, was that the first church had been located in the Old Center on County Road near the Carpenter Inn. That building was abandoned about 1830 and was moved to what was to become Harold Johnson's farm, where it still served as a barn. The story said that the present church was erected in the new center when the center was relocated. I never heard, or read, of any reason given for the relocation of the center.

In 1941, a 100th Anniversary Committee was formed to research and record the history of the existing church building. The committee consisted of: Reverend Ruel Rust, George Howes, Evelyn Beaudoin, Beatrice Taylor, and Henry Glabach. They published an anniversary souvenir booklet, *The Meeting House... The Methodist Church... Leyden, Massachusetts*. That booklet was the major source of the pre-1950s, church information contained herein.

Photos that were taken before 1900 show the building with two separate front entrances. There was one entrance located beneath each of the outer second floor windows. The reason for the two widely separated doors is unknown. Sometime just

Courtesy of Leyden Historical Commission

The New Meeting House, as it originally appeared with two entrances.

before 1900, those entrances were replaced with windows and a new single entrance was constructed in the middle. At about that same time, the original balcony, or choir loft, was enclosed. In the 1950s, the former choir loft was the Sunday School room.

The church had the appearance of an old, but very well kept, building. A few steps and a large slate landing graced the front. Opening the doors, one entered into a foyer with a wide-board wood floor that had obviously been trodden by worshipers for many, many years. Walking could be difficult if one was not careful, due to the raised knots in the very worn floor. Very narrow, steep, circular stairs to the right led to the Sunday School room. Two doors allowed entry from the foyer into either side of the main room. In the winter, heat was supplied from two stoves at the rear of the room, which I remember well. Smoke from the stoves was piped all the way to the front where the chimneys were located. Sometime in the early or mid-1950s, the wood stoves were replaced with oil-fired or propane heat which I do not remember at all.

In the 1950s, there was both a piano and a foot-pumped organ up front. For many years, Judson Ewer was the organist every Sunday. Judson may have been the only person in town with a doctorate. His training was either in music or botany, possibly both, and he certainly knew a lot about both subjects.

He had been an instructor in botany at the University of Massachusetts and was regularly consulted on botanical topics by town residents. Other than the Sunday services, he largely lived a secluded life, west of the church where his parents had lived, and where, I presume, he grew up. Many people believed that he had a secret crush on my Aunt Leta. He would frequently show up at public, and some family, events that she would be attending. He always remembered her birthday with a card and a small gift. However, as far as I know, they never actually dated.

He supplemented his income by teaching piano to local children and a few adults. One summer, Jessie signed both Orilla and me up for piano lessons. She thought that would be a good use for a lot of our spare time until school began in the fall. Orilla took to it immediately and became quite a good pianist. It seemed to me that the piano was a girl's instrument and I resisted the whole thing making almost no progress and glad of it. Finally, near the end of the summer, Judson stopped by the house and told Jessie that she was wasting money paying for piano lessons for me, as I had no musical talent whatsoever.

The roof of the church was all slate, something that may have saved the structure when the original Town Hall next door burned in 1929. In the late 1950s, there was still a cracked window on the east side due to the heat from that fire. The church had a bell tower or steeple base which contained the large "call to service" bell given to the church in 1905. Uncle Bill Glabach would always ring that bell about 10 minutes before the start of Sunday Service. I heard stories telling that there was also a smaller bell in the tower that was intended as a fire bell, but I never saw it or heard it rung.

An odd feature of the church was that it had no steeple. There was a belfry, or steeple base, but it was not topped by a pointed steeple as was the almost universal practice in old New England churches. The anniversary booklet, published in 1941, contains no clues as to why there was no steeple. However, I do remember being told more than once that the church originally had a steeple. One story was that it had been blown off in the hurricane of 1938 and was never replaced due to the cost and lack of insurance. If that was true, when the committee wrote the church history in 1941, with the 1938 hurricane fresh in everyone's memory, it seems that the loss of the steeple would have been mentioned. Yet, no mention was made in that booklet of any hurricane damage. I have no idea what the original source of the hurricane story was, but it was not true. In the limited research that I did for this chapter, I came across several photos of the church, dated as early as prior to 1900, which show the church with no steeple. There is even one showing the building with its original two front entrances, but no steeple.

Henry's brother, Wilhelm (Bill), and wife, Doris Glabach, lived in a house they built diagonally across from the church. They were the caretakers for the church for many years, just as Henry was caretaker of the Town Hall. As with nearly all other aspects of the town, Henry was active with the church although he didn't attend Sunday services all that often. He was chairman of the board of trustees for many years and headed up the committee in charge of repairs and improvements that were made in the 1940s. He was also one of the authors of the 1941 history booklet.

Jessie was a very active member of the Leyden Methodist Church. Unlike Henry, she rarely missed a service, but she never chided Henry for his spotty attendance. She realized that Sunday was his only day off after putting in 60 to 70 hours working Monday through Saturday every week. Actually, his "day off" was usually spent working on small projects in the shop or around the house. As kids, Orilla and I were usually not given any choice, and were expected to accompany Jessie most Sundays. As the church treasurer, Jessie came home each Sunday with the offering safely stashed in a cloth sack inside her large purse. After counting and recording everything, the bills and checks were deposited into the church's bank account within a day or two. The coins, that sometimes represented the lion's share of the offering, were dumped into a large glass bowl that sat in the lower middle drawer of her dining room buffet, to be rolled and banked at a later date.

About every other month, Jessie would declare a coin wrapping night. In those days, banks did not have automatic coin counters and would not accept buckets of loose change. Jessie, Orilla, and I would sit for hours counting and wrapping coins. We would often find a few old or unusual coins among the common ones. Silver dollars, Indian head pennies, Mercury dimes, and coins with pre-1900 dates were common, as were Canadian coins. Generally, Canadian coins, in small quantities, were accepted by most businesses, and even banks, as equivalent to their US counterparts. Jessie seemed to know quite a lot about coins and sparked my interest. Often, when we would come across something especially unusual, she would let me run up to my room and return with a more ordinary coin of the same value to make an exchange. The morning after the wrapping session, I usually helped Jessie take them to the bank. After our counting and recounting to be sure of having the correct number of coins in each roll, it amazed me that the teller could always tell by the feel of a wrapped roll of pennies if it was over or under by as little as one penny out of the proper fifty.

Nearly every Sunday, a small piece of tightly folded white paper would be found among the coins, bills, and checks. It was always an IOU written out for exactly 50 cents each week. Often there was a small drawing of a flower, bird, or animal in one corner. Written along the bottom edge it always said, "To be paid when I have it." Jessie was well aware of the financial condition of the donor, so she never presented the IOUs for collection, and she never divulged to anyone who the author of those IOUs was. Each week, the new slip of paper was added to an envelope containing all the previous editions. The envelope was then safely tucked away underneath the bowl of coins.

Jessie and Henry always helped with all the church activities. For many years, Jessie was on the committee for the church's food booth at the Franklin County Fair. The fair ran for about a week each September and it was common knowledge that year after year, the Leyden Church Booth had the best food of any booth on the grounds. There were numerous places where a fairgoer could get a hotdog or hamburger, but the Church Booth was the only place to get "real food."

Notes compiled by Katie Ainsworth indicate that the original food booth was built in 1938. Henry built the walls in his shop, and with several helpers, quickly fastened the building together on the fairgrounds. The original booth was little more than a shack with a dirt floor and canvas roof. Customers sat around the outside on some of Henry's empty horseshoe kegs before proper benches were added a few years later. Some of the cooking activities took place out of doors for lack of room inside. Ruth Herron spent untold hours sitting by a tree stump peeling onions and potatoes for the booth's famous beef stew which I am told is still made from the original recipe over 70 years later. That recipe may be found in Appendix D along with a few others.

The Leyden Church Food Booth at the Franklin County Fair,
as it appeared in the early 1950s.

For many years there was no running water in the booth. Water was carried in buckets from the large round water tank by the stock barns next door; something that would probably give a health department inspector a heart attack today. Over the years, several additions and remodelings of the booth took place, which made things more convenient for both the helpers and the customers. Most of the workers in the booth were the women of the church, organized as the Women's Society of Christian Service, or WSCS. However, husbands and even older children were frequently drafted to help out as well. As a teenager, I often worked there as a waiter or cashier on weekends.

Sometimes it was difficult to come up with enough helpers to properly function. One of the most frequent, knowledgeable, and dependable workers every year was Edith Fisher. Over the years, she performed every job that was required in the booth. She peeled vegetables, cooked stews and chowders, washed dishes, swept floors, waited on customers, was cashier, etc. If it needed doing, Edith did it. One day, the lunch hour was approaching and only Edith and Jessie were working at the booth. The promised extra help had not yet arrived, but lunch customers would be arriving soon. "Well, Edith," Jessie said, "A lot of those people are going to want hamburgers and hotdogs. We can't just serve them beef stew and clam chowder! I have no idea how to run the grill, do you?" Edith admitted that the grill was the one job she had never done, but she was willing to give it a try. She soon had the grill in full operation and no customer suspected that his burger had been cooked by a rookie.

During the booth's early years, the most famous menu items may have been hamburgers and cheeseburgers. They were noted for being the most flavorful, and by far the juiciest burgers on the fairgrounds. The secret was a hold-over from the Great Depression years when meat was scarce and expensive. In the food prep area in the back, a cook moistened a few slices of white bread for each pound of ground beef. Then, the bread was worked into the ground beef over and over until the entire mass appeared to contain only meat. When burgers were cooked from this meat-bread mixture, they retained much more juice and flavor than 100% meat burgers.

This came to a halt suddenly one day when some type of government inspector was checking the kitchen and saw the meat being amended. Apparently, it was against a law of some sort, so from then on the Leyden Church Booth had to serve the same 100% meat, (dry burgers) as everyone else.

The booth location near the livestock barns made it very convenient for many of the farmers who were showing their prize livestock. A lot of the 4-H kids lived and slept right there in the barns with their cows or sheep for the duration of the fair. Most of them also ate the Leyden booth's home-cooked food after they got sick (sometimes literally) of the junk food on the midway. If a kid didn't have the money to pay for his meal, Jessie, Edith, or another of the church ladies would often reach into her apron pocket and pay for his meal herself. Woe be it to anyone trying to get a freebee when they actually had the money, however. Somehow the church ladies always knew. I was told that on one occasion, Bud Kennedy gladly paid for supper out of his own pocket for every kid in the 4H cattle barn.

Some years, there would be considerable discussion as to whether the food booth at the fair should be open on Sunday or not. The arguments against being open on Sunday were not based entirely on the old Massachusetts Blue Laws. More importantly, Sunday services were attended by a small cadre of regulars. Many of these regulars were also primary booth staffers. If the booth was open, those working that shift would not be able to attend the service at the church. The minister might not have anyone to preach to! However, Sunday often had the largest attendance at the fair and if the booth was closed they would miss out a lot of potential customers. At least one year, the minister had an idea how to solve the problem. He signed up to work at the food booth on Sunday morning and held an abbreviated service right there next to the hotdog grill and soda cooler. I understand that the attendance was quite good, with a number of the farmers from the stock barns and a few midway workers taking part.

Although attendance at Sunday service was seldom large, in many ways, the church was the social heart of the community. Of course on Easter and Christmas nearly every pew was filled, but what really drew people were the church events that took place outside of the building itself. The suppers, the food booth, serving refreshments at Town Hall events and Old Home Day, and other WSCS activities affected the lives of numerous residents who were not inclined to listen to Sunday sermons. I imagine that wasn't a lot different in 1950 that it was in 1850, or maybe even today.

Chapter 22

BLUEBERRY SUPPERS

Blueberries like to grow in high rocky fields where there is abundant sunshine, acidic soil, and not a lot of competition from other nearby vegetation. East Hill had numerous pastures which provided just these conditions. Henry used to tell of when he was a kid, picking berries on his father's farm and selling them in Greenfield. By the 1950s, only the Herron farm turned blueberries into a profitable enterprise. Wild blueberries are much smaller than the cultivated type found in grocery stores these days, and they are a lot tastier. Donnie Herron's farm was probably the largest in town. He milked a herd of about 125 dairy cattle, sold firewood, and raised a few crops with the help of his wife, Ruth, and their sons. They were well known for their wild blueberries, not only in Leyden, but in other towns as well. Donnie and the boys put a lot of time and effort into creating ideal conditions for growing the berries. He and his family picked and sold most of the crop commercially. The Herrons used cranberry scoops to pick the berries and had a special machine that sorted out the good berries and discarded the unripe ones along with leaves, twigs, and the occasional bug.

The Herrons nursed about 125 acres of "wild" blueberries. Mostly the plants looked after themselves, but Donnie felt it was important to burn over each field about every three years on a rotating basis. Among other things, the fire may have helped control the fungus that sometimes preys on blueberries. Sometimes this "farming by fire" created interesting challenges for the Leyden Fire Department. Birds were always a threat to pick the ripe berries before they could be harvested. To minimize his losses, Donnie used some sort of propane fired "bird bomb" that set off a loud "BANG" about every three minutes.

Most of Donnie's plants were of the low bush type, which grew only a few inches off the ground, and you had to just about sit on the ground to pick them. Here and there, you could usually find a few high bush plants that could be harvested standing up. However, there was general agreement that the high bush berries were not as flavorful as the low bush kind.

Each summer, for a few days, he would open some of his blueberry pastures for do-it-yourself picking. Every year Jessie would take Orilla and me blueberrying at least once or twice. You brought your own containers and paid by the quart when leaving. There was no charge for the handfuls we kids carried out in our bellies, even though the evidence was all over our faces. We would often return home with 10 to 20 quarts of berries which were turned into blueberry pies, muffins, or just a big bowl of berries with sugar and cream. Jessie, of course, would can or freeze large quantities of berries so that we could enjoy them well into the winter months.

Other berries were often in good supply as well. Several Leyden residents raised and sold red raspberries, but my favorites were the small black raspberries that grew wild. I had a favorite patch in a local farmer's pasture that I don't think the farmer knew about and I wasn't telling. When the berries were approaching ripeness, I would check on them several times a day. If I didn't get to them on exactly the correct day, birds would eat the entire crop.

Later in the summer, it was time to search out a good blackberry patch. Blackberries tended to grow best in formerly wooded areas that had been logged over a few years before. They wouldn't grow there at all for decades below the trees, due to too much shade, I suppose. Yet, when the trees had been harvested, and the shade was gone, blackberry plants would often show up the very next year. Jessie claimed they were planted by the birds. There were seldom just a few plants in a location; usually there were lots of them. I guess they were waiting there all those years for just the right conditions. Blackberries must be very patient plants.

These days, we can all go to our local grocery stores, or warehouse club, and buy fresh blueberries, strawberries, blackberries and other fruits year around. Some are flown in by gas hawk from wherever they are in season. Others are grown in greenhouses under very controlled conditions, producing strawberries ten times the size of those I used to pick in the cow pastures. In the 1950s, everything had a season and we looked forward to each one in turn. It seemed that fruits tasted better then, maybe because of the anticipation, or because they were local, and completely natural.

Every year, the Herron family would donate all the blueberries needed for the church's annual blueberry supper. This usually amounted to about 200 quarts. The only string attached to the gift was that "The meal is not to cost more than a working man with a family can afford." I remember helping Jessie deliver berries all over town for the ladies to make pies. If someone signed up to bake, say, four pies for the supper, they would usually be given enough berries so that they could make a fifth pie for their family. On the afternoon of the supper, we would return to each house, collect the pies, and transport them to the Town Hall. Somebody had made a set of pie racks that fit across the back seat of a car so that about 20 pies could be safely transported at once. I always thought it interesting that each pie baker had her own style and I got so I could often identify the baker of a blueberry pie by its appearance, and certainly by its flavor.

Although the pies were baked a day ahead of time, several ladies of the town, including Doris Glabach, Bill's wife, and Dottie Howes, George's wife, baked batch after batch of blueberry muffins the afternoon and night of the supper. Hot blueberry muffins were rushed from their kitchens directly to the dining room tables in the Town Hall. If the reader would like to try an original Leyden recipe for blueberry muffins, or blueberry pie, they can be found in Appendix D.

Reservations were required for the supper, and once the date was set and publicized, people called in from all around. There were always at least two sittings in the dining room of the Town Hall, and if it was an especially good year for blueberries, a third sitting might be added. People who called in on the last day or two were usually disappointed to learn that all the available reservations had been filled. The next year they were sure to call sooner.

Edith Fisher, who was very involved with the blueberry suppers for many years, provided me with the following:

> For many years I was in charge of the annual blueberry suppers which were made possible by the Herron family's generous donation of the main ingredient, blueberries. The menu stayed much the same from year to year. For the meat dish, I ordered sliced and tied "football hams" from Foster's Market in Greenfield. The hams were precooked, but we would apply a pineapple juice glaze and re-bake them resulting in a uniquely delicious flavor. Another unique item was the beet salad. It was sliced beets and onions in a vinaigrette dressing. The food editor for the Springfield, MA, Republican would always attend the blueberry suppers and our recipes were printed in that newspaper at least twice.

The entire Herron family, and there were quite a few of them, were always given free reservations in exchange for their donation of the berries. The year just after the fire station was built was a "berry good year" and reservations filled up rapidly. Somebody got the idea that space for a few more reservations could be added if the Herron family was to be seated as a group in the new fire station next door instead of in the Town Hall dining room. So the station was cleaned up all Spic and Span, the fire trucks were parked outside, and plenty of tables and chairs were added so that the entire Herron clan could be seated at once. Apparently, they had a pretty good time based on the amount of blueberries that were swept up the next day.

As with the Sugar Supper, the main course was not what mattered. The object of it all was the blueberry muffins, bowls of blueberries with sugar and cream, and especially as many slices of blueberry pie as you could eat. Nobody ever went home hungry from a Leyden Church Supper.

From a fairly early age, Orilla and I were drafted to help out the night of the supper. At first, it was just setting tables, taking out trash and cleaning up. We would rush around between sittings getting things ready for the new crowd that was waiting upstairs. Tables were set up in groups of two or three, end to end. A few days before the supper, somebody would stop at the *Greenfield Recorder-Gazette* and pick up several free roll ends of newsprint. These had about 100 feet or more of blank newsprint still on the core. It was exactly the correct width for covering the tables quickly. One kid would thumbtack the paper to one end of a row of tables and then give the roll a push to the other end. As we grew a little older, Orilla and I became full-fledged wait staff, but I wanted to go back to the cleanup crew after I spilled a pot of hot coffee on my hand.

Just about everyone who attended the suppers was delighted with the meal they received. However, from time to time there would be a disgruntled patron who refused to be satisfied no matter how we tried to please them. The meat was too tough, the beans were dry, the coffee wasn't hot enough, some other church put on better meals, etc.

One night there was a particularly difficult out-of-towner to deal with at one of the tables that I was serving. He seemed to complain excessively about everything. In addition to being a major source of irritation to me, he was upsetting everyone else around him, including those that had arrived in his party. Finally, he demanded to see the cook and said he was going to tell him just what he thought of the meal.

Of course there wasn't just one cook, lots of people were involved in preparing the food. I retreated to the kitchen wondering what to do and had the great fortune of bumping into Bud Kennedy, who had just arrived. His given name was actually Cornelius, but nobody ever dared to call him that. Bud was always involved with all the food events the church put on and was very versatile. Bud always had a knack for solving all sorts of problems, so I told him about the complainer and asked him what I should do. Bud told me not to worry because the guy would be leaving soon, and asked me to point him out. Telling me to stay in the kitchen, Bud started toward the dining room. Now Bud was a very nice, easy-going guy who just liked to help out with whatever the project or problem of the moment might be. I believe it was during his stint in the Navy that a fire partially disfigured one eyelid. If the occasion called for it, Bud could take advantage of that eye and put on a rather fierce appearance. This occasion qualified for the full treatment.

Before entering the dining room, Bud cocked his old sailor's hat forward, took off his outer shirt, and rolled up his cigarette pack into one sleeve of his T-shirt. Donning a long white chef's apron, and carrying a large wooden spoon, he sallied forth to take on the complainer. Approaching the table, he politely asked how everyone was enjoying their meals. As expected, the complainer launched into a tirade of everything that he found inexcusable.

"Sir, if you will follow me into the kitchen I will take special care of you," Bud said.

Taking the complainer's arm, Bud led him into the kitchen through the door that was away from the stove area. Crossing the room quickly, he opened the outside door and turning with one smooth motion pushed the complainer out the door and slammed it behind him. Apparently the complainer got the message since nothing more was heard or seen of him the rest of the night.

Chapter 23

WASPS DON'T MAKE HONEY

It must be difficult for children, and parents of children, of the 21st century to understand how we kids of the New England hills in the 1950s, lived our lives and entertained ourselves. It is probably even more difficult for them to relate to the level of personal freedom that we enjoyed. I guess some of the things we did would be considered dangerous today, but we didn't think so; we learned when, where, and how to be careful.

Today's arranged "play date" at the park, under several mothers' watchful eyes, can't compare with walking up the road to a friend's house and spending the day together playing outdoor games, hunting for tadpoles and salamanders in a swamp, or just poking around in the woods. Sometimes a group of us would get together for a pickup game of baseball with no need for adults being involved. As long as we didn't stray too far from home, a parent did not feel a need to know what we were doing every minute, where we were doing it, or who we were doing it with. It was not uncommon to go out the door after breakfast and simply return for lunch a few hours later, dirty, exhausted, and hungry with exciting tales of adventures. Adventures seem to be a lot less common these days.

In the early 1950s, very few homes had TVs, and of course nobody had an iPod, PC, or video game machine, because they did not exist. Instead, we spent our free time playing games that exercised more than our thumbs, fishing, or exploring in the woods. Much of our playtime was spent in make-believe, pretending to be characters from a movie, a book, or our imagination. Sometimes we were knights of King Arthur's Round Table. We would spend hours in Henry's shop making wooden swords when he was off shoeing. Mock sword fights followed with metal trash can lids for shields. Other times, we were the heroes of WWI dashing out from the trenches to annihilate the Kaiser's hordes.

My favorite, by far, was to play Cowboys and Indians. The older kids would assume the role of their favorite movie and comic book cowboy: Tom Mix, Gene Autry, Hopalong Cassidy, Wild Bill Elliot, or my personal favorite, Roy Rogers. For several years, I would not wear a short sleeved shirt because I had never seen a photo of Roy in anything except long sleeves. Incidentally, I was sad to learn while writing this, that the Roy Rogers Museum has closed and the contents have been sold at auction. I guess nobody remembers Roy, Dale, Trigger, and Bullet anymore. Worse, many of today's idols have strayed far from the upright, moral values that our 1950s role models exuded.

The younger kids were usually required to play the parts of the bad guys, or Indians, and they, of course, were always vanquished by the older heroes. They didn't feel taken advantage of, because they knew that when they were older, it would be their turn to play the good guys. We all decided among ourselves what was fair, and what was not. When we reached adulthood, we faced the world with a firm foundation in decision making, and knowledge of right and wrong.

Very rarely, would one of our gang ever do anything terribly dangerous, or that we shouldn't do by the standards of the day. We were simply having fun. Meeting a stranger was not something to be feared, but rather was an opportunity for a new experience or to learn something new. Going to a friend's house, or just an extended walk in the woods alone, required not so much permission, as simply a notice to a parent as to where we were planning to be. Unless the friend's house was a long ways away, there was no expectation of being given a ride. We were healthy, and good walkers.

Every boy carried a jackknife in his pocket, all day, even in school. It was always kept quite sharp because we knew that a dull knife could slip and cut something it shouldn't, possibly a part of one of us. Mostly the knives were of the simple two-blade folding kind with none of the gimmicky blades such as in a Swiss Army type. The large blade was used for everyday utilitarian tasks. The smaller one was reserved for clean purposes, such as peeling an apple or digging a sliver out of a finger. The knife was used for thousands of tasks such as preparing a new fishing pole from a small sapling, trimming a fishing line, tying on a new hook, or a makeshift shoe repair. It was the only tool we needed to skin a squirrel, or rabbit, or dig a huge beetle out of a rotted tree trunk in order to inspect the creature more closely.

In the course of our activity, there were always a few scraped knees, bruised elbows, and sore muscles, but they were just part of growing up. You got up, shook it off, and continued on. Most of us carried a Band-Aid or two in a pocket because nobody wanted to suffer the indignity of going home to Mama with an injury.

Emulation of the Indians and early New England pioneers was always a favorite activity of mine. Nabisco Shredded Wheat boxes had great pioneer and Indian craft "how-tos" printed on the cardboard dividers between the layers of their steel-wool-like cereal. I didn't especially care for shredded wheat, but I put up with it because I wanted the dividers. Henry had shown me his trick of pouring a little hot water over the brittle lump, before adding milk and sugar, which helped a lot.

It was usually just me, but sometimes a friend, or visiting cousin, would join me in the woods following Nabisco's instructions and trying to construct some Indian or pioneer item out of the simple materials at hand. One summer day, a few of us decided to build a replica of a woodland Indian's wigwam in the woods. There was a particularly good stand of thin, tall saplings growing at the edge of the woods by Gerry's field where the forest was gradually reclaiming the land that used to be a vegetable garden. We "borrowed" a small ax from somewhere and along with our pocketknives soon had a good supply of thin green saplings. We dragged them to the selected building site and began sticking one end in the ground and then slowly bending them until both ends were well planted, anchored with small stakes and tied off with used baler twine. Next we gathered a lot of hemlock boughs farther up the hill for roofing and sides.

We were dragging the boughs to our building site when somebody heard a buzzing above our heads. Looking up, we discovered a good sized bee nest hanging from a small branch of a tree. There were hundreds of bees buzzing around the nest and a lot of others seemed to be coming and going.

Many of the bees seemed to be arriving from and returning to the general direction of the apple trees downhill from Henry's shop. "They must be making honey!" somebody whispered as if the bees understood English. "I bet there is a lot of comb honey in that nest."

Raw honey, still in the beeswax comb, was a favorite delicacy. You didn't eat the whole thing. You would bite off a chunk and chew it to extract the honey. When the comb was fully chewed, you would spit out the wax and take another bite. Once we tried our hand at making candles from the beeswax, but that didn't turn out too well when we spilled our pot of melted beeswax all over Jessie's kitchen floor.

That bees' nest was practically daring us to find out if it contained any honey, and we never turned down a dare. We had all been the victims of a bee's wrath on more than one occasion and with hundreds of bees at this nest, great caution and careful planning was called for. After considering several options, none of which was to leave the nest alone, it was decided that the best plan was to have one of us climb the tree, and use the ax to cut off the branch the nest was hanging from. The rest of us would stay well away from where the nest was expected to hit the ground. The kid who did the cutting would be safe up in the tree because all the angry bees would be down near the ground with their nest. All we would have to do was to wait for the bees to lose interest and leave. If they didn't, we'd get a couple pails of water and soak the hive down really good to chase them away. It sounded like a foolproof plan.

With a great deal of bravado, the tallest kid took the ax in one hand and started climbing the tree while the rest of us backed off to what we felt was a safe distance. The plan might have worked if the nest had dropped straight down, but Murphy saw to it that it did not. The vibrations caused by chopping on the branch got the bees very riled up even before it fell. When the branch was cut a little more than halfway through, it cracked and started to fall. However, it was still anchored to the tree by the underside bark, causing the branch with the bee nest still attached to swing downward in an arc and strike the trunk of the tree just a few feet below the young woodsman.

A seemingly cloud of bees erupted like smoke from their smashed nest as they darted out seeking revenge in all directions. On the ground, we scattered, running as fast as we could, but bees can fly a lot faster than boys can run. The unfortunate tree climber got the worst of it. As he dropped to the ground, he knocked down what was left of the nest. It hit the ground first and he nearly landed on top of it.

Fortunately, the bees didn't chase us very far. As quickly as we could get there, we were all rolling on wet muddy ground across the road from the woods. The old wives tale about dried-on mud relieving bee stings is just that, an old wives tale. I went home covered in mud and bee stings and the other guys headed off having had enough fun for one day.

Jessie made me get out of all my muddy clothes and into a bath tub of cold water to which she added a whole box of baking soda. I don't know if it really helped the bee stings, or if the shock of soaking in that cold water made me forget my other pains. When Henry came home, I told him my story, trying to make what we did sound as wise and logical as possible. "Well," he said, "you didn't learn how to build a wigwam, but you sure learned something about bees. First of all, honey bees don't build a nest hanging from a branch. Second, paper wasps do, and they don't make honey."

The next day I cautiously went alone up to the tree to check out what was left of the nest. All the wasps were gone, and Henry was right, as usual. There was no sign of any honey.

Chapter 24

GYPSY MOTHS AND OTHER PESTS

It seems like there is always some insect or disease just waiting to wipe out formerly healthy trees by the millions. Pine bark beetles and spruce bud worms are currently killing square mile after square mile of lodgepole pines and other evergreens in Colorado and other western mountain states. A hundred years ago, one of the first species in the east to be essentially eradicated was the glorious chestnut tree. It is estimated that around 1900 the eastern and southern hardwood forests consisted of about 25 percent chestnut trees. Chestnuts were so common, and made such good lumber, that even barns were built from them. Today, few people have ever seen a chestnut tree.

It was beneath a "spreading chestnut tree" that Longfellow placed the village smithy in his famous poem. When he wrote it, he likely envisioned that village smithies and chestnut trees would endure forever. However, within 50 years of his death in 1882, chestnut trees and village smithies were both on the highly endangered list. In about 1904, just four years before Henry Ford changed the world forever with his Model T, the chestnut blight was introduced to North America. It was a fungus, the modus operandi of which is still not understood. Whatever the mechanism, by 1940, the chestnut trees were dead. In less than 40 years, the fungus had killed several billion trees.

In the 1950s, the fate of the chestnut trees was still a sometimes topic of conversation around the shop. From time to time someone would discover a young chestnut tree growing in isolation. Some would survive long enough to produce a crop or two of seed, but they would die of the fungus within 10 years. The eradication of the American Elm trees was also well underway by 1950. Elm bark beetles arrived on the east coast in 1928, and by 1960 had spread as far as Chicago.

Massachusetts, along with several other eastern states, waged a war against the gypsy moth throughout much of the 20th century. That war may still be going on, and if it is, my guess is that the moths are still winning. In the 1950s, that war had been going on for nearly 100 years since the intentional introduction of the moth in Medford, MA, in about 1860. The original intent was to hybridize it with the silkworm in order to produce a hardier silk producer. I don't believe that gypsy moth silk ever lived up to its commercial expectations. The moths escaped and have been expanding their territory ever since, defoliating trees as they go.

The Leyden town budget contained a small amount of money every year for gypsy moth control and the state and county contributed as well. In years that the infestation was greater than normal, roadsides might be sprayed with pesticides.

The moths overwinter as tan or white egg masses laid on tree branches or trunks or in any hospitable location. One control method used in Leyden every year was the painting over of the egg clusters to keep them from hatching. In late winter or early spring before the eggs hatched, "bug hunters" would go forth armed with a small paint brush and a can of creosote. They would walk the roadsides all through town looking for egg clusters and painting creosote over any that were located. If the painting or spraying had any real effect, it was only near the roads. There was no control effort at all in the forests where the bulk of the trees were, and presumably the bulk of the gypsy moths as well.

I remember one year, about 1958, when Junior Fisher, Billy Glabach, Pete Snow and I did most of the gypsy moth painting. In teams of two, we walked and walked searching for egg nests, but most days we found very few. Finally, one day as Pete and I were sitting on an old stone wall eating our lunch, Pete knocked a stone over and was surprised to find the underside covered with gypsy moth egg clusters. We spent the entire afternoon tearing down that stone wall and painting over thousands of egg clusters.

Feeling very proud of our accomplishment, at the supper table I was bragging about all the egg masses we had destroyed that day. "That's good," Henry said, "but what about the stone wall?"

"What about it?" I asked. "We turned over every stone in that wall. We didn't miss an egg."

"But did you rebuild the wall? That was somebody's stone wall and you guys destroyed it."

The next day we didn't find any egg masses. We were too busy building a stone wall.

A tent caterpillar's goal in life is to defoliate any tree that the gypsy moths might have missed. While the gypsy moths seemed to prefer oaks, the tent caterpillar's favorites may have been fruit trees. Certainly the apple orchards and chokecherries had their share of bug nests. The caterpillar phase builds a multi-layered silk tent around the forks of a small branch. A single tent was often home to thousands of caterpillars, and an infested apple tree might contain a dozen nests or more. The caterpillars would venture forth daily from their nests to eat as many leaves as possible.

Spraying didn't seem to have a big impact on the tent caterpillars, but we discovered a sure-fire (pun intended) method of destroying the nests and roasting a gazillion caterpillars along with it. We would go to Henry's scrap lumber pile and find some narrow sticks of wood about 10 feet long. Next we would wrap one end of the stick tightly with many layers of rags securing them with wire. After filling a pail with a mixture of kerosene and used motor oil, clutching a few matches, off we would go to the apple orchard.

The rag end of the pole was dipped in the oil and then lighted forming a very long, hot torch. We would go around an apple tree holding a torch up close under each nest we found.

The silk would catch fire and singed caterpillars dropped like stones. So many caterpillars would drop it seemed like rain. Orilla used to like to help with this until one day she stood too close under a nest and it rained caterpillars into her hair, down her neck, and generally all over her.

There was another type of caterpillar which received special attention, but I only remember doing it one year, and I can't recall its name. The adults of this species would lay an egg mass that was a smooth, rounded, reddish-brown lump surrounding a twig. The overall size and shape resembled an olive speared by a toothpick.

One year an official of something or other came to the school to announce a bug nest contest. Prizes would be awarded to the students who could collect the largest number of these bug nests. The idea was to find infested trees and brush, snip off the bug nests, and collect them in a bag. The contest was to run for a few weeks with each student bringing his or her bag of bug nests to school each day for counting. The eighth grade students were to be enlisted to count the bug nests in order to determine the winner.

The first Saturday of the contest, I went bug hunting and found a bug nest gold mine in some brush well down the Greenfield Road, or down on the mountain as it was called. By the time I was done with that area, I had 1337 bug nests in my bag. I showed Henry my take and told him I couldn't wait to go to school Monday with all my nests.

"Are you sure you want to take all of them in the first day?" he asked. "After all, the contest has just started and you don't know what everybody else is doing."

Ignoring his advice to "play it cool," I took all 1337 bug nests to school on Monday and had by far the greatest number turned in that day. The next day, very few kids had any bug nests to turn in, but one kid turned in what he claimed was 5,000. Devastated, I looked at the size of his bag which was considerably smaller than mine had been the day before.

"How can you have 5,000 bug nests in that bag when mine yesterday had only 1,337 and mine was a much larger package than yours?" I challenged.

He stood by his number. I said that we would see what the eighth grade counters had to say about it. Unfortunately, the counting of my 1,337 the day before had taken so much time away from class work that Miss Rhodes forbade the counting of this batch. Her edict was that the number stated on the package would stand at 5,000 without a verifying count.

When I told Henry what had happened, he told me that I had just learned one of life's lessons: "When you are playing poker, you don't show all your cards up front."

As the 1950s moved on toward the 1960s, an increasing topic of conversation at Henry's garage was the condition of many of the town's old maple trees. It was not simply a curiosity concern because the maples were important to the town's economy by providing the essential ingredient for making syrup in the spring. They were also the trees most responsible for the town's reputation as one of the best foliage viewing areas in the autumn.

To many longtime residents, a large number of the oldest maples did not look nearly as healthy as they used to. Branches were dying, they did not leaf out as early in the spring, and their autumn colors were consistently less brilliant than in years past. A common observation was that it seemed to be the trees close to the roads which were the most impacted by whatever it was that was causing the change. Of course the gypsy moth was blamed by some, but others pointed out that the affected trees didn't always show any sign of defoliation by insects. Some were convinced that the problem was most acute along roadways which had been paved. The speculation was that paving the road had disrupted the water runoff pattern that trees had grown up with over the decades or centuries.

I'm not sure if there was ever any consensus as to what the cause was of the change to the maples, or even if the change was real. It certainly appeared that a lot of old maples which had withstood the onslaughts of nature and people for decades, or centuries, were going into rapid decline. A goodly number of the conversations on this topic tended to point a finger at the salt and calcium chloride used to deice the roads in the winter. The amount of deicer chemicals being used had certainly increased over the years. One needed to look no further than the increasing numbers of rusted-out cars and trucks to know that. The theory was that, after being spread on the road in order to reduce the amount of ice for a day or two, the salt and calcium chloride were dissolved by melting snow and ice and leached into the soil and ground water where it remained, maybe forever.

Since the 1950s, studies have indicated several causes of the maples' decline in the northeast. Manmade causes have been identified as partly to blame including road salt, paving, and soil compaction. One of the most disturbing causes is Verticillum wilt. I believe this is the same fungus that kills tomato plants if they are planted in the same location too often. It is a fungus that lives in the soil and gradually moves upward from the roots through the sapwood. There is no known cure other than cutting down infected trees, or pulling up infected tomato plants, and hoping others don't get the disease. Sounds eerily like the chestnut problem of 100 years ago.

Chapter 25

THE MYSTERIOUS HUNTER

It sounds to him like her mother's voice,
Singing in Paradise!
He needs must think of her once more,
How in the grave she lies;
And with his hard, rough hand he wipes
A tear out of his eyes.

Longfellow

Fall was many people's favorite time of the year in much of New England. The weather was often bright and crisp, the sky was blue, and the heat, humidity, mosquitoes and thunderstorms of summer were gone. Usually there would be at least one pretty good frost by about the middle of September settling the hash of the season's last crop of biting insects. Following the killing of everyone's tomato plants by an early frost, a very nice Indian Summer would often set in. In many parts of New England, the local economy took a pretty nice surge during the fall as the colorful foliage attracted a lot of tourists. Although Leyden's foliage was usually among the best around, there wasn't a lot of economic impact in town due to a total lack of motels, restaurants and other tourist facilities. There was no Chamber of Commerce advertising the sights. You can't get an economic boost from tourists if there is nowhere for them to spend money. Most years, we still managed to have a lot of "flatlanders" driving through, but stopping for directions and buying a token amount of gas was about all that could be expected of them.

As soon as a few leaves began to turn color, speculation would begin as to how good the foliage season was going to be. Residents stopping by Henry's shop would always comment on the changing of the season even if they had stopped by yesterday and made the identical comments.

The conversation would start off something like, "Well, Henry, I noticed a couple of maples up on East Hill this morning that are already starting to turn. If we get a frost soon, looks like it could be a good season for the leaves. I'm betting on a hard winter."

Most people in town had their pet theory or indicators used to make foliage predictions. Most considered frost to be a strong factor in leaf color. It was far from a sure thing, but there certainly seemed to be a correlation between the arrival dates of the first frosts of the season, and the degree of color in the maples. Others felt that the amount and frequency of rain during the summer had a lot to do with it. As I recall, the usual claim was that too much rain would hurt the colors. Scientists in big cities and universities claimed that frost had nothing to do with the color change of the leaves. Leyden folks living in the hills, and experiencing the change every year, knew better.

Along with their foliage predictions, many residents enjoyed speculating as to how harsh the coming winter might be. Some observed how actively the squirrels gathered their acorns. Others noted how soon, or late, the birds started to head south. One old timer kept track of the first day every year that he heard geese flying south high overhead. Jessie's favorite predictor of winter harshness was the length of the black center stripe on the wooly-bear caterpillars: the longer the black portion, the harsher the coming winter. I don't know of anyone who actually kept track of the various predictors of winter versus what actually happened. In any event, it made for great conversation around the shop.

Once it arrived, the quality of the foliage season was largely judged by the amount of deep orange and intense red color the maple trees showed. Many trees, such as the oaks, were rather boring in that every year they changed to the same dull brown or yellow. Hard maples were the kings of the show, the same trees that would supply the sap for maple syrup a few months later. Some years they simply turned yellow like some other varieties. Other years they might be almost crimson. The season was considered a bust if the predominant maple color was yellow and it was a super season if there was a lot of red everywhere. The better the season, the more traffic in town as the leaf hunters cruised around in search of that perfect viewing spot. We could always count on selling a little more gas at the shop during those weeks. Sometimes we had to deliver that gas to wherever a leafer's tank ran dry.

Many of the Leyden roads were not well identified with signs in those days and few, if any, detailed road maps of the town existed. One fact about Leyden Roads was that if you started out from the Center in any direction on any road and kept turning the same way every time you came to an intersection, you would always come back to the Center. These "features" contributed to no end of stories to tell over supper after observing confused or lost leaf viewers who were not familiar with the town. Every weekend during foliage season there would be at least one out of town car stopping at the shop for some gas and the driver would ask for directions to Leyden. They always reacted with shock when told that they were smack dab in the middle of it.

I remember one time when I was helping Henry with something in the shop and we noticed a shiny new Ford slowly drive past the garage. An hour or so later it drove by again in the same direction. On its third pass it pulled up to the gas pumps and the driver asked for a fill-up. A fill-up was always a big sale, possibly $3.00 or even $4.00. The locals normally bought a dollar's worth at a time. As I pumped the gas, the driver casually asked for directions to Colrain. I told him to go the way he was headed, up the hill and just keep going. He said he had tried that twice, but kept going past here instead. I gave him more detailed directions and sent him on his way.

Close by the shop and our house were several huge old rock maple trees. The trunk of each was at least four feet in diameter. Given the slow growth rate of maple trees, those giants must have had their roots in Massachusetts soil before the Pilgrims touched their famous rock. The maple closest to the house was the termination point for Jessie's clothes line. There was a large cavity in the trunk where an ancient limb had existed at one time. Some years that cavity would be home to a family of raccoons that often found the buffet of Henry's garden to their liking, especially the corn.

After the trees dropped their leaves in the fall, they would be nearly knee deep beneath those huge maples. Every year we used some of those leaves to insulate around the foundation of our house before the first snowstorm. Henry would build a wall of batten boards around the house foundation about two to three feet high and spaced out from the house about a foot and a half. Then we would collect load after load of maple leaves in his truck and pack them tightly between the house and boards. Henry would pour in bushels of leaves and Orilla and I would walk back and forth on them packing them down as more and more were added. In the spring, the boards were taken down and the leaves scattered in the apple orchard.

After the house had been banked with leaves, the next order of business was to install the storm windows. The house's windows were all single pane, double hung units. Those that weren't painted shut let in some pretty good drafts and the single thickness of glass was of little insulating value. The storm windows were brought up from the barn area below the house and thoroughly washed to remove the dirt, spider webs, and assorted dead critters. Then they were attached by screws directly to the house completely covering the double hung units. Come spring, a similar operation was conducted to replace the storm windows with screens.

I don't believe that it was generally realized in the 1950s, that much of the heat loss in a home was through the roof. Many older homes, including ours, had little or no attic insulation. This was the direct cause of the formation of icicles and ice dams along the eaves. Some years when the weather was right, outside a living room window, a huge icicle would grow all the way from the eave to the ground.

Another big topic of conversation in the fall was the approaching deer hunting season. Deer season in Massachusetts was always in early December. In October and November, hunters began swapping stories of where they had seen the animals lately and telling tall tales about the big buck they nearly harvested last year. Many farmers often encouraged hunting on their property because of the amount of damage deer caused to crops, especially corn. Although there was no restriction as to buck or doe in Massachusetts, a hunter who bagged a large buck with a big rack of antlers definitely had more bragging rights than another hunter who settled for a doe.

No rifles were allowed for deer hunting in the state. You had to hunt with a shotgun, which made sense to some bureaucrats I suppose. A shotgun slug would carry nearly as far as a rifle bullet in the thick New England woods, would do at least as much damage, but it traveled with a whole lot less accuracy. The other ammunition choice was buckshot. Buckshot loads for a 12-gauge came in several sizes. The smaller the shot size, the more pellets per load, but less energy per pellet. Most buckshot users settled on 00 buck which gave nine pellets of about .33 caliber each.

Some town residents also hunted in Vermont, which required purchasing an out of state license. No shooting of does was allowed in Vermont, but in at least some years a hunter could harvest two bucks. In theory at least, the chances of getting a good sized deer were greater in Vermont because of fewer hunters and less populated terrain.

Vermont permitted hunting with rifles. Some would-be Vermont hunters did not own a rifle, but Henry had a nice one. It was a Winchester model 1894 carbine in .30WCF (30-30) caliber that he received in a trade with Charlie Bolton. It was light and easy to carry and very accurate. It was a special order gun, serial number 887351, with a half-length magazine and a rifle style stock instead of carbine style.

Henry always liked to tell the story about how he had the gun in the shop with him one day soon after he obtained it.

As he was busy repairing something for a couple of waiting customers, one of the men spotted a crow land in Zimmerman's newly planted cornfield south of the library. Seizing the opportunity to do a little good-natured needling, he said, "Hey, Henry. I'll bet you five dollars that you can't get that crow with your new rifle."

Without saying a word, Henry set aside the part he was working on and picked up his rifle. Walking to the open door, he calmly leaned his left shoulder against the side of the opening and slowly brought the gun up to his right shoulder. He fired one shot. The crow exploded in a cloud of black feathers. Without saying a word, Henry set the gun down and went back to work. The astonished customers were quiet also. When their bill was written up, it contained an additional item, "Lost bet: $5.00."

To my knowledge, Henry never hunted in Vermont, so I have no idea why he traded his shotgun for that rifle. Actually, he very rarely hunted in Massachusetts either. About every other year, a potential Vermont hunter would stop by the shop or house a few days before Vermont's opening day and ask to borrow Henry's rifle. He always was glad to lend it to a friend and never expected anything in return. If the borrower was successful, and usually they were, the hunter would drop off a hind quarter or some prime cuts of venison when he returned the Winchester. We always loved dining on venison steaks and stew.

When I turned 15, I became eligible to hunt in Massachusetts and pestered Henry to take me deer hunting. I finally convinced him, and we began making our plans. Our biggest problem was that we had no shotguns to hunt with. Henry called Edric Cook who was well known for hunting all types of game animals all over New England, and owned a large assortment of guns. Henry asked if he had a shotgun that I could borrow. Edric agreed to lend me a Winchester 20 gauge Model 12 and showed me how to use it. One day, Casper Zimmerman was at the shop and heard of our plans. Cap was not a hunter, but he said he had a 12 gauge pump that Henry could borrow. It was a larger version of the gun I had borrowed from Edric.

Now we were armed, but we needed some ammo and

other supplies, so off we went to Clark's hardware store in Greenfield. Clark's was the best all-around hardware store in the area and in the basement they had a sporting goods shop. In those days you could buy ammunition by the piece and we purchased 5 slugs and 5 buck shot for each gun. We also bought a few pieces of the required red hunter safety material and red hats.

Back home, we were admiring our purchases, when we realized that we didn't have hunting knives. I don't recall Henry ever carrying a pocketknife, but from somewhere he scrounged up a rusty old folding knife that he would use. I didn't think I would look like much of a hunter if I just had my pocket folder. I wanted a real hunting knife. A few days later, when Jessie said she was going to Greenfield to buy groceries, I begged her to buy me a hunting knife. She didn't think that was necessary because, "You two probably won't even see a deer." However, when she returned, she had a short hunting knife. I was a bit disappointed with the size of it, but it had a leather sheath so I could wear it on my belt like a real hunter. I still have that knife to this day. It has a Solingen steel blade and can be sharpened up so fine that you can shave with it.

On opening day off we went, well before sunrise. We drove in Henry's truck down to the farm and parked along the road near the north end. On the drive down, we had discussed our strategy. Jessie had made us promise that we would stay together, but she never defined what "together" meant. Besides, she wasn't there to enforce it. I had no clue whatsoever how to hunt deer, but it seemed to me that the best place would be in the thick woods on the hill to the east of the hayfield. Henry wanted to be in more open country, so he took up a stand in the pasture on the west side of the road.

I walked into the woods as quietly as I could which wasn't very quiet. There was no snow on the ground, and the woods were dry, so every step I took made a loud crunching, cracking sound. I finally figured out that I would never be able to surprise a deer while making all that noise so I found a small open area to watch and stood still, hoping a deer would find me. After a couple of hours a deer did appear! It stood looking at me, and in spite of my amazement, I managed to fire the 20 gauge. When I recovered from the recoil, the deer was nowhere to be seen. I ran over to where it had been and to my surprise I found some blood. I walked in what seemed like the logical direction and soon crossed a barbed wire fence. Just past the fence there lay a young buck.

Henry had given me instructions on what to do to dress the deer if I got one. He had impressed on me how important it was to gut it out immediately. It seemed like a disgusting thing to do, but I had shot a deer and now I had to follow through.

The next problem was getting it back to the truck. It was far too heavy for me to carry, and there was that fence to cross. I had remembered to stuff a length of rope in a pocket so I tied one end around the antlers and started pulling. I could move it, but it was an awful lot of work. I thought of leaving it there and going to get Henry to help, but I was afraid that somebody might steal my deer, although I wasn't aware of anyone else hunting on the farm.

Just as I was dragging my deer up to the fence and wondering how I was going to get it across, a man appeared beside me. I neither saw nor heard him coming, but suddenly there he was. He wore a wide-brimmed slouch hat and carried an old double-barreled shotgun. It was the kind with external hammers that had to be cocked with your thumb before it would fire. His boots were of the high lace-up leather type with the legs of his pants tucked inside. The only safety red he wore was a dirty red neckerchief. He knew my name, and did not introduce himself, acting as if he had always known me, and me him. There seemed to be something very familiar about him, but I didn't think I had ever met him before, and I know I haven't seen him since. He admired my buck and told me that I had done an excellent job of gutting it. When asked where I was going with it, I told him I needed to get it to my Dad's truck, trying to make it sound like Henry was a lot closer than he really was. Without a word, the man lifted the deer over the fence and then took my rope and started dragging it. Was he stealing my deer right in front of me? I followed along behind wondering what I should do. Somehow, he seemed to know exactly which way to go to the truck without me giving any directions.

After a time we exited the woods and continued across the hay field directly to Henry's truck. I didn't see another vehicle anywhere around, yet the hunter seemed to have known exactly where Henry's truck was parked. The stranger lifted my deer into the truck, shook my hand and quickly walked back into the woods. I got into the truck (nobody locked their vehicles in those days) and ate my lunch. After an hour or so, I saw Henry approaching through the pasture. When he arrived at the truck he admired my deer and asked if I had much trouble getting it to the truck. "No," I told him. "I didn't have any trouble at all."

Although deer hunting was the most talked about, several other species were also actively pursued by at least some of the local sportsmen. A few, such as Edric Cook, traveled far northward to find moose or black bear in other states or even Canada, but most hunters stayed pretty close to the home town. Sometime in the late summer or early fall was 'coon season'. As with woodchucks in the spring, most farmers were delighted to have hunters go after raccoons on their land because a family of coons could devastate a vegetable garden or cornfield in the course of a single night.

Raccoons were the only species that were legal to hunt at night with the help of lights and a good pack of hounds. The hunt would usually start about when it got dark by slowly driving near a cornfield in the hope of seeing a coon cross the road. If none was spotted, the vehicle would be parked and the hounds turned loose to do some sniffing. The dogs always thought this was great sport and took off in various directions, noses to the ground and being very vocal. When a hound picked up a scent, it would begin baying louder and faster. All the other dogs would rush over to join in the chorus and all the hunters would come running with their flashlights. The chase was on!

If it was a young coon, the hounds would usually tree it fairly soon. The hunters would run up huffing and puffing and if somebody had a steady enough hand after all the running, a shot from a .22 would usually put the coon in the bag. If it was a crafty old coon, the outcome might be totally different. Sometimes it seemed as if the coon was enjoying the chase as much as the hounds. If there was a stream nearby, an experienced coon would often head for it and then wade either up or down steam causing the dogs to lose the scent. The hunters would take dogs both up and down stream trying to pick up the trail again. One time a coon went upstream a ways, came out and left a short scent trail on land and then returned to the same place that it had left the stream and continued upstream. After it had gone a ways, it once again came out onto the shore before returning to the water and continuing. When the hounds found both scent trails, considerable confusion resulted, providing the crafty old coon with plenty of time to get well away.

It may have been Doug Barton's coon houndss that once had a large coon treed after a chase of a mile or more. When the hunters reached the tree, they found a huge coon scowling down at the three hounds, all of which were jumping at the tree and making quite a racket. Just as a hunter prepared to shoot, the coon dropped straight down and landed on the back of one of the dogs. It held onto the animal's ears with its front paws and the hind claws dug into the skin of its sides. The dog bucked like a wild mustang, and rolled in the dirt, but could not dislodge the coon. The other two dogs joined in the fracas, but were getting more mouthfuls of their buddy than of the coon. The hunters couldn't shoot for fear of hitting the wrong animal. Suddenly the coon jumped to the ground and took off running. The dogs had had enough and simply watched it go as they licked their multiple wounds.

Raccoons were quite at home in the water and if there was a pond in the vicinity they would often head for it when being chased. An experienced coon hunter was always careful about allowing his dogs to chase a coon into deep water where the coon could often get the upper hand. Some dogs liked to swim, and some didn't, but no matter how good a swimmer it might have been, it was always a mistake to follow a coon into deep water. Once in the pond, a coon would turn briefly to do battle and then lead the dog into deeper water. Once the water was deeper than its opponent was tall, the coon would try to drown it. Often they were successful. One technique was to face the now swimming hound and bite its nose. With a solid grip on the nose, the coon would then drag the surprised animal's head under water. Another method was to get onto the dog's back and then work its way up to the head. The weight of the coon on its head and neck would force the dog's face below the surface.

I didn't go on too many coon hunts, but the ones I did participate in were a lot of fun. I don't remember who took me along on my first coon hunt. I was permitted to bag a small young coon even though I had done the least amount of work on the hunt. The other guys said that it would be great eating. Back home, proud as a peacock, I walked into the house carrying my coon by the rear legs.

"What are you going to do with that thing?" asked Jessie

"We're going to eat it for supper tomorrow," I said. "It will be great eating."

"Just because other darn fools eat coon doesn't mean we are going to."

Henry was sitting at the kitchen table doing his logbook and came to my defense. "No sense wasting free meat," he said. "Let's give it a try. Take it out to the shed and I'll help you gut it and skin it."

Now there are a few good reasons that you don't find too many coon steaks and roasts at your local supermarket. A major reason is that no matter how well it is skinned and cleaned, COONS STINK!

The next afternoon Jessie gamely tried to concoct a coon recipe. It seemed like the more she cooked my coon, the worse it smelled. Finally she had had enough.

"Take that thing outside and bury it," she said. "Make sure it is deep so the dogs don't dig it up. And don't you ever bring home another one of those things!"

Chapter 26

WHEN A TREE FALLS IN THE WOODS

In the 1950s, the majority of the Leyden residents were farmers, at least part time. Even if they had a primary job out of town, many did a little farming on the side. Most of the farms were small, and today would probably be classified as subsistence farms. Due to the rocky, hilly terrain and thin soil, few vegetable crops were raised in Leyden except those grown in small garden plots to be consumed by the family. A fair amount of acreage went into growing corn, but it was mostly chopped into silage and stored for use during the winter as cattle feed.

I don't recall anyone having an actual tree farm in town, but logging of the natural tree growth was a significant occupation for a number of people. Logging had been an important industry in Leyden since the settlement's earliest days. When the Deerfield captives struggled northward in 1704, nearly the entire town was covered with huge trees. Later, when settlers began arriving, one of their first tasks was to clear the trees off some of the land in order to plant crops and raise livestock. Trees were cut down, stumps pulled, and slash piles burned. Sawmills were located along major streams in order to make use of water power to convert the huge logs into useful lumber. The lumber sawn from those old growth trees often included boards as wide as 30-inches or more, something unheard of today. Evidence of those wide boards can still be found in some of the oldest houses in town, although often covered with modern plaster or dry wall.

As the meadows and fields became cleared, the tree harvesting areas moved farther back into the hills and away from the permanent sawmills in the valleys. However, lumber was still much in demand and a lot of it was delivered to towns outside of Leyden. The advent of the steam engine, and later the internal combustion engine, provided the opportunity to build temporary sawmills back in the woods closer to the log harvesting areas. These temporary mills could be set up in a few days and relocated as needed.

In the early 1950s, the use of living horsepower was still very common around the lumber camps. One or two sturdy draft horses could be hitched to a large log using a chain cinched around one end of the load. Horses had a knack for finding the best route between trees, something the smartest tractor has yet to learn how to do! They could step over boulders or deadfalls and didn't get stuck in mud holes.

As the decade progressed, the use of small crawler tractors for logging increased and the use of draft horses became less common. Nearly all the old, large trees were gone. Instead of handling logs individually as before, the smaller logs could be stacked on a logging sled and hauled as a bundle along bulldozed roads to the sawmill. As one old time logger put it, "You don't need to feed a tractor if it's not doing any work, like you do a horse."

Being a lumberjack was one of the more dangerous ways to earn a living. By comparison, the most risky farming tasks seemed rather tame. Gasoline powered chainsaws were becoming common in the woods, but a lot of work was still being done with the two-man crosscut saw and double bitted ax. No matter what tool was being used to fell a tree, it was necessary for one or two loggers to be right there at the base of the tree when the moment of truth arrived and the tree began to topple to the ground.

An experienced logger could do a pretty good job of causing a tree to fall exactly where he wanted it, but a number of things needed to be taken into consideration when selecting where and how to make his cuts. These included the lean of the tree, the slope of the land, direction and strength of the wind, and the locations of other nearby trees. The highest priority was to predetermine exactly what his escape route would be once the tree began to topple. The moment the tree started to fall, the logger needed to be elsewhere, FAST! Things could go wrong at the last minute and sometimes did. A sudden gust of wind could greatly alter the direction of fall, the falling tree might bounce off another, or no matter how well planned, a tree just might not drop where it was supposed to.

One of the most dangerous situations was just as the tree was starting to fall. It might suddenly twist and the trunk could jump sideways off the stump while the rest of the forest giant was still well up in the air. One time, a logger was felling a large oak and had nearly completed his final cut. The tree gave a shudder and just as it started to fall, it suddenly twisted almost a quarter turn and the nearly upright tree jumped sideways off the stump. The severed trunk came down squarely on the logger's left boot breaking nearly every bone in his foot.

Another time, a widely branched tree was about to come down when something went totally wrong. Instead of falling away, the tree moved directly toward one of the men. Unable to get away in time, the logger was slammed to the ground by the branches of the tree. Fortunately he was not hit by anything large and the branches kept the heavy trunk propped up above him. He wasn't too badly hurt, but it took many minutes of careful cutting of branches before the other loggers could remove him from his woody prison.

A few of the loggers in town worked at it almost full-time. However, many were farmers who had a large wood lot and sold a few logs for lumber or cut firewood for sale. Others had out of town jobs and logged on weekends. Much of the logging was done in the winter months for a couple of reasons. First, winter was the slowest time of the year for most farmers. Second, with snow on the frozen ground, it was much easier to drag logs and haul heavy logging sleds than it was in summer.

Slab wood was a byproduct of lumber cutting at sawmills.

Slabs were the outermost cuts from each side of the log and as such contained tree bark on one side. These were very much in demand as firewood. They burned well, and the price was generally lower than that of purpose-cut firewood.

A definite downside to logging was the impact it had on the forests, but most of the environmental movements were still far in the future. Logged-over areas took decades to recover. Temporary logging roads were bulldozed without regard to their impact on the area. Unsold piles of slabs and slash were left for Mother Nature to deal with. I'd bet that many of the slash piles created in the 1950s are still in evidence today. Fortunately, clear-cut logging, as practiced in some other parts of the USA, in which every tree in an area is harvested regardless of size, was not common in much of New England.

By the 1960s, local logging had decreased significantly. It was often cheaper to haul in lumber from the huge operations in the south, northwest, Vermont, or even Canada. In addition, accessible trees of significant size were becoming scarce in the Leyden hills.

As both farming and logging declined, Mother Nature began the slow process of reclaiming some of the land which had been denuded decades before. Today, many hillsides that were once thinly treed, and meadows that were once hay fields, are becoming forested once again. Everything goes in cycles.

Chapter 27

THERE'S IRON IN THEM THAR HILLS

By the time we reached our early teens, most of us boys had developed an interest in guns. In the 1950s New England hills, this was simply one more step toward manhood. My first shooting experience was on a Sunday afternoon at my Uncle Howard Wood's home in Saxton's River, Vermont. Uncle Howard was strongly interested in collecting antique guns of all types. In the 1950s, their value was many times less than they are today and good example pieces were easy to find. In his work as an electrician, Howard crawled around in a lot of attics and basements of old Vermont houses and would often come across an old firearm or two that the owner didn't know existed. Howard would bring them to the owner and would usually be able to buy them for just a few dollars. Sometimes, the owner would throw in the guns as a tip for a job well done.

Whenever our family went to Howard's house, he would always show Henry and me his latest treasures. One day he was showing us an old Winchester Model 1890, 22 rimfire. It was a pump action repeater of the type used in shooting galleries that were still common at fairs and carnivals in those days. Howard suggested that we go outside and give the old gun a try.

The hillside behind his house had a pretty good crop of long stemmed yellow daisies. After a few test shots to confirm that the gun was not likely to blow up in our faces, Howard suggested that we play "pick the daisy." The game went something like this: We stood about 10 or 15 feet from the hillside and when it was a shooter's turn, he would point out which daisy he was going to pick. Picking involved shooting not at the daisy itself, but at its stem so the flower was picked as if snipped off with scissors. Given that the width of a daisy stem, and the bullet diameter, were pretty close to the same, it was a bit of a challenge. Howard went first and his shot snipped off a flower, but he admitted it wasn't the one he aimed at. Henry went next, but his bullet went a little high and destroyed the flower head. When it was my turn, Howard gave me lots if instruction before I was allowed to fire a shot. When I did, no daisy that I shot at was in any danger. Howard proceeded to pick off daisy after daisy, impressing Henry and me with his marksmanship. On a later occasion, Howard divulged his secret to me. "The secret to picking daisies," he said, "is to select one that, from your vantage point, has a stem that is perfectly vertical. That way it doesn't matter if your bullet goes a little above or below where you aimed, you will still cut the stem if you are anywhere on it, left and right."

Part of growing up, for most of us, was honing our shooting skills and learning how to stalk and hunt small game. As beginners, most of us were usually restricted to .22 rimfire rifles by our parents. The only .22 that Henry owned was a heavy Winchester Model 75 target rifle that he had used when he was an active member of the Leyden Rifle Club. To steady his aim, Henry had inserted lead into parts of the stock so that the thing weighed over ten pounds. His theory was that the heavier the gun, the more steady his aim. Heavy as it was, I loved carrying it through the woods and over the fields in search of targets of opportunity. One day Junior Fisher and I were shooting bottles and cans at Henry's dump down at the farm. It was an excellent location in the woods well away from the road, no houses nearby, and a steep hill for a backstop.

Suddenly we heard someone yell, "Hey you boys. You're not supposed to be doing that. Put those guns down." We looked up, and coming down the hill, with their hands on the butts of their holstered handguns, were two Massachusetts game wardens in full huff and puff. Never before having encountered officialdom, we did as instructed. We were sternly lectured and they confiscated both guns. We walked home worrying about what our fathers were going to say.

Henry didn't get mad very often, but that evening when I told him what had happened, he became very angry. Thankfully, not mad at me, but at the game wardens who he felt had far overstepped their authority. The next morning he was busy on the phone. I don't know all of whom he called, but they sure got an earful. First, he explained that we were target shooting, not hunting, so it was none of the game wardens' business. He then pointed out that we were on his land, with his permission, doing what he had said we could do. He also pointed out that the game wardens had been on his land without his permission. His threat of legal action had some effect, because a few days later a game warden dropped off Henry's gun at the shop. I don't know if Junior Fisher ever got his gun back.

After I was a few years older, I would spend as much time as possible in the spring hunting woodchucks. The farmers encouraged woodchuck hunting because the chucks dug deep holes in the fields that could cause a broken leg if a cow or horse stepped into them, and their dirt piles could damage haying equipment. A den always had a main hole with a lot of dirt piled up around it, but there would usually be several back doors as well. The back doors were excavated from below and were often difficult to spot, especially if the grass was tall. A woodchuck was a very wary animal and was seldom far from a hole. At the slightest hint of danger they would dive into the den, often to peek out of another hole to see what the danger was. For me, the most interesting part of chuck hunting was to see how close I could get without scaring the critter into its hole.

Sometimes Eddie Carron would go chuck hunting with me. I had a scope sighted .222 Remington that could easily put any woodchuck's life in mortal danger within 200 yards or so. Eddie used an old single-shot .45-70 that he had found in the attic of the old house where his family lived. That old gun fired a huge 500 grain bullet at such a low velocity that Eddie often had to aim several inches over a chuck's head to allow for the bullet drop.

I used to love to watch Eddie shoot that rifle. He would crawl on his belly toward his intended target, hiding behind every scrap of brush or clump of grass. When within range, he would touch off a round that sounded like a bomb. The recoil would push Eddie backward a little, and after a perceptible delay, there would be a big eruption of dirt in the general vicinity of the woodchuck. I don't recall Eddie ever actually hitting a chuck with one of those huge bullets, but he may have scared a few to death. Of course if he had made a hit, there wouldn't have been much evidence remaining, I suppose.

There used to be a barn across the road from where Eddie lived. Eddie's father wanted to build a corral for a few cattle at the south side of the barn. He obtained a quantity of posts from somewhere that were supposed to be locust wood which had the reputation of making very durable fence posts. He then commissioned Eddie and me to dig all the post holes and set the posts. The digging wasn't too difficult because the soil on that side of the barn was always damp from a natural spring. Luckily, and strangely for Leyden, we encountered few rocks. It took us two or three days to set the posts, after which Eddie's father nailed on the rails to complete the corral.

The odd thing was, the following spring several of the posts sprouted small twigs and leaves. By the end of summer, they were beginning to resemble actual trees. The corral didn't last too long, partly because Eddie and his family moved to a farm north of the center and the new residents had no need for a living fence. Although most of it was torn down, what had been one corner post was left and grew into a very respectable willow tree.

In my teenage years, one of my favorite things to do was to get out into the woods someplace in town and just walk around to see what I could find. I found numerous interesting natural and man-made places that only I knew about and possibly I am the only one to know of some of them even today. I located Balancing Rock which had been "lost" for many years. According to stories told by some of the old timers, Balancing

Rock (called Tipping Rock in Arms' book) used to be something of a local tourist attraction. It was a huge, sort of potato-shaped boulder weighing many tons. It sat atop a larger flat rock or ledge in such a fashion that the stories claimed the pressure of just one hand would make the rock tip back and forth. When I found it, there were two small trees that had grown up closely on the south side of the boulder and restricted its movement somewhat. However, even with the trees there, a little bit of a push was enough to make the boulder rock back and forth a few inches. Balancing Rock was near the end of a line of very large boulders that were part of a lateral moraine left there by a glacier as it retreated from the Leyden valleys thousands of years ago. A few of the boulders were nearly the size of a small house. Even the largest boulders had rounded corners and edges indicating that they had been tumbled around a lot before coming to rest where I found them. In some areas, just above the line of boulders was a steep cliff that still bore the horizontal scars from moving ice.

For several years, I had heard stories of a Leyden mine that produced high grade iron ore prior to, and during, the Revolutionary War. The stories claimed that the Leyden ore was very rich, and when smelted down it made first-rate iron for musket barrels. Being located far back on the 18th century frontier, the Boston-based British army was unlikely to discover the mine. Nobody I talked with seemed to know much about the approximate location of where the mine might have been, or even if it ever actually existed. Some told me that they had heard that the mine had been located over the line in Bernardston. In fact, an early Bernardston history book says exactly that. Other than a few gravel pits, there were no active or inactive mining operations in Leyden in the 1950s, so I didn't have a lot to go on. Leyden's valleys and gentle slopes held the homes and farms of the residents, and nobody ever mentioned discovering any iron diggings on their property. Bert Whitney claimed to have done some mining in his younger days near his place in West Leyden, but it was for copper, not iron, and he seemed to be quite vague as to the exact location. Old Bert always had a lot of stories.

So, where should I start looking? In the 18th century, a lot of firearms manufacturing activity sprung up in the lower Connecticut River Valley due largely to the availability of reliable water power and the Connecticut River "highway" for transportation. Iron ore is heavy, and you need to process a pretty large quantity of ore to get a little iron. It seemed logical that the Leyden ore would have been transported down the Connecticut River to a smelter. So, it also seemed logical that the mine would have been located somewhere such that the transportation of the ore to the river would have been mostly downhill. I decided that the likely place to look was near the top of East Hill which would have provided easy downhill hauling to the river in Bernardston. I didn't expect the location to be very near a modern day house or farm because somebody would have already known it was there. Of course, it was possible that somebody did know the location, but wasn't telling.

I didn't have much of an idea what high grade iron ore looked like, but I figured it would look different than the igneous rock that formed most of the town. I also thought that if there was a lot of iron around, my compass should behave oddly just as it did around Henry's shop. Maybe my compass would lead me to the "mother lode." I was encouraged by stories I had heard of early airplane pilots claiming that they couldn't trust their compass while flying over Leyden. Gee, is that why the name LEYDEN had been painted on the shop roof?

I spent many days, walking many miles, in the woods carefully noting the terrain although I had no clear idea what it was I expected to see. Every few feet I stopped, noted my location on a map as best I could, and recorded any deviation of my compass needle from the expected magnetic north. After days of searching and finding nothing that resembled what I thought a mine should look like, I plotted all my compass readings on a more detailed map. There it was! Many of the compass deviations tended to point toward a common location!

The next morning I was out in the woods, before breakfast, headed for the convergence point on my map. It turned out to be surprisingly easy to find. There was a place where the compass went crazy and couldn't decide which way to point. Moving just a short distance would cause the compass to shift noticeably. I figured I must be close. Near the foot of a steep ledge, covered in underbrush, was a depression about 100 feet across and several feet deep. Near the depression were several piles of broken rock. The rocks in those piles had sharp and jagged edges, so I knew they were not a result of glacial activity. I had brought a WWII entrenching tool with me, and after a bit of digging near the rock piles I unearthed a few pieces of rusty iron which I imagined could have been the remains of old mining tools. It certainly looked as if there had been a lot of digging there for some reason long ago. I was convinced I had found the mine.

Like most of Leyden, the depression I had located was on private property. I went straight to the owner and told him of what I had found. In my enthusiasm, I fully expected the land owner to be excited also and return with me to the site for a more extensive investigation. I couldn't have been more wrong.

"What were you doing poking around on my property without my permission?" he demanded.

"I didn't mean any harm," I stammered, "I was just trying to find the old iron mine, and I think I did. Would you like me to show you where it is?"

"I know my property and there ain't no mine on it. Now get out of here and don't tell anyone what you found. I don't want a lot of snoopers around here."

So I dejectedly left and never returned. I kept my word not to tell anyone that I had found the mine. I'm still not going to divulge its location, but I will say it is on the southeast side of East Hill, and definitely in Leyden, not Bernardston. I still often wonder what it was that the property owner didn't want found around that old mine.

There are actually quite a few mineral outcroppings in Leyden. Few, have ever been commercially exploited, as far as I know, and most are probably not large enough to be worth the expense. Poking around in the woods, I found a number of what, out west, would be called prospect holes. Often, they were associated with a good vein of quartz. I suspect that somebody thought that the quartz might contain some gold or silver, which it often does, at least in the west.

I once heard a story about a few rough diamonds being found somewhere in town. Diamonds are usually associated with a certain type of vertical volcanic core called kimberlite. Leyden geography isn't very volcanic, but who knows what might be back there in the woods where nobody goes.

Pete Snow once showed me where there was a wonderful outcropping of garnets not far from where he and his family lived. Garnets are also often associated with kimberlite, so that might be the source of the Leyden diamond stories. The outcropping was at the top of a small rounded hill that was nearly barren of vegetation due to the very thin soil. Digging around just below the surface produced quantities of perfectly shaped garnets. Garnets are sometimes indicators of more valuable gems to be found nearby, but I don't know if anybody has ever found any. Or, maybe nobody understood what the raw gemstones looked like. Or, maybe nobody is talking!

Chapter 28

THE RIPSLED RIDERS

Toiling, --rejoicing, --sorrowing,
Onward through life he goes;
Each morning sees some task begin,
Each evening sees it close;
Something attempted, something done,
Has earned a night's repose.
                                    Longfellow

One of the best things about New England was that each year there were four very distinct and very different seasons. Many of Leyden's residents probably felt that winter was by far their least favorite season, but I always liked it. I'm a snow fan and did Leyden ever get snow!

One of the numerous challenges of a fierce winter was that of staying warm. In the 1950s, some homes were heated by fuel oil or kerosene; others burned coal. However, most of the Leyden homes in those days, were heated with wood. A big advantage of wood stoves was that they kept right on working in the event of a power failure. Anyone who has never experienced the warmth of a wood fire, on a biting cold day, has missed one of life's great pleasures. Coming in from the snow into today's 68 degree, uniformly heated, home cannot compare to thawing out next to a fired-up wood stove and feeling the heat penetrate first your clothing, then your body, all the way to your bones.

Henry's shop, the Town Hall, the Town Shed, the library, and the church were all heated by wood fires. If a resident didn't have his own wood lot, several farmers or loggers could be counted on to sell good quality hardwood or slabs cut to stove length. If splitting was needed, that was usually up to the user on an as-needed basis. A good supply of firewood would be obtained in the early fall and hopefully would last all winter. If it did not, there was always a lot of dead wood lying around in the nearby forests. The familiar quotation: "A wood fire warms you twice, once when it is cut and again when it is burned" has been attributed to various people ranging from Henry Thoreau to Henry Ford. Whoever first said it was spot on. You sure could work up a sweat out in the wood lot or woodshed, no matter what the temperature.

A lot of homes had several wood stoves in various parts of the house instead of central heat. Some, however, such as at our house, had a wood burning furnace in the basement that distributed warm air throughout the house by natural convection, except for the kitchen. The Town Hall had two huge wood burning furnaces, a black monster of a wood burning range in the kitchen, and a small wood stove in the selectmen's office. One furnace heated only the main hall on the second floor. The other could be used to heat the dining room on the first floor as well as helping to heat the upstairs. During cold winter weather, both furnaces would be fired up to capacity. There were no thermostats or other automatic controls on the furnaces, so it was pretty much a judgment call as to whether both furnaces would be needed or if one would suffice, and how large to build the fires in them. Once started, a measure of manual control could be maintained by the amount of wood added from time to time, and the opening or closing of the combustion air damper. Sometimes, when a mid-winter, Saturday night dance was being held, it was necessary to open the outside doors and windows to relieve the excess heat even if the outside air temperature was way below freezing.

Henry was the Town Hall janitor for many years (at the huge salary of $100 per year), and it was his responsibility to fire up the wood furnaces prior to any event that was being held there in the winter months. Starting when I was about 12 years old, the responsibility for Town Hall heating was often delegated to me. On a cold day, it was necessary to start the furnaces in the early afternoon for an evening event in order to have the building warm when people arrived. Henry often didn't return from shoeing until early evening, and it was time for me to start earning my keep. In addition to the heat, I often had to shovel away as much snow as possible from the entrance and then walk over to the Town Shed to get some sand to sprinkle on the ice.

To build fires in the furnaces, I would first crawl into the woodshed attached to the furnace room and toss a quantity of firewood close to where it would be used. Then I would select one or two chunks that had straight grain, with no knots, to split into kindling. Henry had taught me to split wood using a large headed, very dull, ax because a sharp ax would cut into the wood instead of splitting it, would wedge itself in, and be difficult to remove. Kindling was piled in a criss-cross on top of wadded paper in the firebox. Next, a few smaller pieces of firewood were laid on top. For good measure, a cup full of kerosene or used motor oil was sometimes poured on top. The furnaces had such great draft, that they would often blow out a match before the paper at the bottom of the pile caught fire. I soon learned that the easy way to get the fire started was to roll up some newspaper and light one end outside of the furnace. That temporary torch worked great to get the fire started and luckily, I never burned down the Town Hall using it. Once the fire was going well, full size wood chunks could be added every few hours as necessary.

Uncle Bill had the same responsibility for the Church that Henry had for the Town Hall. Instead of a furnace, there were two large wood stoves, one in each corner at the back of the room. The stove pipes gave off additional heat as they traveled the entire length of the room to the chimneys up front. Sometime, maybe in the late 1950s, the wood stoves in the church were replaced with oil burners.

Henry's shop was heated by a stove that he built himself from two large steel drums. A large 55-gallon drum was laid horizontally and a door was fashioned into one end. A smaller drum was welded vertically at the center of the horizontal drum to extract additional heat before the smoke made its way to the chimney. To protect the thin steel of the drum from burning through, several inches of sand and gravel were placed in the bottom. Although it was intended to be a temporary heat source, that stove was used daily every winter from about 1950 until Henry sold out in 1986.

One of the best things about snow was the crust. These days snow doesn't seem to form a crust like it used to, or maybe I'm just not as aware of it. After a good snowstorm, there would often be a day or two of relatively warm sunshine. This would cause the top inch or so of snow to partly melt. Overnight, or when the temperature dropped well below freezing again, this heavy wet snow on top would freeze solid. Sometimes it would form a crust strong enough for a grown man to walk on without breaking through to the fluffy soft snow below.

A lot of sleds in those days had narrow metal runners. Those sleds didn't work well at all on deep, soft snow, but a good crust meant GREAT sledding! It was difficult to control where a sled might go on crust, but it sure went fast. Once in a while the sled runners would cut completely through the crust causing the sled to suddenly halt, but the rider's momentum kept him going down the hill on his belly or the seat of his pants. Sometimes we would dispense with store-bought sleds all together and slide down hill on a piece of cardboard, an inflated truck inner tube, or whatever else was handy.

One of our best sledding places was the hill directly behind George Howes' barn at the south edge of the Center. The hill started near the road and dropped quickly into a small depression then rose slightly to an old stone wall and line of trees that marked the edge of the Zimmerman farm. Beyond the stonewall, the hill pitched down again all the way to the lower valley. We never slid all the way down because it was way too far to walk back up. Unless the snow was especially deep, the top few layers of stones in the wall were usually visible. The speed gained from sliding down the hill behind the barn was usually more than enough to get you to the stone wall at a pretty good clip. There was a gap in the wall that was maybe six feet wide. If you felt lucky, you would try to maneuver your sled through that gap. If you successfully shot through, you were a hero to your buddies. If you missed, you risked a close encounter of the painful kind with a few big chunks of granite!

An experienced sled rider knew exactly where he had to bail off the sled if it looked like he was going to miss the hole. Big sleds offered an opportunity to play our version of chicken. Three or four kids (yes, girls did it too) would sit tightly together on a large sled or toboggan. The first to "chicken out" and bail was taunted by "Chicken, Chicken." Sometimes, if it was obvious that a heavily loaded sled was headed for disaster, the kid on the tail end would jump off, but keep hanging onto the sled using his body as an anchor to slow everybody down.

The ultimate achievement was to hit the hole in the stone wall while riding a tube or cardboard, which was nearly unsteerable. In an anti-hero sort of way, the most admired slider of the day was always the one who stayed on his or her ride until actually colliding with the stone wall. Oddly, I don't recall there being too many serious injuries. One time a sledder, possibly Eddie Carron or Glen Hine, proudly navigated the hole in the wall at top speed. He lifted both arms in celebration and promptly slammed into a small tree just past the hole. His "Red Badge of Courage" included a bloody nose and a chipped tooth.

We didn't do it that often, but some of the most exciting, and dangerous, sliding took place directly on the road riding the ripsled. The ripsled was useless on the usual sliding hills, even if there was a hard crust. The weight of a load of kids would cause its narrow runners to cut through the crust and it would bog down in the loose snow. The place to ride the ripsled was in the road on hard packed snow and ice. Any hilly road in town with packed snow, and some good curves, was prime ripsled territory!

I don't remember who owned the ripsled. It just seemed to appear from time to time. Cousin Bill Glabach recently suggested that it may have belonged to the town and was stored in the old hearse house. A rip was a long sled, somewhat resembling a toboggan. It held several riders sitting on a seat elevated above two sets of runners. The long pair of runners toward the rear was fixed and the shorter pair at the front could be angled left and right to steer by pulling on ropes. To add to the excitement, we liked to ride the ripsled at night, especially if there was a full moon so that we could actually see where we were going. The justification we gave to our parents, when they questioned our sanity, was that it was easier to see cars coming at night due to their lights reflecting on the snow; actually that was true.

A few adults were into ripsledding also. Usually we had an adult or two along, partly to satisfy a few of the mothers who felt that what we were doing was just a bit dangerous, especially without some adult supervision. Another reason was to increase the weight on the sled to reduce its tendency to side-slip or tip over on icy curves. One adult always drove a car following us down the road, partly to prevent us getting run over from behind, but mainly to tow us back up the hill after each run. The ripsled was about eight feet long and held five or six riders sitting tightly one behind another. You sat with your feet on top of the runners and wrapped your arms around the person in front of you creating a solid mass of stupidity... err, humanity. The rider in the front had nothing to hold onto because he had to do the steering by pulling the ropes with both hands. I said "he" because I don't recall a girl ever offering to sit in front and steer. Girls usually sat in the middle, screaming, with their eyes tightly closed for the whole run. The second passenger from the front often held one or two flashlights so that the person steering could see where to go, and to hopefully warn oncoming cars that we were there. The rearmost rider got the whole thing moving by pushing and then jumping on the tail end if there was room. Everyone else simply held on for dear life!

Sometimes at night after a snowstorm, if the snow on the road was not all plowed off, and had been well packed by cars, we would gather near George Howes' barn. However, instead of sliding behind the barn, as we did during the day, we slid down the road. Much of the downhill section was rather steep and extended for a half mile or more before leveling out. If we hit the flats at top speed, and the road didn't have a lot of bare spots, we could sometimes coast for close to another half mile. As many kids as possible would pile onto the ripsled with the biggest kid, or an adult, at the rear. Slowly at first, the ripsled started down the road aided by a firm push. By the time we reached Darwin Hine's house we had a little speed up and that was where the hill began to really get steep.

By the time we passed Orr's house, the sled was moving faster than any car had ever traveled that road. This was the start of the only really difficult curve. Upon approaching the curve, the person up front would yell out "Lean to the right!" This was a critical maneuver. If we were going to have a disaster, it usually happened right there. If everyone did not lean to the right, the top heavy sled could tip over sending us all skidding headfirst across the ice into the left snow bank (if we were lucky.) If we leaned too much, the runners would skid sideways and, still on the sled, we would slam into whatever was at the side of the road. Not everyone always knew their left from their right, so the rule of thumb was to simply lean the direction the kid in front of you leaned and hope the one up front had it correct. All the while we were on the lookout for an oncoming car with few options as to what to do if there was one. As long as we kept moving, cars behind us were not much of a concern as we were going much faster than they were.

The next potential disaster point was at the foot of the hill just as the roadway leveled out. Here the Brattleboro Road came in from the left. The danger was that a car might come out of that road directly into our path. There was no stop sign there in those days. Much of the view of our road was blocked by a low hill and a lot of trees, so a car's driver might not see us coming at all. With no brakes, there was no way we could stop, short of steering into a snow bank in what would hopefully be a controlled crash with bodies strewn everywhere.

One night we had an especially good layer of snow on the road. It had been packed hard by numerous vehicles before the snowplow pushed the softer stuff to the sides. The night air was cold and crisp with no wind and stars were shining brightly. The conditions were ideal for ripsledding! That night we only had one adult and he was driving the following car to pull us back up the hill. The steerer up front was one of us boys.

We piled the maximum number of bodies onto the sled, partly to keep warm, and partly because our theory was that the heavier the load, the faster the sled would go. Off we went. We were making a terrific run right from the start. The cold wind we created blew so hard in our faces that our eyes watered and it was difficult to breathe. None of us had any doubt that we were going the fastest we had ever gone on that rickety sled. We maneuvered the curve perfectly, but as we approached the intersection with Brattleboro Road, we saw car lights reflecting off the snow ahead. A vehicle was approaching the intersection on the other road and we were on a collision course! There was a guard rail and a pretty good drop off to the right and steering left would either propel us into a thick stand of trees, or move the sled directly into the path of the oncoming car.

With no way to stop and no place to go except straight ahead, on we went. We all yelled and screamed as loud as we could. The rider with the flashlights waved them frantically, hoping the car's driver would see them. No such luck. The car slowed at the intersection and then pulled out onto our road just a few yards in front of us and moving much slower than we were. Luckily the road was wide and the kid in front was a good steerer. Just as the hill flattened out into the valley he suddenly steered to the left side of the road. We passed that car like it was standing still! It would have been priceless to see the expression that must have come across the face of the car's driver as his headlights caught the sight of that sled full of kids passing him and pulling ahead.

For quite a few years leading into the early 1950s, the road boss was responsible for maintaining the roads most of the year, but he was not in charge of the winter snowplowing. Instead, Henry was in charge of keeping the roads open with the town's only snowplow. I'm not sure why that odd arrangement existed. It may have had to do with the fact that Austin Dobias, who was the regular road boss, may have been too busy preparing for the annual sugaring season which was a large source of income for him. And, the winter was often Henry's slowest horseshoeing season, so he had some time available.

Snowplowing was a new activity that came about in the early decades of the 20th century following the increasing numbers of automobiles in town. Before cars were common, winter transportation was by way of horse drawn sleighs or other wheel-less conveyances. Henry often told stories of the large, oxen-pulled roller that was used to pack down the snow in the roads making for better sleigh travel. "If you think we have bad Mud Seasons now," he would say, "you should have seen how bad the roads were when all that packed snow started to melt."

Old Rosie, Leyden's first town tractor and snowplow.

The town's first real snowplow was a small crawler tractor with a double wing V-plow. It was nicknamed Old Rosie. Following a snowstorm, Henry would start out with Old Rosie to clear the roads so that people could get to work and kids to school. The plowing would continue until all the roads were cleared. It was often necessary to replow roads if the wind came up, creating large drifts. During one storm, Henry and Old Rosie plowed for 34 straight hours with only three breaks for food and fuel. As the years passed, Henry did less of the snowplowing himself, but would schedule drivers who mostly were farmers or summer road gang members who were glad for an opportunity to make a few dollars during the slow winter months. When someone was out plowing for the night, Henry would leave the shop unlocked so that the plowmen could have a place to go inside and warm up.

Sometime around the late 1940s, Old Rosie was retired and replaced by a larger and more powerful Caterpillar D4. Rosie was a great snow mover with her V-plow on the front and a wing on each side, but sometimes she was a bit over matched by deep hard packed drifts. And, she was getting a bit tired. Chances are the D4 was purchased used, as was typical of most of the town's equipment. There never was enough money to buy brand new equipment in those days. I don't know when Leyden's D4 was made, but Caterpillar began producing them probably in the mid-1930s. Today, D4s that are 70 years old, or more, still bring a good price at auctions. It was the town's primary piece of road maintenance equipment, and only snowplow, for several years. Each year around the end of September, the D4's bulldozer blade was exchanged for the snowplow and the wood and glass operator's cab was attached. The machine was fueled up and sat by the Town Shed waiting for the first snowfall. Most years it didn't have long to wait.

The D4's plow setup was similar to Old Rosie's except the V-plow was a little larger and the wings were hydraulically operated, which was a major improvement. The side wings on Rosie's plow had been controlled manually by chain falls and winches, which could be difficult and tedious to operate. Or, the wing adjustment devices could become iced up and impossible to adjust until they thawed out.

The Cat's heavier weight, and greater horsepower, permitted it to plow a wider swath then Rosie could. The Cat's wings sat a little behind the V-plow and could be angled out, angled upward, and raised up and down. With the wings down, a much wider path could be cleared than with just the V-plow alone. Other times they would be raised up a bit and used to take some of the snow that was being pushed to the sides by the V-plow and push it farther away thus lowering the height of the snow bank and keeping the snow from falling back into the recently plowed roadway. This also created space into which the next storm's snow could be plowed.

Plowing the Greenfield Road was always the first priority. In those days it was simply called the Main Road or The Mountain. After several inches of snow had fallen, the D4 would be driven from the Center down to the Greenfield line and back clearing the way for at least some residents to get to their jobs or to a grocery store in spite of the storm. School bus routes were the second priority although a major storm was sure to cancel school for a few days. Plowing generally worked its way out from the Center until eventually all the roads in town were passable. With the slow D4, this often took several days, especially if there were big drifts to buck.

The last priority was to plow driveways, unless another storm had come along in the meantime. In the 1950s, very few people owned a 4X4 vehicle. The few that were in town were war surplus Jeeps and army trucks. Private snowplows were nearly unheard of, but a few farmers used the front end loaders on their tractors to open up the roads near their houses. You couldn't count on when, but eventually the D4 would show up at your house to help you clear your driveway. This practice was dropped sometime in the '60s.

The Caterpillar D4 was a rugged, reliable machine, but it was not totally problem free. Starting the engine in very cold weather could take a while, sometimes 15 minutes or more! It was equipped with a small 2-cylinder gasoline powered engine that served as the starter for the diesel motor. To begin the starting process, a lever was pulled, releasing compression from all cylinders of the main engine. The small gasoline engine was started using a pull rope as on an old power mower. Once started, the gasoline engine was used to spin the diesel, building up its oil pressure and warming it. The exhaust from the small engine was piped through the diesel motor in order to help with the warming. In addition, the gas and diesel engines shared a common cooling water jacket which also helped to pre-warm the diesel, making it easier to start. After several minutes, with the diesel engine still spinning, the compression lever would be closed, and the diesel fuel valve opened. If the gasoline engine had been run long enough, the diesel would usually start up fairly easily.

One very cold day, the D4 was plowing somewhere in the Beaver Meadow area. At lunchtime, a nearby local resident came out and invited the very chilled driver into the house to warm up and have a hot lunch. The delighted plow operator gladly accepted the offer and immediately parked the D4. Since he was concerned about the amount of diesel fuel remaining, he turned off the engine. Following his lunch of fish chowder, hot coffee, and apple pie, the thoroughly fed, and thoroughly warmed, driver returned to the now cold D4 and went through the starting procedure. The gasoline engine fired right up, but even after a half hour of trying, the diesel refused to pop even once. The driver's long lunch break, and the very cold temperature, had caused the diesel fuel to gel somewhere in the fuel line blocking the flow to the engine.

Several hours later, after sunset, Jessie heard a strange noise coming from just past the Gerry house. Looking down the road she thought she saw the D4 coming very slowly with its plow up, wings folded back, and no lights. Going over to the shop, she told Henry, "You better come and look, I think something is wrong. The snowplow is coming back, but it is making a very strange sound and it's barely moving."

Unable to get the diesel engine started, the resourceful plow operator had the machine limping home using only the small gasoline starter engine for power. Luckily there were no steep hills or snow drifts along the route! Henry used a blow torch to warm the diesel fuel system and soon the D4 was back on the job with the operator instructed to keep it running.

The crawler tractor with the big double-winged V-plow was somewhat unique to Leyden. By the 1950s, most towns had evolved to using angled snowplows on large dump trucks and road graders for most of their snow removal. However, if a heavy snowstorm hit with high winds, drifts could be created that would stop any truck mounted snowplow in its tracks. From time to time, Bernardston, Guilford, or Colrain would call and ask if Leyden's D4 would come over and deal with the snowdrifts on a few of their hilly back roads. I have personally seen that big V-plow go through drifts that were higher than the plow was tall. The operator would fold both wings way back, raise the V-plow well off the road surface, get a good head start and smack into the drift. Sometimes the driver would have to clear piled-up snow from in front of the windshield before he could see well enough to hit the drift again. It might take a few passes before a major drift was fully tamed, but the D4 was never beaten.

Sometime in the 1950s, the town purchased a Ford, four-wheel-drive, dump truck which was equipped with a modern angled snowplow in the winter. This unit usually did a much faster and cleaner job of plowing the roads than the D4 as long as the snowfall wasn't too deep or the drifts too large. With two snowplows working, the roads were now cleared much faster. The Ford would begin plowing the Greenfield Road, and other roads around the center, and the D4 would immediately head for the back roads. One time, during the first winter of plowing with the new truck, it was being used to open up the road somewhere along the south end of East Hill. Everything was going fine when, coming around a curve, there appeared across the road ahead, the deepest drift of the day. Undaunted, the driver surged the truck forward only to shudder to a stop just a few feet into the drift. The driver backed up, put the pedal to the metal once again, and slammed into the drift a second time.

Now a V-plow, as used on the D4, pushed snow both to the right and left. Since the forces on the tractor were equal, there was no tendency for it to get pushed to one side when hitting a deep drift. Not so with the truck's angled plow. It was built such that the snow was pushed in only one direction. As the snow was pushed to the right, that same angle would tend to force the truck to the left which was exactly what happened when the truck slammed into that drift the second time. Some snow moved to the right, but a lot of truck moved to the left, all the way left into the ditch where it, its plow, and the driver became very stuck. Luckily, it happened not far from the Croutworst farm, so the driver walked there and called Henry's shop to explain his problem. About an hour later Henry arrived driving the D4. "I'll pull you out of that ditch in a minute," he told the driver. "But first let me get this little drift out of your way!"

Winter scene at the Old Hearse House, just past the church.

Because road conditions in the winter could be so snow covered and icy, the use of tire chains on a vehicle's powered wheels was very common. It seems as if chains are seldom used these days, but in the 1950s, some residents put the chains on when the first storm arrived and would leave them on until spring. Others performed the nasty job of putting chains on and off several times a season. Chains provided greatly improved traction, especially on icy roads, and were much superior to snow tires. They were vastly better than today's all-season mud & snow tires. There were some downsides to chains, however. For one, they were difficult and messy to put on, or at least to put on correctly, so that they didn't come off or strike the inside of the car's fenders as the wheels turned. For another, they wore out fast if driven on dry pavement. And, you were limited to about 30 mph, or your chains might come apart. It was not at all uncommon to hear a car coming with a broken chain going "clank, clank, clank." Henry always did a pretty good business of replacing broken tire chain cross links each winter.

The main road from the Center to the Greenfield line was always better maintained than other roads in town. Snowy and icy roads in other parts of town would often change over to well plowed and sanded roads at the Center. A few residents, who lived in West Leyden, on their way to work in Greenfield, would stop at Henry's shop on their way, with chains on their rear wheels. There, they would remove the chains, or ask Henry or Bill to do it, before proceeding. On the return trip they reversed the process. I clearly remember one commuter who I thought had the best system. He had two sets of rear wheels and tires for his car. One set of wheels had chains installed and the other did not. On his way to Greenfield, he would stop at the shop and replace the chained wheels with the no-chains pair. On the way home he would do the reverse. It was much easier and faster to simply swap the wheels than to install and remove chains.

The relative isolation of winter with its short days made residents look forward to spring more and more as the season wore on. People trapped in their houses by the winter weather began to get a real case of "Cabin Fever." Nothing resembling today's instant world-wide communications was even envisioned. Most houses did have a radio capable of picking up WHAI in Greenfield and, if the weather conditions permitted, maybe a station or two from quite some distance away. Few if any homes in town had a television set in 1950, but ten years later, they were almost universal. With a roof-top antenna, decent reception of the Hartford, Springfield, and Holyoke stations could be obtained. One year, somebody's parent got the idea of showing movies for us kids on Saturday mornings at the Town Hall. They were a welcome break from the winter blues. For a dime, or 25-cents, we watched two movies, usually a singing-cowboy western and a cartoon. A lot of books got read, especially comic books among us kids. Whenever one of us went to Greenfield, we would come home with one or two new comics. Once read by the owner, they were passed back and forth quite a bit. By spring, they were pretty dog-eared. In good condition, many of those comic books might be valuable collector's items today.

On clear winter nights in Leyden, far removed from the light pollution of any city, we could sometimes get an exciting view of the Northern Lights. Sometimes they were saber-like shafts of colored light stabbing through the sky from the north: blues, greens and yellow. I don't remember ever seeing red. Other times, they resembled sheet lightning which was usually faint yellow. The show never lasted very long, usually just a few minutes. Some winters we did not see them at all. It seems that they became less and less common as the years marched on.

Chapter 29

CHRISTMAS IN THE HILLS

In the 1950s, the Christmas season did not start before Halloween the way commercial and media interests force it onto us today. Not a lot of thought was given to Christmas until Thanksgiving was over. Thanksgiving was a top tier holiday in its own right and was a time for gatherings of friends and family and having fun. It was truly a day to be thankful for what we had, and be hopeful for what may lay ahead. Jessie was one of five siblings and the honor of hosting the Turkey Day feast for the entire Wood family was rotated annually among them. After the meal, somebody wrote the name of each adult on a slip of paper and a drawing was held in order to determine for each adult, which other adult he or she was to buy a Christmas present. It was very secret and hush, hush, only to be revealed on Christmas Day and sometimes not even then. Although each adult received only a single present, each of the children received presents from every adult.

By early December everyone began to focus on the upcoming Christmas celebration. All the kids started behaving a little bit better just in case Santa Claus really was keeping a list. Christmas was a wonderful time of year and everyone looked forward to it no matter what their religion, or lack thereof. It had not yet become the months-long retailing extravaganza and media hyped "holiday season" that we endure today.

We always had a real tree for Christmas, never an artificial one, although they did exist. "If we are going to have a real Christmas, we need to have a real Christmas tree," Henry would say. Usually, we would all ride down to the farm in his pickup and tromp through the woods, getting cold feet from snow in our boots, trying to locate the perfect tree. Actually, two perfect trees, as we always supplied the tree for Frank and Bertha Wood, my maternal grandparents, as well. Of course no perfect trees existed, so extra boughs were cut to be inserted into holes bored in the tree's trunk to fill out some of the bad spots. When the tree was put up in the house, the worst side faced a wall. If the bad side was large, the tree would be located in a corner of the living room.

At least half of the decorations on our tree were homemade. Hours were spent stringing popcorn and macaroni dyed with food coloring to make garlands. Orilla and I cut strips of colored paper to make paper chains. We had a few strings of tree lights with large bulbs and a few bubble lights. However, we could never count on the lights because all it took was one bad bulb and everything would go out. Some years the lights never came on once through the entire season. I remember one year that Henry finally gave up in frustration after he had worked and worked on the lights trying to locate the bad bulb or the short in the wiring. We had a nice Christmas even without the tree lights being lit. The funny thing was, around New Year's Day as we were beginning to remove the decorations from the tree, suddenly the lights came on and stayed on until we had removed all the ornaments.

As the schools' Christmas break neared, more and more time was spent in the class room practicing for the annual Christmas program. Every year the town put on a Christmas party at the Town Hall which was a joint effort between the Methodist Church, the schools, and the town officials. In those days the byword was <u>cooperation</u> of church and state, not separation. I guess nobody realized that such cooperation was a big threat to the republic.

On the day before the big party, some residents would bake cookies or make popcorn balls while others would wrap children's gifts purchased by money that the selectmen managed to find in the town budget. I suspect that in many years, much of the money for gifts came out of their own pockets and those of other prominent citizens. A very careful count was taken to ensure that a gift would be under the Town Hall tree for each and every child living in Leyden, no matter how young.

Henry and Jessie were usually in charge of decorating the Town Hall for the big event. There was always a real tree that a farmer had cut and donated. State law said that in order to have a real Christmas tree in a public building, the tree had to be fireproofed. Henry would make up a solution of detergent, salt, and borax, and he used a fire extinguisher to spray the tree heavily outdoors until it was drenched. This is basically the same chemical mixture used today to "fireproof" the shredded newspaper marketed as cellulose insulation for new houses. After it had dried, the tree was carried inside and decorated. Lights were prohibited (fire danger again), but many residents donated all sorts of ornaments, usually handmade.

On the night of the big event, every seat in the main hall was filled and most of the standing room spots were taken also. The event started with a community sing of favorite Christmas Carols. This was followed by a flock of nervous school kids putting on their program. Some years the school kids just sang, other years we put on a short pageant or skit.

When I was in about the 5th grade, part of the school program consisted of Marilyn Croutworst and me singing a duet. I was scared enough over the prospect of having to sing in front of everyone in town, but the part I really dreaded was that the teacher insisted that, at the conclusion of the song, I should lean forward and kiss Marilyn who would be sitting on a stool in front of me. I had nothing against Marilyn, but to kiss ANY girl, and in front of all those people? I might have been convinced to go along with the plan if it had been Shirley Johnson, but any other girl, NO WAY! However, my days of protests continued to fall on deaf ears. Jessie, who I could usually count on to back me up when I didn't want to do something, was firmly in the teacher's camp.

There seemed to be only one way out. I was never a

strong church-goer, but I did, and still do, believe in a higher intelligence. For several days ahead of the event, I prayed and prayed for something, anything, to save me from this fate.

The day of the program, I was being pretty miserable about the whole thing until Jessie had finally heard enough. She sat me down and let it be known in no uncertain terms that I was going to do what I was expected to do and I was going to do it with a smile on my face. With that, she sent me upstairs to take a bath and then get dressed in my costume. As I pulled off my shirt, I noticed a lot of red spots on my chest and belly.

"Hey Mom," I yelled. "What are these red spots on me?"

"My God," she exclaimed after examining me, "You've got the measles! You can't go to the program or everybody will catch it."

Doing my best imitation of disappointment, I silently prayed "Thank You," as Jessie called the teacher with the bad news.

Another year the school and church cooperated on putting together a living nativity. The curtain rose showing Mary and Joseph at the manger as "angels" sang. From the back of the room the three wise men slowly walked in wearing their aluminum foil crowns and pointing to a construction paper star dangling overhead. Following them were two shepherds, wearing bath robes and towel hats, leading a live sheep. Everything was going great until the sheep arrived at center stage and while munching on the manger's hay, proceeded to take a dump right in front of the Christ Child.

The highlight of the Christmas party was always the arrival of Santa Claus and his distribution of the gifts to all the children. He arrived wearing a patched and faded suit that once must have been bright red, but had aged to a color resembling Campbell's Tomato Soup. Knee-high barn boots, a knit hat, and a cotton-batten beard completed his ensemble. Santa carried with him a huge burlap sack of real gifts to be added to the ones already under the tree.

After all the gifts had been distributed and opened, Santa wished everyone a Merry Christmas and departed, telling us he had several more parties to attend that evening. We kids were never allowed to look out the door or windows to watch him leave. We were told it was bad luck to see Santa's reindeer before Christmas Eve, so we had to be content with the sound of sleigh bells coming from outside. Soon everyone else headed out as well with kids being hustled into cars before they had time to scout for deer tracks or sleigh runner marks. The tree that had so painstakingly been fireproofed and decorated the day before was taken down and given to a needy family along with some left over gifts to make their season just a bit brighter.

As keeper of the town's Santa costume, Jessie was responsible for twisting someone's arm every year to wear it. It was always a closely guarded secret as to who this year's Santa impersonator would be. Sometimes she would fool everyone by bringing in a Santa from another town. At the party, all the men of the town were present or accounted for, so who could that Santa be? Even a few adults started to wonder if he might actually be the real thing! Naturally, Orilla and I had no idea what Jessie was up to.

Back then, Santa seemed a lot more mysterious and real than he does these days when there is a Santa in every store, on every street corner, and in every TV commercial starting soon after Halloween. Santa only appeared at Wilson's Department Store in Greenfield and he was there only for just a few days in early December. After that he went away for a while, supposedly returning to the North Pole to prepare for his big evening.

Jessie kept all sorts of things in a large closet that was just off my bedroom. I was forbidden to go into that closet, which made it all the more appealing. One year in early December, when I was very young, I was poking around in that closet just to see what I could find. I opened an old chest and there on top was the Santa suit and beard.

I recoiled in horror and ran downstairs to Jessie crying "Mom, Mom, Santa Claus is dead! He won't be coming this year!"

"Such foolishness. What makes you say that?" she asked.

"I saw his clothes in my closet!" I blurted out without thinking.

"The closet you're not supposed to go into?"

Instead of a lecture, she took my hand and led me back upstairs. She showed me that it was just a suit of clothes. We looked all around and Santa's body was nowhere to be found. Not convinced, I pointed out to her that Santa certainly would go to Heaven when he died, so of course there was no body in my closet. I was a very relieved little boy when Santa showed up at the town party a few weeks later.

Chapter 30

SUGARING OFF

With Christmas and New Year's behind them, some of Leyden's farmers started making preparations for the upcoming maple syrup season. Buckets had to be repaired and washed, the evaporator pan scrubbed, and a lot of firewood cut and split to fuel the big fire in the sugar house. As the late winter thaws began, the maple trees started to pump sweet sap upward from their roots where it had been stored over the winter. The sugar was pushed all the way up to the branches and twigs in preparation for their annual task of producing leaves. Syrup producers bled off some of that sweet sap, from mature hard maple trees, which was the only ingredient needed for production of maple syrup.

The basic method of producing maple syrup was in use by the Native Americans in the North-East when the European settlers arrived. Then, as in the 1950s, the process involved collecting the sweet sap from maple trees in the late winter and then boiling off much of the water it contained. Although the province of Quebec, Canada, produces at least three-fourths of the world's supply of maple syrup each year, many people tend to associate that sugary liquid with Vermont. "Vermont Maple Syrup" rolls easily off the tongue in much the same manner as "Maine Lobsters" or "Idaho Potatoes" regardless of the actual source of the item in hand. Although their contribution to the world's supply was minimal, production of maple syrup was a big factor in the economy of several of the farms in Leyden, even though they were just a bit south of the Vermont line.

Shortly after the first of February it was time to start tapping trees. Only hard maple trees were tapped (also called sugar maples, rock maples, or black maples.) Soft maples or silver maples (the ones that have deeply indented leaves) were not usually used for syrup production because the sugar content of the sap was much lower. Trees that were candidates for tapping had to be fairly mature, generally with a trunk at least 10-inches to a foot in diameter. Since maple trees are quite slow growing, this meant that a tree was at least 40 to 50 years old before it began to be used for syrup production. Usually only one or two buckets would be hung on a small tree while a very large, centuries old giant might have six to eight.

Using a hand auger, about a half-inch hole was drilled into the trunk two or three feet above snow level. Care was taken to make sure that the new hole was not in vertical alignment with scars from the holes of previous years. A short, tapered metal spigot was then tapped into the hole and a covered bucket was hung on it. Almost immediately, a slow trickle of sap would emerge from the spigot and begin to drip into the bucket.

On a warm day, during a good run, sap would drop into each bucket at the rate of about one drop each second. A good sap run might produce 1 1/2 to 2 quarts a day from each spigot. After the buckets had been hung in the sugar bush (maple tree grove) for a day or two, it was time to start gathering sap. The length of time between gatherings depended largely on the weather. The best runs usually occurred on a warm day following a cold night. Melting snow provided moisture for the roots to supply the sap to the trees' capillaries.

In the 1950s, most of the spigots and sap buckets used were made of galvanized steel. Ten years later, some farmers had eliminated buckets all together and started connecting the taps directly into a hose that led to a tank at the sugar house. However, I remember when I was very young, my grandfather, Frank Wood, still used the old wooden buckets that resembled half a whisky barrel, but were much smaller. They were built from carefully fitted wood staves held tightly together by iron bands. He spent untold hours during each winter repairing damaged and leaking buckets in preparation for the upcoming sugar season. A week or two before they were to be hung on the maple trees, the wooden sap buckets were soaked for several days in water. The soaking caused the wood to absorb moisture and swell, closing the seams tightly so that the buckets would not leak.

I got my start in sugaring at the age of eight. I borrowed some buckets from my grandfather and tapped a few of the maple trees near our house. I gathered the sap in a pair of 40-quart milk cans strapped to my sled and talked Jessie into boiling it down for me on her kitchen stove. A rough rule of thumb was that it required about ten gallons of sap to produce one gallon of syrup. Thus, boiling down one of my 40-quart cans of sap released about 35 quarts of water into the house as steam. After a few days of living in a swamp-like atmosphere with moisture condensing on all the windows and running down the walls, Jessie informed me that enough was enough. She insisted that I come up with some other way of doing my boiling, and somewhere other than in her kitchen.

I talked over my problem, and Jessie's edict, with Henry and, as usual, he came up with a solution. He located a small section of an evaporator pan that was about the size of a very large desk. I think it was originally the section that preheated the sap at the start of the process in a sugar house. For me, it was going to do the entire job. He created a stove out of a large oil drum laid on its side with the upper part cut away to fit under the pan. He set me up outdoors near the shop and I was in business after a few raids to the shop's firewood pile. I ladled sap into one corner of the pan and drained syrup into some of Jessie's canning jars at the opposite corner.

The process worked quite well except when it snowed heavily or especially when the wind blew. I frequently couldn't boil under those conditions and I had nowhere to store my sap which continued to flow into the buckets on my trees. I had an inventory problem! After some persuasion, I convinced

Even Youngsters Boil Sap

Courtesy of Greenfield Recorder-Gazette

*The author, making maple syrup on his small outside evaporator,
when he was eight years old.*

Henry to let me move my operation into the large garage shed
attached to the house in order to boil every day. There would

be a roof over my whole process, and the big front doors could be opened wide to vent the steam. Henry's big concern was the wood floor and walls that were adjacent to where my stove would be burning red hot. To keep me from burning down the house, he lined the floor and nearest wall with several layers of sheet metal.

When I was not busy gathering sap, or boiling off, I was up and down the road with my jars of syrup selling to the neighbors or to gas customers at the shop for $1 per quart. Soon more and more people took an interest in my operation. Residents and even some out-of-towners stopped by frequently to watch, take photos, and purchase some of my product. One day a reporter from the *Greenfield Recorder-Gazette* showed up to photograph me and my operation for his newspaper. I never understood what all the fuss was about. After all, I was just doing the same thing that hundreds of farmers all over New England were doing. Of course, most of them were more than eight years old. As my fame and customer base grew, I needed a larger supply of sap. My raw material inventory problem had swung from too much to too little. Soon I had several buckets hanging on nearly every maple tree in Leyden Center.

One night at supper, when my inaugural sugaring season was winding down, Jessie said that it was time for us to talk business.

"What kind of business?" I asked.

"Well," she said, "every business has expenses that have to be paid. For example, if somebody buys a dollar's worth of gas at the shop, the dollar he pays us isn't all profit that we can put in the bank. Most of that dollar was already spent by us buying the gasoline from the oil company. Our profit is the difference between what we pay for the gas and what we sell it for."

"I understand, but I don't see what that has to do with me."

"Well, for one thing, before canning season next summer I'm going to have to get hold of a lot of new canning jars.

You've been giving away one of my best jars with each quart of syrup you have sold."

"Oh, I get it. You want me to get back all those jars."

"That's one possibility, but it might be a lot simpler and easier to just buy me some new ones using some of the money you collected. They aren't terribly expensive."

I sat quietly for several minutes. I hadn't thought of it before, but she was right. I had been using up her jars and Henry's firewood while pocketing every dollar that came in. Suddenly that stack of dollar bills I was accumulating didn't look so large. Such was my introduction to the world of business.

For a couple of years, while I was in high school, I worked for Austin Dobias gathering sap and generally helping with the sugaring process. Austin was a very interesting character and was typically New England. He insisted on things being done his way because he knew the right way do them. I must admit that most of the time he was correct. He was also very fair and a good boss to work for.

Austin had one of the larger sugaring operations in town. We used a crawler tractor or team of horses to pull a heavy sled on which a large metal tank was fastened. The tank held maybe 200 or 300 gallons and had a small opening on top. Two of us each used a pair of 5-gallon pails to gather the sap from the buckets on the trees and then dumped them into the tank on the sled. Austin, or his son, Arthur, drove the tractor or horses. Often there would be ice on top of the sap in the buckets. A prevailing theory was that the sugar content of the sap would not allow freezing, so the ice was assumed to be pure water and was thrown away. This theory was easily disproven by melting a piece of the ice in your mouth and tasting the sweetness, but Austin was not to be argued with.

When the tank was full, or all the buckets had been emptied, we returned to the sugar house. Our sled tank was emptied into the storage tank that sat uphill of the sugar house providing gravity flow to the evaporator. Then it was time to go into the sugar house to warm up before heading out for another load. Austin was always in charge of the actual boiling process and often worked at the evaporator alone while the

Courtesy of Polly Dobias Streeter

Austin Dobias' sugar house in Beaver Meadow.

rest of us were outside gathering sap or hauling in firewood to feed the fire under the boiler pan.

As a rule, the best syrup was made from sap collected during the first few days of the run. The sugar content was probably higher then and less heating was needed to make the final product. Dark syrup did not bring the best price and had to be sold in large drums to candy manufacturers. Premium syrup was a light amber color, contained no carbon flakes, and was sold in metal cans or glass jugs up to and including one-gallon size. Some were sold to local residents and to stores on the Mohawk Trail west of Greenfield. Some of the Leyden producers had a contract with a company that sold their Massachusetts-made syrup as genuine Vermont Maple Syrup at tourist shops all up and down the Connecticut Valley.

The sugar content of the raw sap varied from year to year and also from the start of a season's run to the end a few weeks later. The lower the sugar content of the sap, the more water had to be boiled off to make syrup. The main processing device in the sugar house was a large flat pan evaporator. It had three main sections. The first section was the preheater where a steady flow of raw sap flowed in by gravity and was heated before moving into the main evaporator pan. The pan was built with a series of channels so that the heating and evaporating liquid was always flowing back and forth from the entrance toward the exit. The syrup had to be kept moving. If it stopped, or flowed too slowly, it would carbonize or burn-on resulting in a very low grade product. From the main pan, it flowed into the final small section which did not receive as much heat. There the amount of remaining water could be better controlled. At the discharge end of the final section the hot syrup flowed into containers where it cooled. The main control parameters were the incoming flow rate of raw sap and the heat of the fire.

The entire pan was heated from below by a large wood fire burning in what was called the arch. Some sugar houses had been converted to burn fuel oil, but Austin's still burned wood slabs procured from a sawmill. The sugar house was built such that the rising steam from the open pan evaporator would go out through a large vent in the roof yet snow and rain could not get in. When the evaporator was boiling, huge clouds of steam rose continually from the opening in the roof.

In addition to evaporation of the excess water, the other function of the heating was to caramelize a portion of the sugars, giving the syrup its distinctive flavor and color. It was essential to not heat the solution too quickly, or get it too hot, resulting in dark, burned-tasting syrup. I don't remember Austin ever trusting anyone except himself to run the evaporator, probably a very wise move. If the sugar content was too low (i.e., not enough water had been evaporated out) the syrup would taste weak and would tend to spoil. If the sugar content was too high, crystals would form in the bottom of each container of syrup. Somehow Austin had the knack of adjusting the sap flow and the heat of the fire so that top grade syrup kept flowing into the containers. He did make a few concessions to science however. He had a thermometer fastened to the discharge end of the evaporator and checked it constantly. As water was evaporated, the syrup became more concentrated and the boiling point would rise. Austin wanted the temperature of the exiting syrup to be exactly 219 degrees. If the syrup contained too much water, the exit temperature would be below 219 degrees. If too much water was being removed, the temperature would rise above that mark. From time to time he would also measure the density of the syrup using a laboratory style hydrometer to measure the sugar content, but Austin had more faith in the thermometer.

In the fall of the year, Austin often produced a lot of apple cider. It was the old-fashioned kind of cider made by pressing washed apples without benefit of any other process. There was no filtration other than a canvas sack, and certainly no pasteurization. The cider was stored in wooden barrels along one wall inside the sugar house. As it aged, the cider fermented, became hard, and carried quite a kick. Before the advent of factory-made beer, hard cider had been the most common "adult" beverage in New England, especially in Vermont.

By February, when we were making syrup, the cider made in September seemed like it could grow hair on a billiard ball. Some of us referred to it as paint thinner. While we were making syrup, from time to time Austin would go over to the exit end of the evaporator and fill a large coffee mug with hot syrup straight from the discharge pipe. He would then drink that nearly boiling hot syrup down in one big gulp. Austin called it part of the testing process. Then he would go over to one of the wood barrels and fill the cup to the brim once more, this time with hard cider. One more gulp and the cider was downed as a chaser. He sometimes offered the opportunity to the rest of us to "test the syrup" in the same manner, but nobody else could handle it.

After only a few weeks, the daily temperature had risen, and most of the winter's snows had melted away, signaling that the end of the sugaring season was not far off. Soon the sap runs would dwindle down to such a low level that it wasn't worth it to gather sap anymore. Finally, Austin announced that it was time to take down the buckets, scrub the evaporator pan, and haul away the accumulated wood ashes. Each year, before all the canned syrup was shipped away, several gallons were set aside for a very special occasion: the annual Sugar Supper!

On a day soon after a deep snowfall of the light, fluffy kind, and with Old Man Winter on his last legs, several Leyden men would get out the snow barrels and haul them to a location back in the woods where the drifts were deep and the snow was very clean. There, they shoveled the barrels full of snow and packed it in tightly. Lids were secured on each barrel and they were then hauled to the freezer locker plant in Greenfield for storage until spring.

After winter's icy grasp was loosened, and spring was definitely in the air, it was time for the ladies of the Church to begin making plans for the upcoming Sugar Supper. The supper was held after the roads had mostly dried from Mud Season, and often flowers were starting to bloom. The Sugar Supper ranked, with summer's Blueberry Supper, as one of the best community suppers put on anywhere. It was a town-wide effort, and was another example of the cooperation that existed in small New England towns. The Church, the local government, and members of the community at large all pitched in and worked together for the better of all.

Leyden farmers who had made a good crop of maple syrup that year would each donate a few gallons of their best product. If it had been a poor sugaring year, they would often still donate, but it might be lower quality syrup or some left over from the previous season. The ladies of the church donated their time to cook up large amounts of food for the main course. As with the Blueberry Supper, the main course was really not the object. What really mattered was the dessert: Sugar on Snow!

Once again, Bud Kennedy's culinary talents were called upon, and he was always responsible for cooking down the syrup to the right consistency. The object was to boil off even more of the water from the syrup so it would congeal on the cold snow, but not so much that it would quickly harden at room temperature. If it was not cooked down enough, the hot syrup would not quickly stiffen when poured onto the snow, and would just melt its way to the bottom of the bowl. If cooked down too much, it would turn into maple sugar crystals. Bud had the knack for getting it just right. His primary measure of the correctness of a batch was if the hot syrup would "apron" down the surface of a large spoon when dipped in and quickly pulled back out. When it was very close, Bud would call for a bowl of snow for the final test.

The barrels of snow were kept in the coolest convenient location that could be found near the Town Hall kitchen. If the weather was cold, they were outside the kitchen door. Other times they were kept in the woodshed. To prepare the feature dessert, a bowl was heaped over with snow, and a clean dish towel was draped over the mound. The bowl was inverted, the snow packed flat against a table top, and it was ready for use. Each diner was given a bowl of packed snow and every table had one or two small pitchers of hot syrup.

The syrup was poured onto the snow in small puddles about a teaspoon full or less in each spot. It would cool rapidly and immediately start to stiffen after melting in only a very short distance. The diner would then take his or her fork and twirl it to wrap the stiffened syrup around the tines and then, down the hatch. A bowl of snow would be reused until nearly the entire flat surface had been melted, then it was time to ask a waitress for a new bowl.

Eating the syrup was great at first, but because it was so very sweet, most people could not stand it for very long. After eating a few forkfuls of Sugar on Snow, it was time to "cleanse the pallet." The eater would take a big bite of a dill pickle which would reset the taste buds and set him or her up for another bowl full of syrup. An experienced Sugar on Snow eater could be identified by the fork in one hand and a dill pickle in the other.

After the diners had eaten their fill, many wished to stir some syrup into maple sugar. They would be given a small empty bowl into which they would pour about a third to a half cup of syrup. Taking a spoon or fork, they would begin stirring as rapidly as possible while the syrup cooled. After a few minutes, sugar crystals would start to form as evidenced by the syrup changing to an opaque light tan color. The more rapid the stirring, the finer the crystals would be and the higher the quality of the maple candy. Before long the bowl contained a lump of the best maple sugar candy on earth. It bore no comparison to the commercially made rock-hard maple leaf shaped lumps sold in the tourist shops in Vermont and on the Mohawk Trail.

After the final sitting was over, the kitchen and wait staff sat down to tackle the leftovers. There was usually at least a half barrel of snow left over which seldom went to waste. Those warm weather, after dark, snowball fights were the highlight of the event for some of us!

Chapter 31

WHO NEEDS A STOP SIGN?

The legal age to obtain a driver's license was 16, but you could get a learner's permit at 15 1/2. The purpose of the learner's permit was to allow the teenager to get sufficient driving experience in order to pass the driving test when he or she turned 16. That may have been necessary for kids in the big towns and cities, but in the backwoods and hills of New England, many of us were very accomplished drivers by the time we were around the age of 12 or 13, at least we thought we were. Of course when we reached the proper age, we were obliged to take a driver's education course in order to get a reduction in our insurance rates.

Most of us got our introduction to driving on farm equipment out in the fields. My first learning tool was a gray Ford farm tractor. These were smaller and lower than the John Deere and Farmall machines. They were just about standard equipment on farms from the '30s at least through the '60s. They were solid, well built, machines and it is very common to see them still in use today although many are well over 50 years old. I began driving the Ford pulling a hay wagon slowly through the field while men tossed hay onto the rack. I was paid 25 cents per hour and thought I was making big money. After cutting my teeth in the fields, I was later permitted to drive to and from the barn as well, sometimes on the roads. Backing the loaded wagon into the barn required a totally different skill level altogether, as attested to by the numerous scrapes, digs, and splinters around the barn door, not all of which were put there by me. It seemed to me that when backing a wagon, you always had to do the opposite of what you thought was the correct thing to do.

You had reached the big time when you were first allowed to drive a farm truck. The truck was a bit more of a challenge than a tractor. First of all, instead of a hand throttle and a fixed motor speed as with a tractor, you had to keep a foot on the gas pedal and adjust the motor speed as needed. That could be quite a challenge for a kid who could barely reach the gas pedal. You had to make sure to slide yourself forward enough so that your foot was on the gas pedal and still sit high enough to see over the steering wheel! Second, the tractor would start up and go in any gear, while the truck had to be put into motion in a lower gear and then shifted on the fly; no automatic transmissions in those days. Generally the truck's gears were not synchronized, or the syncros were worn out, so unless the skill of double-clutching had been learned, a lot of gear grinding was heard and led to a lot of razzing by the more experienced drivers. Of course the big difference was that it was way too easy to get the truck going too fast, especially downhill.

From a farm truck in the fields, it was a natural transition to driving a pickup or even a car on the public roadways. Of course, in the fields there usually wasn't another vehicle coming at you from the opposite direction. From about the age of 13 on, Henry would often let me drive his truck with him as passenger as long as we were going to stay within town. Leyden had no real police force, and needed none. The state police passed through town only about once a month, often on the same day of the month, and always took the same route up the Greenfield Road, through the Center, and on toward West Leyden, so they were very predictable. Thus the risk of getting caught driving without a license was very minimal. Needless to say, when I eventually took the driver's education class at PVRS, I didn't learn much I didn't already know about the mechanics of driving, but I had a lot to learn about the rules of the road.

Our driver's education car was a brand new 1959 Chevrolet, the model with the X-frame which caused the cars to break in half whenever they got hit in the area of the driver's or passenger's door. Even a mild bump in the right place was known to put a bend in those cars; just the type of thing you want beginners to be driving! I don't remember the car having seat belts, but maybe it did. Seat belts started becoming standard equipment sometime in the early '60s as I recall. Actually, I'm not sure it would have been a good idea to be strapped into a car that was likely to break in half directly under where you were sitting!

When it was class time on-the-road, three or four of us students would pile into the Chevy, along with the instructor riding shotgun with his foot hovering over the panic brake in front of him. The idea was for the passengers in the back seat to learn by observing the mistakes made by the current student driver. I'm not sure we learned much back there because we were usually too busy laughing and poking fun at the hapless kid up front.

Stop signs and traffic lights were something new for me, as the Town of Leyden did not contain a single traffic control device. Heck, you could drive around town half the day and never see another vehicle on the road. The concept of coming to a full stop at an intersection just because there was a red or yellow (yes, yellow) octagonal sign or a red light was very foreign to my way of thinking. "Why do I need to stop at an intersection when there is no other car in sight?" I asked the instructor over and over. I think he got very tired of explaining and using the passenger side foot brake to keep us all from being hurled into oblivion whenever I was driving.

Somehow, we all managed to pass the driving test; I even remembered to stop at all the stop signs during my exam. I even made one extra stop. The tester had me turn left at an intersection controlled by a traffic light. As we approached the intersection, the light was green, so I entered and started my left turn. Just as I was completing my turn I looked up and saw the red light. Of course it was red in that direction to stop the cross traffic, but I had had it drummed into my head never to drive through a red light. So I hit the brakes and stopped right there in the middle of the intersection. I guess I did everything else correctly because I got my license. With our licenses safely in our pockets, we moved on to the next level, that of hounding our parents to allow us to drive to school instead of riding the bus. "Nobody with a driver's license rides the bus," I pleaded to deaf ears around the supper table every night.

Of course once a new driver had permission to drive to school, the next requirement was to have something to drive there. It couldn't be just any old car or truck either. Fords were generally preferred by a lot of the guys due to their history of powerful V-8 engines. Chevies from '55, '56, and '57 were popular too, especially if they had a V8. We might have treated them better had we known then that those Chevies would become collector's cars in high demand a few decades down the road; no, we wouldn't have!

Nobody wanted to have a straight six engine because you couldn't properly squeal the tires when leaving school or peeling out from one of the drive-ins. Another item high on the want list for a car was a four-on-the-floor transmission. If your car had a three-speed column shift, it was definitely second class. A really low first gear upped the tire squeal potential, so many a transmission got an upgrade or the rear end ratio was changed. Of course any car with an automatic, slush-box tranny wasn't even a consideration.

A lot of work went into making a car look just right. Whitewall tires were a must. If you couldn't afford them, you could get add-ons that installed over your black walls, but you had to watch your tire pressure closely because the add-on whitewalls didn't always seal tightly on those new-fangled tubeless tires. To be in style, and have "the right look," the rear of the car had to be lowered way down. If the driver was short, he might have to sit on a pillow to see over the up-tilted hood, but that didn't matter as long as his car had "the look." With the rear end properly lowered, next it was important to install a pair of fender skirts that filled in much of the rear wheel opening. A first-class setup showed as little rear tire as possible with the rear bumper almost dragging. Speed bumps had to be avoided of course, and even a pothole might result in a trail of sparks.

Putting together the whole package at once wasn't always the best idea. One guy had a good after-school and weekend job and put most of his earnings into modifying his car. He had a big souped-up V8 engine, very low first gear, racing slicks, etc. The lowered rear caused the front of the car to stick up so high that it was difficult for him to see anything close to the car. In spite of Principal Leonard's rule against "peeling rubber" on school grounds, this guy just had to show off as he headed home every day. One day he hit the gas and popped the clutch right in front of the school with Mr. Leonard watching. With the slicks squealing, the torque of that big engine caused the lowered rear bumper to drag causing a huge shower of sparks as he went. It was a while before he was permitted to drive at all on school grounds.

If you didn't want to go to the time and expense of installing a lowering kit, a quick temporary fix was to compress the rear springs by weighting down the rear of the car with a couple of bags of cement, or a few concrete blocks, in the trunk! I finally got permission to drive Jessie's '55 Chevy to school most days, but it didn't look nearly as classy as Billy Pratt's '57. Henry wouldn't hear of the rear being lowered, so I had to take the alternate approach. I ended up with some explaining to do one Saturday when Jessie took the car to Greenfield to buy groceries. When she opened the trunk to load her purchases, she found it filled with all sorts of scrap iron from the pile behind Henry's shop!

In the evening it was "way cool" to drive around slowly with only your parking lights on, even it if was well past sundown. To enhance that look, some of us installed colored lights behind the grill in front of the radiator. The ultimate grill lights were red and blue which, of course, were illegal being reserved for emergency vehicles. That just added significantly to the thrill of getting away with it. Wise installers always put the grill lights on a switch so that they could be quickly shut off when driving through areas frequented by the police.

If a car looked right, it also had to sound right. Massachusetts had some pretty strict laws about mufflers. Excessive engine noise could cause a car to be rejected for a semi-annual inspection sticker or result in a second citation if you were stopped for speeding. Dual glass-pack mufflers pretty much gave the ideal sound, but they could be expensive and a lot of inspection stations would fail a car if they knew it had glass packs even if the car wasn't terribly loud. Some guys would punch a few nail holes in a stock muffler to "improve" the sound. Just before inspection they would insert sheet metal screws to seal off the holes and take the screws back out afterward.

Everybody's big fear was the "registry cops." These were special officers empowered to enforce the rules set down by the Massachusetts Registry of Motor Vehicles. The local police and state police weren't much of a problem unless they observed a moving violation. The registry cops, however, ignored the probable cause law and would stop a vehicle just because it looked like a teenager's car. Today, that would be called profiling, which is forbidden even to stop a terrorist. Once stopped, the registry cop would give the car and the driver a thorough going over looking for the slightest violation. If a violation was found, no matter how small, a ticket was always issued. The rumor was that these guys were paid based on the number of tickets they wrote every month.

I remember hearing about a guy who was stopped by a registry cop while he was on his way to get his spring inspection sticker. His car had a single muffler, but it was pretty much a straight through affair, so the car was quite loud. In an attempt to mitigate the noise, before leaving home for the inspection station, he had used a broom handle to shove a good sized wad of steel wool up the tailpipe. He hoped the steel wool would muffle the sound sufficiently to pass inspection. His plan was to fish the steel wool back out once he had his sticker. Of course, the steel wool blocking the exhaust pipe caused the motor to run quite poorly, but emission testing was years in the future.

As soon as he saw that he was being pulled over, he parked and immediately turned off the engine. After checking over the car, the registry cop told my friend to start the engine, which he did very carefully trying to make as little noise as possible. Standing behind the poorly running car, the cop told him to step on the gas. Beginning to sweat a little, the guy increased the engine rpm only slightly. "Floor it!" commanded the registry cop who was standing directly behind the tail pipe. Just as the gas pedal hit the floor, the wad of steel wool shot out of the tail pipe, accompanied by a loud "bang," and slammed into the cop's leg. The cop didn't say a word; he just took out his ticket book.

Chapter 32

THE WRONG WAY FIRE TRUCK

Leyden had become legally incorporated as a separate town in February of 1809, when it was split off from Bernardston. Actually, Arms says that it had existed as a separate district since 1784 when no less than John Hancock, President of the Commonwealth of Massachusetts, and Samuel Adams, created it. From that time forward, Leyden had existed as a separate entity. However, at its formation, Leyden did not contain enough residents to qualify for sending its own representative to the General Court (legislature.) So it continued to share a representative with Bernardston and therefore was a district instead of a town. In May of 1808, the residents voted to petition the General Court to complete the separation and it was accomplished the following year. Thus the sesquicentennial was 150 years later in 1959. Incidentally, the 1809 year was roughly the same time that Leyden experienced its all-time peak population of over 1000 souls.

As the 1950s moved steadily toward the 1960s, there was increasing talk in town about what should be done to celebrate the upcoming landmark birthday. In about 1954, William T. Arms and his wife Marsha got the idea to write a book, *The History of Leyden, Massachusetts 1676 - 1959*. Their objective was to have its publication coincide with the town's upcoming birthday celebration. Unfortunately, with a population under 500 and less than 200 households, there wasn't a lot of money in the town budget for a big party. Regardless, nearly everyone agreed that something needed to be done. Several other towns in the area had recently celebrated their 200th birthdays with lavish parades and other events. Nobody wanted Leyden to look like a piker, but financing a big party would be a major financial burden for the town. As 1959 grew closer and closer, ideas for a celebration became a more frequent topic of discussion between Henry and visitors to the shop.

At the annual Town Meeting, the town voted to plan an observance of the birthday with no idea of what the celebration might be. A committee was appointed by the selectmen and the sum of $100 was appropriated. Even back in 1958, $100 wasn't much money to fund a town-wide celebration, but it was a start. In addition to the usual expenses that year, the town was spending $3200 to purchase a fire truck, and $1200 to complete construction of the fire station. Another $2500 had already been spent toward the birthday by funding the creation of Arms' town history book. The town paid the publication expenses and also purchased a copy of the book for each family in town. There just wasn't much room in the budget for a big birthday party.

The selectmen called together some of the leading residents and challenged them to put together a low budget, yet impressive, plan. The committee members were Mrs. Arms, Mrs. Clifford Howes, Mrs. Wilhelm Glabach, Town Clerk Harold Campbell, and Malcolm Bailey. None of the selectmen were on the committee, possibly to protect their political futures in case the plan was a bust. Henry was asked to be a member of the committee, but declined saying that his business was very heavy that summer. In reality, Henry was protesting the minuscule budget amount that the selectmen had provided. He was afraid that lack of funding would make Leyden's celebration look absurd in comparison to what other towns had been doing. However, after one of the original committee members resigned, Henry agreed to get on board and assumed responsibility for putting together a first class parade with a nonexistent budget.

The Arms' had spent several years gathering historical

facts about the town and writing their manuscript. As 1959 approached, they became very involved in the celebration planning. A major contribution was identifying historical families living in town and numerous pioneer sites. The Arms, Dottie Howes, and several other residents began writing articles for a special edition of *the Greenfield Recorder-Gazette* which was to be published the day before the big celebration.

In spite of having no budget, Henry and Jessie set about trying to line up entries for the parade. After doing a lot of arm twisting to obtain entries, Henry felt obliged to enter a float himself. Another reason might have been the realization that if he wasn't in the parade, he would be expected to be the parade announcer. Public speaking was one of the few things that he feared. So, the job of announcing the parade entries from the huge slate slab outside the church was delegated to me.

Henry's float was a mobile blacksmith shop. He arranged with one of the local farmers to help him build it. On a large flatbed truck, they put together a working blacksmith shop complete with a real horse that Henry actually shod as the parade rolled along. Henry's portable forge, the one that was seldom used in reality, was fired up and poured out smoke and sparks along the route.

Various other towns, individuals, and organizations also created floats including one with a log cabin and a family depicting Leyden's first settlers. Several equestrian groups, an ox team, old cars, twirlers, and kid's decorated bicycles were joined by a band and numerous fire trucks to create an impressive parade. I believe the only money prizes went to the kids with their bikes.

Jessie had put together the parade sequence and supplied me, the announcer, with a copy to read from. My instructions were to simply read the next title and description into the loudspeaker as units passed the reviewing stand between the church and Town Hall. The same list was given to those who were in charge of lining up the units along the road between Judson Ewer's driveway and the old Center School.

It was a good plan, but unfortunately, as soon as the parade started, and units began to approach the church, it became obvious to me that entries were not appearing in the same order as on the sheet I was to read from. The descriptions on Jessie's list didn't at all match what I saw approaching. I later found out that as units had arrived, each entry simply fell into line behind whatever unit arrived ahead of it. At first the parade marshals tried to sort things out, but before long they realized it was impossible due to new units continuing to arrive, the narrow road, and limited opportunities to turn units around. Once everything was in line, there wasn't time to provide me with a revised sequence list. Fortunately I knew most of the locals in the parade and for the others I quickly scanned down my list and picked a title and description that sounded at least close to what I saw approaching the reviewing stand. I'm sure that several units were surprised to discover that they had been rechristened with new names and descriptions in front of the church!

Several local fire departments entered trucks in the parade. One came from somewhere south of Deerfield, I believe, and the firemen with the truck didn't know quite where Leyden was. They lost considerable time wandering around the Greenfield area before finally getting on the correct road. By the time the lost truck crossed into Leyden, it was nearly time for the parade to start. So, taking advantage of being an emergency vehicle, they turned on their red lights and siren and floored it, trying to make up some lost time. Somewhere around George Howes' barn, the wrong-way fire truck rushing north, met the lead unit of the parade marching south. The truck continued on, weaving in and out between parade units. Spotting the on-coming truck, another fire truck that was in the parade, pulled into Leon Beaudoin's driveway to turn around and go help fight the fire that the other truck was obviously heading north to deal with! When the rogue truck reached Henry's shop, the driver gave up and pulled over until the last parade unit went past and then meekly fell in bringing up the rear. According to the *Greenfield Recorder-Gazette* article, over 1800 people attended the celebration on Saturday. Not bad for a town with a population about a fourth of that!

Chapter 33

OLD HOME DAY

As the summer days grew hot and humid, the upcoming annual Old Home Day celebration became a more and more frequent topic of conversation around Henry's shop. Every year, the first or second Saturday in August, was set aside for Leyden's annual Old Home Day, a sort of one day small-town fair. I don't know when the tradition started, but by 1950 it was firmly established. As Henry once explained to me, Old Home Day was held to attract former residents and citizens of neighboring towns to Leyden for a big social event along with all the current residents. It wasn't much of a money making event, but it wasn't heavily supported by tax money either. As was the rule with much of what transpired in small New England towns, all the work of planning and putting on the event was done strictly by volunteers. Most of the supplies and equipment needed for the event were volunteered also, or supplied by the town or church at no cost. I don't remember there being a fee for attending the day's activities, but there was a small fee for parking on the grounds. The daytime activities were held at the Town Field which is now the ball field adjacent to the Pearl Rhodes Elementary School. Some years, the festivities got off to a start on Friday night, with a baked bean supper at the Town Hall. It was always very well attended although the menu was very simple, typically consisting of baked beans, ham, and apple pie.

Members of the Old Home Day committee were unpaid volunteer citizens who just wanted to help out and were pretty much the same people year after year. For many years Henry was the committee chairman. Frequent members included, among others: Bud Kennedy, George and Dottie Howes, Bill Glabach, Wayne and Edith Fisher, Phil Zimmerman, and one or more members of the Barton family. Planning and preparations began sometime in early June. The weeks leading up to the event were filled with mowing the Town Field, repairing the food booth, and fixing up the baseball diamond. The program for the day varied a little from year to year, but the overall plan didn't change much. In the morning, there was always a baseball game pitting the married men against the single men. The single men were younger and usually won, except in the years when they had to recruit a few very young players in order to field a full team. In the afternoon, the official Leyden men's baseball team played a similar team from another town, usually Colrain, Bernardston, or Guilford. The visiting team was usually the winner, partly because the home town team had banged themselves up trying to beat each other in the morning game.

The ladies of the Methodist Church always operated the food booth adjacent to the ball field. The menu usually included beef stew and clam chowder, along with the usual hot dogs and hamburgers with Bud Kennedy (who else?) manning the grill. It was essentially the same menu as would be served at the Franklin County Fair Booth in about a month. Homemade pies were always a high point. One year, a couple of hungry, young Leyden men challenged some men from Bernardston to a pie-eating contest. The man who could down an entire blueberry pie first was to be the winner. There was only one rule: they could not use their hands. The favored technique was to simply plunge your face into the whole pie and start eating. One of the Leyden men easily came in first, but all that pie in his stomach didn't set well with his plan to pitch in the Leyden vs. Bernardston baseball game that started just a few minutes after he wiped all the blueberry pie off his face.

The events which drew the most spectators were the horse

pulling or horse drawing contests. In those days, these contests were regular features of most of the fairs and celebrations all over much of New England. The purpose of a horse pull was to see which team of draft horses could pull the most weight the required distance. In the 1950s, many farmers throughout New England still used one or more pairs of draft horses as a primary power source on their farms. Loggers also used them extensively. Well trained draft horses had several advantages over a tractor. When haying, a farmer could walk beside the wagon loading hay and control the stop, start, and direction by simple voice commands to the horse or horses. With a tractor, he would have to climb on and off the machine or have a helper drive it. Another advantage was that a team of horses could maneuver in the woods, avoiding trees, and easily stepping over fallen logs or stumps that would have to be cleared away for a tractor to pass. And on muddy ground, horses did not get stuck, partly because they had the common sense to step around the mud holes that a tractor might drive right into.

A few non-farmers, and non-loggers, owned a nice pair of pulling horses for nostalgia, or they just liked to have them around. These were show teams and didn't do much real work, but they appeared in a lot of parades and shows wearing fancy harnesses and maybe even plumes on their heads. In addition to his duties as Old Home Day chairman, Henry was always extra busy in the days leading up to the event as many horse owners needed new shoes on their team in order to maximize their traction in the ring. Often, Henry would be found at sunrise on Old Home Day down at the Town Field shoeing a pair or two of horses at the last minute.

A few days before the event, Henry and a couple of helpers would prepare the pit where the pull was to take place. It was a piece of level ground about 50 feet long and maybe 15 to 20 feet wide. The dirt was plowed and harrowed to soften it, and then raked smooth by hand. Logs were laid along the sides serving as out of bounds markers. If a horse stepped over a boundary log while attached to the load, the team would be disqualified. At one end of the pit sat the stoneboat. It was a solidly constructed, flat bottomed, wooden sled with a slight upturn at each end. There were neither wheels nor runners on the bottom. A tractor was used to place several 500 pound concrete blocks on the stoneboat. To compete, the teamster and two helpers would bring their team to the pit and back them to the front of the boat. While it was important to have a team of powerful animals, timing was just as critical. The teamster held the reins as one helper carried each end of a large evener that both horses' harnesses were fastened to. The trick was to get the team to back up so that the ring on the evener could be dropped over the pin on the stoneboat at the exact instant that the horses lunged forward. Experienced horses knew what was expected of them and early false starts were common. If the huge horses lunged forward too soon, they would not be hitched to the load. If the evener was already down on the pin when they lunged they often could not break the sled loose from the grip of the static friction. Coordination between the horses, the teamster, and the two helpers would result in both horses surging forward at exactly the moment that they were hitched to the boat.

Horse pulling contest at an Old Home Day Celebration, mid-1950s.

Once the hitch was made, the helpers had to step to the side, but the teamster did all he could to get his team surging ahead. Shouting and mild slapping with the reins was accepted, but a teamster would be disqualified if the judges felt he was being abusive to the horses. It was essential that the horses work exactly together. This seemed to be one of the secrets to getting the load started. In a well-trained team, both horses pulled exactly together, remaining side by side and moving forward together. If they got into a see-saw motion with one horse out-pulling the other, then the other way around, their pulling power was greatly diminished and the teamster would abort the attempt. Three hitches were allowed in order to try to move the boat the target distance. I seem to recall that the required distance was only 10 feet, but it may have been more. Those that accomplished the feat within the allotted three hitches, qualified for the next go-round, after one or two more 500 pound blocks were added to the load.

After a team had completed their round, a tractor, usually the town's Caterpillar D4 bulldozer, was used to pull the sled back to the starting line. Two men with rakes would then roughen the dirt that had been smoothed and compacted by the weighted sled being pulled over it.

Henry was always the head judge and distance measurer. He had a long stick, marked off in feet and inches, that was the official distance. He would insert a metal pin into the ground at the rear of the boat before the first hitch. Then he held one end of the long stick against the boat and called out the distance as the horses moved the load. Every summer he did this for several other area horse pulls as well, including the Franklin County Fair and the Chester Fair (which still has horse drawing contests, I believe.) As the load on the sled grew heavier, and the horses more tired, it became less common for a team to be able to pull the sled the full distance. If no team went the required distance, the team that pulled the load the farthest was the winner. A small monetary prize was awarded and the winning team did a lap or two around the pit showing off their blue ribbon.

There were usually three different contests with the

categories based on the combined weight of the team of horses. As I recall, the first class was for light-weight teams weighing up to 2300 pounds. The medium-weight class had to weigh less than 2800 pounds and in the heavy class, called the free-for-all, there was no weight limit. Drivers had to get their teams weighed at the feed mill in Greenfield and present a weight slip in order to enter. It was not unheard of for an unscrupulous team owner to hold back water and food from his horses for a day or two before the weigh-in in order to squeak in under the weight limit. If they weighed just over the limit, it was common for the owner to walk them rapidly for a while to sweat-off a few pounds and then weigh again. Occasionally, an owner would trim the horse's mains and bob their tails in order to drop a pound or two.

The crowd's favorite was always the free-for-all class, which had the largest horses and pulled the heaviest loads. Sometimes, the sled would become so loaded that the bulldozer had difficulty pulling it back to the starting line.

The team of matched, large, Belgian horses owned by Ben Henshaw (or Crenshaw?) was always a crowd favorite. Ben lived somewhere in New Hampshire, I believe, and often spent much of the summer traveling the horse-pulling and draft horse show circuit. Those horses were huge, very well groomed and wore fancy harnesses. Their tails were always tied up in a bun which made them look even more powerful. In the first go-round of the free-for-all class, they always were the last to pull, and usually went the distance on the first hitch. This tended to give Ben a psychological advantage over competitors that needed all three hitches to go the required distance. "See how easy it is guys? Nothing to it!" Of course, going last might have helped a bit due to the dirt being well packed by the earlier teams.

One year, a team of Clydesdales unexpectedly showed up that had never entered the Old Home Day pull before. The competition with Henshaw's Belgians promised to be quite a show. Clydesdales and Belgians are both huge draft horses with single animals weighing up to 2000 pounds, sometimes more, and standing from 16 to 19 hands at the withers. Clydes are the showier, and present a more powerful appearance. They usually have long hair from their knees downward over their feet giving them a "bell bottom trousers" look. Clydes are the horses you see these days pulling the beer wagon in Budweiser commercials. The pulling power of both breeds was probably about equal. The Clydesdale's huge feet may have provided a traction advantage, especially in soft dirt, but the Belgians' slightly shorter legs may have put more power on the ground. Teams of either breed with a combined weight of over 4000 pounds have been known to pull more than 15,000 pounds the full distance in big-time draft horse competitions.

As everyone expected, both the Belgians and the Clydes easily pulled the distance with a single hitch in the first go-round of the free-for-all. As the rounds continued, and the boat got heavier, the other teams began to fall by the wayside, but the Belgians and Clydes kept going and going making it look easy. Finally, they were the only two teams left. After the entire supply of 500 pound blocks was on the sled, with both teams still pulling the distance, no winner had been decided. The Belgians were beginning to sweat and look a little tired, but the Clydesdales still pranced into the pit as if they were in a parade. A few beams left over from the chopping contest were piled on top of the blocks to add a bit more weight, and two heavy gents stood on the rear of the boat. Still, both teams pulled the full distance, although both needed all the allowed three hitches to get that far, possibly due as much to fatigue as to the increased load. Henry called for a 15 minute rest and instructed the two drivers to park their teams in the shade and join him in the pit for a conference. He pointed out that there was no practical way to increase the load further and suggested that in order to determine a winner they pull that same weight a second time. If both teams once again pulled the full distance, the team that pulled the farthest on their first hitch would be the winner. The drivers agreed. While the teams were being prepared for one last contest, numerous bets were being placed between members of the audience. The prevailing opinion was that the Clydes would win it because they appeared to be much less tired than Ben's horses.

Ben won the toss and elected to pull last as was his custom.

In this case it also bought his team a few more minutes of rest before having to pull again. The Clydesdales pranced into the pit, circled once and backed smoothly to the boat. Their first hitch pulled the boat three feet forward before bogging down when one horse lost traction and dropped to its front knees. They might have been a little more tired than they appeared to be. The crowd began to murmur. The second hitch increased the distance to eight feet and the crowd mumbling got a little louder. On their third hitch the team see-sawed and their official distance was unchanged. The crowd cheered loudly. There were worried looks on many of the faces that had bet on the tired, sweaty Belgians.

Then it was Henshaw's Belgians' turn. They had already pulled this weight the full 10 feet on the last go-round, but much of their energy reserve had been used up accomplishing that feat. During the break they had been fed just a couple bites of grain spiked with molasses and washed down with a few sips of water. Most of the water had been used to wet them down, so they entered the pit dripping wet. If they could pull the boat just a bit over eight feet, they would be the winners. A hearty cheer arose as the Belgians entered the pit, their thick necks arched, displaying their matching crew-cut manes and bobbed tails. They circled the pit to the left, before backing nervously to the stoneboat. As the helpers dropped the evener over the pin, one horse lunged just a split second too soon, pivoting the boat toward the out of bounds log and nearly being disqualified.

Their first hitch had moved the boat forward less than one foot. The crowd's cheering turned to total silence, but those who had bet on the Clydes had a bit of a smile on their faces. The team was unhooked and the driver walked them around the pit a couple of times to calm them down. The second hitch was difficult because the boat now sat at an angle and Ben didn't want to risk disqualification. Knowing there was no way of pulling the boat forward without a horse going out of bounds, Ben used the second hitch to simply square up the stoneboat and get it pointed in the correct direction. After two hitches, their total forward movement of the boat was little more than one foot. All the Belgians' hopes, and more than a few bets in the crowd, rested on their third and final hitch which had to result in a pull of at least seven feet or lose the match to the Clydesdales.

The crowd was deathly still, and many nails were being bitten. Still very much game, the team circled the pit one more time. A bit of a prance came back into their gait and it seemed as if the horses knew that their reputation rested on that third and final hitch. They backed smoothly to the boat. At precisely the moment when the helpers dropped the evener onto the stoneboat pin, both horses lunged forward exactly side by side. Their lunge was so strong that for an instant, the front of the stoneboat actually lifted upward slightly. Huge muscles in their hind-quarters looked like they would burst and veins like ropes stood out on their sides and bellies. The stoneboat moved, ever so slowly, but move it did. And it kept moving. With both horses' noses nearly touching the ground, the load gradually increased speed. Henry kept his measuring stick against the back of the boat: 1 1/2 feet, 2 feet, 3, 5, 7, MORE THAN 8 FEET finally stopping with the front of the boat resting on a grassy area beyond the prepared pit! The Belgians had pulled the full 10 feet, nine of it in one hitch! The crowd jumped to their feet with a loud cheer and applause followed by exchanges of greenbacks.

But the show was not yet over. The Caterpillar D4 bulldozer was backed into position to pull the loaded stoneboat back to the starting end of the pit to be unloaded. Someone attached the chain, and the dozer started forward. The horses had churned up so much loose dirt in the pit that, once the chain was tight, the D4 couldn't get traction. The tracks just pushed dirt to the rear and the tractor and loaded stoneboat stayed where they were. Several tries were made and the Cat was just digging dirt. The chain was unhooked and the driver used the dozer blade to level the dirt, and then drove back and forth a few times to pack it. Just as the D4 was about to be hooked up for a second try, the losing team of Clydesdales came prancing up alongside. The teamster asked if he could give it a try. The crowd yelled its approval and the officials agreed to let the Clydes give it a go. The D4 was moved out of the way, and the Clydes backed up to the rear of the boat, snorting and sweating. A chain was used to connect them to the boat because the setup on the rear was different than at the front. The length of the chain allowed for more of a forward lunge before the chain went taunt, compared to the hookup at the front. With a single hitch, the Clydes pulled the fully loaded boat all the way back to the starting line to a cheer and ovation just as loud as Henshaw's team received for winning the event!

Another competition held at every Old Home Day celebration was the chopping and sawing contest. In the 1950s, there was still a lot of logging going on in Leyden and in nearby towns. Chainsaws were not nearly as common as they are in the forests today and they were rather pricey. The ax and the cross-cut saw were still common everyday tools to the lumberman, and many lumberjacks came to Old Home Day ready to prove that they were the best of the best.

For the sawing contest, a hardwood log about 12 to 15 feet long and a uniform 18 or more inches in diameter was obtained from one of the local loggers. A uniform log with few knots was ideal and such logs were still available in 1950s New England, but getting more difficult to find every year. The log was laid horizontally resting just off the ground in the notches of a pair of supports. One end of the log protruded two or three feet from its support. To compete, a two-man team took the supplied cross-cut saw that all the teams were required to use and positioned it at the top of the log such that they would saw off a three-inch disk. Each team member grasped the saw handle on his end of the saw and braced himself with one foot pressed against the side of the log. At the signal from the judge holding the stop watch they started sawing.

In addition to having a sharp and well-set blade, there were at least three tricks to efficiently using a two-man, cross-cut saw: First, and most importantly, you only pulled, you never pushed. If you pushed, the blade was likely to bow and bind, making it difficult for your partner to pull it through the kerf to his side. Second, when your partner was pulling, you made sure not to bend the blade to the side. You just kept it aligned with the cut for the same reason. Third, when you were pulling, it was important to pull with your entire body, legs, arms, and back. If you pulled with only your arms, they tired quickly and much of the length of the saw blade was unused. With a team of two strong experienced sawyers, it was amazing how quickly the disk would drop to the ground. One time, the winning team challenged another logger who used a chain saw and they beat him by a couple of seconds.

The chopping contest was for individuals. For this event, instead of a round log, a square cross-sectioned beam about 10 or 12 inches across was used. Unlike the sawing contest, the choppers were permitted to use their own ax. An ax was a more personal tool to a logger than a saw. Most ax-men favored a double bitted ax which had two sharp edges instead of one, and a straight handle. The contestant would stand atop the beam with his legs spread wide. At the "Go!" he started chopping between his feet. The first blows were wide apart and big chips flew. As the cut progressed to the center of the beam, cuts were closer together and the chips smaller. Halfway through the beam the ax man usually turned and faced the other way and continued chopping. The winner usually accomplished his turn by jumping into the air, twisting his body around, switching to the unused blade of his ax head, and landing with both feet on the beam all in one fast, smooth motion.

I never witnessed any accidents in the sawing contest, but I saw several in the chopping. The most common was to have the ax fly out of the chopper's hands toward part of the circle of observers. One time, a contestant came very close to amputating his own toes. He had just turned to face the other way. The ax was descending toward the beam just as his feet touched down. Instead of landing with both feet on the top of the beam, his left foot slid into the center of the cut just as the ax blade arrived. The ax totally removed the front of his boot, but somehow missed most of his toes. It sure was his lucky day. In typical old-time, backwoods, New England style, he didn't make a big deal of his close call, but instead bemoaned being disqualified for not finishing his cut.

The Old Home Day celebration always ended in the evening with a round and square dance at the Town Hall. These were very well attended, drawing dancers from, not only Leyden, but Guilford, Bernardston, and Colrain as well. It was the major social event of the year, even though other dances were often held at the Town Hall on a more or less regular basis throughout the year.

At each event, square dancing accounted for about two thirds of all the dances. There was always a live band, usually consisting of a guitar player, drummer, and piano player. Sometimes there would be a saxophone or accordion player as well. The band would play a well-known old tune while the caller would sing along mixing in the instructions to the dancers with some of the song's original words, using other patter to fill in the gaps. Popular dances included "Redwing", "There'll Be a Hot Time in the Old Town Tonight", and "Little Brown Jug." Henry's brother Ted, from Dummerston, was a caller for many years and often did the Old Home Day dances.

Five or six squares of four couples each would fit on the floor with space around the sides for the onlookers to watch. The square dancing style was the traditional form that dated from the 1700s and early 1800s. The dances that were popular in small towns from the 1920s through the 1950s, only required rudimentary knowledge of about a dozen moves. Today's Western Square Dancing is complex by comparison, requiring weeks of lessons in order for a couple to learn the nearly 100 moves and become semi-skilled. The objective was for everyone to have a good time. Doing everything exactly correct was definitely secondary. Some of the most fun was when one or more couples in a square became confused. If the caller noticed that one or more squares were having a difficult time with the dance, he would often stop the band and slowly walk the people through the correct series of moves before resuming.

In between square dance sets, the band would play a round dance or two. These were always waltzes, fox trots, or polkas giving a courageous guy a chance to hold his partner a bit closer than the square dances provided, and he could have her all to himself for a few minutes and not share her with three other guys. Many dancers would skip the round dances in order to take a break. They'd go outside to cool off, get a beer or two from their car, have a smoke, or go downstairs to sample the refreshments sold by the church ladies. The next morning there would be several hundred beer bottles to be picked up around the outside of the building.

The crowd was almost always very well-behaved in spite of a shortage of official enforcers of the rules. If someone had a few too many beers, or objected to some other guy dancing with a particular girl, the crowd would often deal with the troublemaker. The caller would stop the music, point out the offender, and ask that he be removed from the hall. There was never a shortage of rugged farmers and loggers willing to oblige. I remember one occasion when Cap Zimmerman, and another man whose name I can't recall, each grabbed a drunk's upper arm and elbow, lifted him until his feet were off the floor and carried him outside where they unceremoniously dumped him in the back seat of his own car to sleep it off.

Gradually, as the years moved forward, interest in Old Home Day began to wane and eventually it came to an end. Roads and cars were improving and it was becoming easier to attend larger and more lavish celebrations in other towns instead of the one held in Leyden. Radio, TV, and movies were becoming much more common permitting young adults to become more tuned into the "outside" world than their parents had been. Children were growing up and moving away and being replaced by new residents that were very welcome, but didn't have deep roots in the town. I suppose that another major reason for the decline of the celebration may have been the passing of the old guard. Pretty much the same people had been Old Home Day committee members for many years, if not decades. They were getting tired and burned out. Sometime in the mid to late 1960s, I think, after there had been no Old Home Day for several years, it was decided to have just one more for old time's sake. It wasn't well attended and it just didn't feel the same.

I guess it's true that you can't go home again.

Chapter 34

THE ANVIL NO LONGER SINGS

Thanks, thanks to thee, my worthy friend,
For the lesson thou hast taught!
Thus at the flaming forge of life
Our fortunes must be wrought;
Thus on its sounding anvil shaped
Each burning deed and thought!
                              Longfellow

As Henry approached his mid-70s, he began to think about retiring some day and what would then become of his beloved blacksmith shop, the shop which had been the cornerstone of his life for six decades. Everything around him seemed to be changing. He had never been opposed to changes, but as he aged, he was not quite as receptive to them. Leyden was no longer the same place he had grown up with and he missed the old days and old friends. There was an increasing tendency for residents to use the town mainly as a bedroom community with most of their life's focus directed elsewhere. Increasingly, people were earning their living elsewhere, and they often didn't have the time to involve themselves with the town as before. Social events at the Town Hall had become very infrequent, Old Home Day was gone, and the only sports teams in town were for little kids.

He especially was bothered by the changes he was seeing in himself and the activity at his shop. There was an increasing shortage of local farmers and other residents stopping by to have something repaired and staying to discuss local issues. Many of the former regulars and old timers had retired, converted from farming to a more lucrative vocation, died, or simply moved away. Less and less farming was being done, and once verdant fields and pastures were beginning to be reclaimed by the forests. Just down the hill from his shop, even the Zimmermans no longer did much farming. Instead of milking cows, they earned their living mostly by hauling cattle for others.

Henry had great difficulty accepting the fact that, just like many of the people he had known all his life, he was getting older and was no longer capable of doing many of the things he had done for decades. And, there was less and less need for the type of work he had always done. The blacksmith's trade had already been in decline for decades when he entered it as an apprentice in 1920, and the trend never stopped. However, he had adapted and forged a good living for his family. Now his family too had largely moved on, leaving him and his shop behind.

In the 1970s, the activity at the shop went through a transition. Car repairs were no longer a consideration. "I'm too old to crawl around under cars anymore," Henry said. "Besides, they are making them too darned complicated. It used to be all you had to do was look at and listen to an engine to figure out what was wrong with it. You can't do that anymore."

Horseshoeing activity also changed. There were still a lot of working draft horses to be shod in the 1950s, but their population went into an increasingly steep decline as flesh and blood horsepower continued to be replaced by the gasoline and diesel kind. Horseshoeing became mainly for smaller riding and hobby driving horses for which Henry really never cared. Increasingly, he declined to take on new customers. Nearly all his shoeing work resided outside of Leyden requiring more traveling. And, his arthritic knees were becoming far too painful to have horses leaning on them all day long.

With the decline in horseshoeing, some other activities in the shop increased somewhat, partly because Henry was more available, and partly because people began to realize that if they were going to have the village smithy do a project for them, or simply observe him doing what blacksmiths had done for centuries, they had better "strike while the iron was hot." People began to realize that once Henry and his shop were gone, it would be the end of an era. With the rising wave of nostalgia, interest in all sorts of old items and old methods rose with it. To Henry, these were simply everyday items and techniques that he had grown up with and had used all his life. People would stop by with their cameras and children simply to watch something being made in the forge or a wagon wheel repaired. A common visitor's comment was something like, "I just wanted my kids to see the way things used to be done before it's gone forever."

While astronauts circled the earth, Henry continued doing what he had done for decades, and others before him had done for centuries. Antique wagons, carriages, buggies, and sleighs were brought in to be repaired or restored, some from hundreds of miles away. Sometimes it would just be a few pieces of wood and iron that needed to be repaired or replaced. Other times, Henry would end up essentially building a whole new conveyance. Forge work transitioned from horseshoes and farm equipment to items such as andirons, fireplace tools, and hinges being restored or new ones built and made to look old. He made from scratch, several sets of fireplace andirons, kettle cranes, fire pokers, etc. for various museums such as Old Deerfield and Sturbridge Village. The overall transition at the shop was from working on things that people actually used in their daily lives, to things that "looked the part." Regardless, Henry made everything as sturdy and functional as ever even if he knew it would never really be used.

Eventually the years caught up with him. The stiffness in his joints and numbness in his hands made it more and more difficult, and painful, to do the kind of work he had always done. "Now it takes me several days to make something I could have made before lunch years ago," he once told me.

Finally, pushing 80, he decided to retire. For a couple of years, he had spent more time at the shop sitting and snoozing in his Adirondack chair by the wood stove, than actually working on anything. Visitors still dropped by from time to time, but most of the conversations had changed from local politics and events, to the way things used to be. "I spend a lot of time reminiscing, or helping others to reminisce," he would say. More and more, he found himself living in the past, a past he never really wanted to lose.

Buggy and wagon wheels stored in the horseshoeing area in preparation for the auction.

Henry had hoped that when he retired, the town would purchase the shop, along with all the tools and equipment in it, and turn it into a museum. He was well aware of how unique his shop was, and how time had passed it by. There would never be another like it, and once it was gone, it would be gone forever. He wanted to be the volunteer curator taking visitors on tours and describing to them how things were used. As conscious of the town's health and image as always, he felt that a blacksmith shop museum would put Leyden on the map and attract tourists from all over. However it wasn't to be.

Eventually he decided to have an auction, get rid of everything, and move away. After a few months of sorting and cleaning six or seven decades of history, auction day arrived. Bidders came from all over the northeast and as far away as Virginia and Ohio. The auction was written up before and after in several New England newspapers. Everything in the shop was sold right down to the walls and floor, actually, including the floor in the horseshoeing area. I was fortunate to rescue a few pieces for the family, including the anvil that he had used as an apprentice blacksmith, and later carried on the road for so many years. I also saved his leather apron, horseshoeing tools, and the 72-drawer octagonal cabinet. A few items went to museums, but everything else became scattered to the four winds.

The house was then sold along with the empty shop. The land opposite the library where he grew vegetables for decades was sold to the town to become the new Leyden Town Common. The small plot containing the town vault was officially conveyed to the town although it may have already been on town property for 100 years. Finally, Henry and Jessie moved to the house that had belonged to Jessie's sister, Leta, on Millers Falls Road in Northfield. After being completely immersed in everything about Leyden for so many years, both of them felt rather lonely in Northfield. Quiet, familiar, Leyden had been exchanged for the noisy traffic of strangers just outside their front door. Their friends, and people they had known all their lives, now lived much farther away and visits were much less frequent. Jessie often returned to Leyden to attend church services and see old friends. Henry, however, had less interest in returning. He preferred to remember the town and the people the way they used to be.

In November, 1991, Henry suffered a stroke and died at the age of 86. After a standing room only funeral in the Leyden Church, he was laid to rest in the South Cemetery at a site adjacent to an old stone wall and overlooking a sugar house. The graves of his parents and Jessie's were nearby as were those of many friends and neighbors he had known all his life. Jessie joined him there in January of 1994.

Courtesy of Richard DiMatteo

Cover image of the 1985 Leyden Town Report, one year before Henry retired and sold everything at auction.

A Blacksmith's Prayer

My fire is extinct
And my forge is decayed,
By the side of the bench
My old vise is laid.

My anvil and hammer
Lie gathering dust,
My powerful bellows
Have lost all their thrust.

My coal is now spent,
My iron's all gone,
My last nail's been driven,
And my day's work is done.

Ray Smith, anvilfire.com

Appendix A

AT THE FORGE AND ON THE ANVIL

Forge area of Henry Glabach's Leyden Blacksmith Shop.

The history of blacksmithing can be traced back to the time of the early Greek and Roman civilizations. Hephaestus was blacksmith to the gods in Greek mythology, as was Vulcan to the Romans. Hephaestus' forge was a volcano where he fashioned the weapons of the gods. From the moment that civilization emerged from the Bronze Age into the Iron Age, the blacksmith and his forge was at the center of progress for mere mortals as well. The blacksmith's forge was an essential tool of civilization for centuries thereafter. It not only was required to form shoes for the horses and oxen which were the primary sources of power, it was an important tool whereby iron and steel were transformed into hundreds of essential metal items. Today, due largely to depiction in thousands of movies and TV shows, many people have the impression that a blacksmith was a person who only shod horses. Actually, a horseshoer was called a farrier. Many blacksmiths also adopted the farrier trade when factory-made items began to replace what they formerly made by hand.

The heart of the forge was the firepot where the iron or steel was heated, although in general usage it often referred to the entire blacksmithing operation. Today, many Americans have never seen an actual working smithy's forge outside of a museum, living history display, or artistic blacksmithing shop. Even in the 1950s, real working smithies were few and far between. Because of its uniqueness, Henry and his shop were often the topic of articles in New England newspapers and other publications.

The definition of a blacksmith's shop was pretty much just the location of a forge and anvil and someone called a blacksmith who knew how to use them to fabricate and repair metal items. The basic operation was quite simple. The forge was used to heat iron so that it could be easily shaped by bending or hammering. Once iron was heated hot enough that it gave off a red, orange or yellow glow, it became soft and plastic and could be easily transformed into the desired shape.

Henry's forge consisted of a cast iron forge pot imbedded in what was essentially a concrete workbench with an open chimney on the left, and a coal bin on the right. A hand-cranked blower forced air into the pot from below. The faster the blower was cranked, the more air was fed into the forge pot, and the hotter and broader the flames. The iron or steel piece to be shaped was pushed down into the glowing coals and more fuel packed in around and above it.

The length of time required for the metal to reach working temperature varied with the size of the piece, but it usually took only a few minutes. Following heating, the glowing metal piece needed to be quickly hammered and bent into the desired shape before it cooled. For a large piece, or a complex shape, several heating and hammering cycles would often be required. The color of the heated metal told the blacksmith if it was hot enough. The temperature needed depended on what was to be done to the piece. For most forge work, Henry liked to heat the metal to a glowing bright orange or yellow color. If left in the fire too long, the metal would reach a very bright yellow color, or even a white heat. At those temperatures, showers of sparks like a 4th of July sparkler would jump from the hot metal as it was removed from the fire. A lot of sparkling indicated that the piece was approaching the melting temperature, which for iron is about 2800 degrees F.

Usually, only a few inches of a metal piece would be heated with the remainder protruding from the fire. If it was long enough, say, 24 inches or more, one end of an iron could be glowing yellow, but the other end could be comfortably grasped by a bare hand. Shorter pieces, such as horseshoes had to be handled by large tongs. Henry had several sets of forge tongs, all handmade. Some of Henry's tongs had been formed by his mentor, Ed Howes. Others, he had made himself as learning projects in 1920 when he was an apprentice.

Henry would simply hammer the hot metal to the desired shape on the 250 pound anvil that stood next to the forge. If a special shape was needed, such as a half-round, instead of the anvil, he would hammer the soft, hot metal into one of a variety of holes in a large swage block (or fuller block) which sat on a stand just past the anvil. Often it was necessary to repeat the heating and hammering cycle several times before an object was complete. Once a metal part had attained the desired shape, it would be quickly immersed in a large container of water to cool it. Following a few seconds of hissing and steaming, the entire part would be cool enough to handle with bare hands.

Certain types of work required the metal part to be

tempered. Tempering increased the hardness and strength of the metal and was essential for any part that was to hold a sharp edge such as a knife, hoe, or any type of cutting tool. For a hardened metal piece, it was necessary to make it from high carbon steel, not iron. Hardening, or tempering, would set up a rigid carbon matrix in the steel giving it much greater strength than common iron. In a way it was similar to a certain carbon atom arrangement that gives a diamond its extreme hardness. It's amazing stuff, carbon, the basis of all life on earth.

To temper a piece, first it would be heated in the forge and shaped into whatever the required form might be. Once shaped, the piece was heated one more time. This time, the piece, or portion of the piece to be tempered had to be uniformly heated to just the right temperature as indicated by the color. Once the correct color was obtained, the piece was quickly plunged into water to cool it. The degree of hardness obtained was controlled largely by how hot the metal was when it was quenched in the water. If the steel was a bright orange or yellow, it would be very hard, but it could also be brittle. For most tempering work, Henry liked to heat the part to a "good cherry red" as this would usually give the necessary hardness without causing the metal to become brittle.

As the 1950s wore on and became the 1960s and 1970s, repair and restoration of a wide variety of antiques became a larger and larger portion of the work done at the shop. Often this would require a bit more artistic blacksmithing than that needed to form a horseshoe, repair a wagon wheel, or mend a broken plow blade. For example, perhaps a twisted square shaft was needed to restore an old fireplace set. To make the twist, a square cross section rod was heated in the forge. Only the portion of the rod that was to have the twist was heated. This might mean heating the middle portion of the rod while keeping both ends out of the fire. The trick was to uniformly heat the section to be twisted. Once properly heated, the rod was quickly removed from the forge and one end was clamped in a vise. The other end was simply turned with a wrench until the desired degree of twist was obtained. You had to get it right the first time because once twisted, it was virtually impossible to change it and end up with a good looking shaft.

Due to the invention of the electric welder, forge welding had become pretty much a lost art by the 1950s. However, due to the aforementioned surge in antique restoration, it enjoyed a bit of a revival in later years. Henry was always a firm believer in the older, simpler ways of doing things. However, if a newer method was clearly superior, he would gladly adopt it. Electric welding was quickly accepted. However, if an original antique piece was to be repaired or matched, no evidence of electric welding was acceptable. To forge weld two pieces of iron together, it was first necessary to shape the individual mating parts so that they shared a uniform contact area. Next, the two were heated together in the forge so that the weld area became bright yellow. It was important that no metal scale existed on the mating surfaces, and the fire had to be made from clean burning, low ash coke or coal to avoid impurities in the weld that would weaken it. When the desired temperature was reached, some welding powder was sprinkled on all sides of the weld area. This powder was part flux and part powdered metal. This was followed by more heating to melt the powder into the joint. Finally, the yellow-hot joint was hammered on all sides on the anvil and cooled with water. Even with all his experience, Henry often had difficulty making what he considered a satisfactory forge weld. The main culprit, he felt, was the lack of good clean coke or coal for fuel. If ash clung to the pieces to be welded, a weak weld would be the result. "Years ago," he would say, "It was easy because you could get what they called smithy coal. It was clean burning and low in sulfur. Too much sulfur in the coal can make the hot iron tend to come apart and not hammer out well. Nowadays, you can't get smithy coal anymore. I guess that's progress." For cleanliness, and control of the flame, most of the blacksmiths who specialized in making decorative wrought iron had switched to using a gas flame. Henry, however, always liked doing things the old-fashioned way, or "the right way" as he called it.

The anvil was an essential tool for the blacksmith and the worldwide symbol of his trade. It was the object against which hot softened metal from the forge was pounded into shape with a heavy hammer. Not only horseshoes, but all sorts of iron and steel items were hammered into shape on anvils. Of necessity, an anvil was a very heavy object with a lot of inertia so that it would not move a lot in response to all the pounding.

Henry had two large anvils. Both were of the classic London style. The larger weighed over 250 pounds and stayed in one place in the shop. It was always located on a wooden block to the right of the forge. That was the anvil that had been used by his mentor, Ed Howes. The smaller anvil weighed 150 pounds and was originally located beside the second forge. It was used by Henry when he was an apprentice. Later, it was his traveling anvil that he took with him shoeing horses all over New England for more than 50 years. I have no idea how old Henry's anvils were. I only know that he told me they were the same ones that were salvaged from the ruins of the old blacksmith shop that had burned in the early 1920s. It is possible that those same anvils had been singing their songs in Leyden since before the Civil War.

The pointed end of the anvil was called the horn. It was of a more or less round cross section tapering to a point with most of the taper occurring along the underside (called the shoulder) rather than the top. The horn was used whenever a curve was required in the piece being made, or if a hole had to be opened up a little. Henry was right handed and he always had his anvils set up so that the horn was on his left. In the shop, the anvil was mounted on the end grain of a large wooden block with the anvil face about 28 inches off the floor. The large flat top surface that received most of the pounding was called the face. Between the horn and the face was a smaller flat surface called the step or table. The surface of the step was a little lower than the face. Some people claim that the purpose of the step was to provide an area for metal cutting to avoid damaging the face. I never saw Henry use the step for cutting. What he did use it for was in situations in which he needed to create a good square corner on the hot metal. He would pound the metal at an angle into the corner of the step.

The end opposite the horn was called the heel. Toward the right end of the heel were two holes. The larger was square and was called the hardy hole. It had many uses, but its primary purpose was to hold a variety of anvil accessory tools. The most common accessory was an anvil chisel, or hot chisel. The chisel was set in the hardy hole with the blade facing up. The hot iron from the forge would be held onto the chisel and then struck with a hammer blow to cut it. While shoeing on the road, Henry often needed to widen the heel of a horseshoe without benefit of a forge. He would insert one of the heel ends into the hardy hole, set the other end firmly on the face, and strike a hard blow on the toe end of the shoe. The very rounded edges of the hardy hole on Henry's anvil provides testament to its decades, if not centuries, of use in that fashion.

The smaller hole was of round cross section and was called the pritchel hole. Its primary purpose was to provide a backing for punching operations. New horseshoe blanks usually needed to have the nail holes punched and enlarged. Used shoes needed to have the old nails punched out so the shoes could be reused. Henry's 150 pound anvil has three pritchel holes; two are about a half-inch in diameter and the third a quarter-inch.

A good anvil was never made of cast iron. Cast iron was brittle and could not be trusted to hold up to all the necessary pounding. In addition, it was somewhat spongy and didn't respond well to hammer blows. Rather, as befitting a blacksmith's tool, the anvil was made of wrought iron. A good anvil was always made from a nearly molten chunk of iron that was pressed and hammered into the required shape.

When shoeing on the road, it was often necessary to make minor adjustments to the horseshoes without the benefit of a forge. Sometimes the adjustment was simply to make the heel of the shoe a bit wider or narrower. Other times it was necessary to change the degree of roundness at the toe. Henry used a very heavy hammer to slightly reshape cold shoes without benefit of heat. Somebody once gave Henry a small portable forge, thinking that he could use it on the road to more easily make adjustments to shoes or even prepare shoes from scratch on site. He carried it in his pickup for a while, but I don't think he ever used it. He said that it was too much trouble to carry kindling and coal with him, wait for the fire to get hot enough, and then wait for it to cool down before loading it back into his truck. As fire chief, he was also very concerned about firing up a forge in, or near, a barn full of highly flammable hay. The rolled over edge on the face of his traveling anvil, which is in my possession, is clear evidence of a lot of cold hammering.

Appendix B

WE USED TO SAY...

One thing that I notice more and more these days is how our language has changed over the last 50 or 60 years. I don't just mean the addition of words naming new inventions, new slang words, or the deletion of words that are no longer relevant. Maybe it has to do with where I now live, but it seems that I rarely meet anyone anymore who has a real identifiable accent. Some areas, such as around Boston, New York City and the Deep South have clung to some of theirs, especially among the older crowd. But for the most part these days we all sound pretty much like the guys and gals on the TV news. It seems that our language has been distilled to a mediocre dull brown by the dual onslaughts of Hollywood/media dialect and political correctness. In the 1950s, you could often tell which part, of which New England state, people were from just by listening to them talk for a few minutes.

It wasn't just the accent that used to make people unique; it was also what they said. There has been a wholesale loss of colorful, straight to the point, idioms and sayings that used to be common. There were hundreds of colorful expressions that I constantly heard Jessie and others quoting when I was a kid. Some of the sayings were in common use and had been for a long time. Others were strictly Jessieisms that I never heard anyone except her use. It seemed like she always had a saying that cut to the core of whatever the current situation might be.

The origin of many expressions was obscure. Some seem to have been pulled from the writings of Benjamin Franklin, Chaucer, Aesop, and the Bible. I think many were actually of southern origin so I have no idea how they arrived in New England. I'm sure Jessie was actually the author of a few of her favorites.

A lot of the old sayings were actually condensed, to the point, expressions of values and ideals that were generally still held in high esteem in the 1950s. Today, many of the old expressions are no longer heard in everyday conversations.

Here, in no particular order, are some of the sayings that I still remember. I even use them from time to time. There were many, many more.

"Waste not, Want not." I must have heard this one 5000 times while growing up. It pretty much summed up Henry and Jessie's frugal, common sense lifestyle. It applied to such diverse situations as Orilla and me cleaning up our dinner plates, to Henry's hoards of scrap iron, and to Jessie's stash of unused, but expired, WWII ration coupons.

"They don't have a pot to pee in," Refers to the financial condition of a family or couple in a somewhat negative fashion.

"They are poorer than church mice," or **"They don't have two pennies to rub together,"** Additional expressions of someone's financial condition who was not too well off. These were always used in a sympathetic sense and never derogatory. I have no idea why anyone that did have two pennies would want to rub them together!

"He's three sheets to the wind," or **"He's higher than a kite."** Refers to someone who may have imbibed a bit too much adult refreshment.

"Farther than Timbuktu," A location much farther away than the speaker was willing to consider traveling. As a kid, I never realized that Tumbuktu was a real place: a city in Western Africa.

"Hotter than Hell-a-lu-ya," Refers to a hot summer's day. Could also be expressed by a cook removing something from the oven while using a worn out oven mitt!

"Too dry to spit," Refers to the impact of continuing hot dry weather and lack of rainfall.

"Too mad to spit," Described the speaker's complete dissatisfaction with someone or something.

"Jimminy Christmas," and **"Gee Hosafat"** Expressions of surprise. Generally the speaker was not too happy with the surprise.

"Goodness Gracious," A somewhat lesser degree of surprise and usually it was a good thing.

"Blowing like '38," Compared a wind storm to the very destructive hurricane of 1938 that went up the Connecticut River Valley creating havoc and destruction as it went.

"Quicker than you can say 'Jack Sprat'," Something that happened very quickly. I presume this referred to the Jack Sprat in the nursery rhyme, but I have no idea why.

"Cuter than a bug's ear," An expression of cuteness reserved for a very young child or possibly a kitten or puppy. This is an example of a saying that really made no sense, but through usage took on a meaning of its own.

"Smaller than a gnat's eyebrow," Something very tiny indeed. Gnats' eyebrows were the subject of other comparisons as well. An unusually accurate rifleman might be described as **"He can shoot the eyebrows off a gnat."** Another variation was **"Like shooting eyebrows off a gnat,"** which referred to something the speaker felt was impossible to accomplish.

"Lower than a snake's belly," Described someone who was quite underhanded and not to be trusted.

"Raining cats and dogs," A good rainstorm.

"A gully washer," An even harder rainstorm usually accompanied by wind.

"Still water runs deep," Expressed the frequent observation that someone who tended to keep to himself, and did not talk a lot, often possessed a lot of intelligence and good character traits.

"Slower than molasses flowing uphill in January," This referred to something that was happening at an impossibly slow pace and needed to be speeded up.

"Not worth a tinker's dam," Referred to something insignificant or worthless. I'd bet that a lot of people who have used that expression have no idea where it came from. A tinker was a traveling tinsmith who repaired pots and pans. If the bottom of a pail or bucket contained numerous leaks where it had rusted through, instead of fixing the leaks one at a time, the tinker would create a dam of dough-like material all around the outside bottom edge. He would then flood the bottom with melted solder to seal off all the leaks at once. The dam held the solder in place until it cooled. The dam was then removed and discarded as it was no longer of any value.

"Holier than thou," A comment about someone who tried to give the impression that he was a notch or two better than the average person.

"Tighter than a vise," Someone who was not generous and didn't spend much money, although the general opinion was that he had an ample supply. A similar expression was **"Tighter than bark on a tree."**

"Time and tide wait for no man," Meant that you better get moving. You were in danger of events getting ahead of you.

"A watched pot never boils," Summed up the frequent observation that the more you want, or need, something to happen soon, the longer it seems to take.

"Slick as a whistle," Something that went much more smoothly than expected.

"Sharper than a tack," A person who was very smart or very quick to catch onto things.

"When pigs fly," Expressed an opinion that whatever the topic was, it just wasn't very likely to happen.

"In a pig's ear," Indicated strong disagreement with the topic under discussion. Sometimes "ear" was replaced by a different part of a pig's anatomy.

"Duller than an old hoe," The extreme expression of dullness. It might be applied to anything from an actual dull instrument, such as a knife or ax. It might apply to a lecture or speech, or to the person giving it.

"Lord willing" or **"Lord willing and the creek don't rise,"** Indicated that a task was expected to be completed on time barring unforeseen circumstances.

"Money doesn't grow on trees," An expression I heard numerous times whenever I asked for something my parents didn't think I needed. (Today Jessie would be the first to point out that Washington seems to believe that money does in fact grow on trees.)

"Scarce as hen's teeth," Could refer to anything in short supply. Could refer to a material object or to a character trait.

"Useless as teats on a bull," Referred to someone, or something, believed to be totally without value to society.

"Strong as an ox," A person with unusual physical, intellectual, or moral strength.

"More slippery than goose poop on linoleum," Described a person not to be trusted in financial or any other dealings.

"Dragged through a knothole backward," An expression of feeling or looking very tired and worn out.

"Dead as a doornail," Over, done with, finished.

"Two ax handles wide," This may have originally been an expression of the width, and therefore strength, of the hind quarters of a very strong draft horse or ox. It came to be applied as a not so kind reference to a person who was considerably overweight.

"Skinny as a rail," The extreme measure of thinness.

"Like a fish out of water," This was used to describe a person who was generally quite capable, but had no clue how to proceed with the current task at hand. An alternate expression might be **"A square peg in a round hole."**

"Chief cook and bottle washer," A term for the person in charge. This expression might have been used to sum up the duties of the chairperson at the county fair food booth, or the individual in charge of a church supper.

"Tastes like stump water," Originally referred to very weak coffee or some other disagreeable drink. It came to be often used to express total disagreement with something being said. An alternate expression was **"Leaves a bad taste in your mouth."**

"Tough as shoe leather," This was another expression that originally meant one thing and became something else. It originally referred simply to a piece of meat that was terribly difficult to chew. Later it was used to refer to an especially resilient individual who kept bouncing back from adversity.

"Putting the cart before the horse," Doing things in the wrong order. Taking credit for doing a job before it was finished.

"Shiny as a new penny," Could refer to a child all cleaned up and dressed up, to a newly polished car, or to a proposal that sounded way too good to be true.

"Neat as a pin," A person, house, etc. that was very clean and orderly with nothing out of place. Could also apply to a well thought out plan for attacking a problem.

"A chip off the old block," Referred to a child who had much the same desirable qualities as a parent.

"The acorn (or apple) doesn't fall far from the tree," Referred to a child who had much the same undesirable qualities as a parent.

"Not worth a hill of beans," Could refer to almost anything or anyone considered to be useless, but I have no idea why. Beans were often planted in hills and they certainly were not without value.

"Madder than a wet hen," Someone who was very mad, usually because of the actions, or inactions, of another.

"You can't get blood out of a turnip," Referred to someone who just refused to face up to his financial or other obligations.

"Not in a coon's age," Something that was going to take a very long time indeed. Maybe coons had a reputation for living to a ripe old age.

"A hard nut to crack," Referred to a person who was exceptionally difficult to convince of something.

"Where there's a will, there's a way," Expressed the opinion that if you wanted something bad enough and were willing to work hard for it, chances are that it would happen.

"If he was a knife, he couldn't cut warm butter," Expressed the opinion that there was no way that someone was up to the task at hand.

"Like a hot knife through butter," Something happened very easily, in fact, much easier than expected.

"Kicked the bucket," Someone, or something, died unexpectedly. Probably originated from the tendency for a dairy cow to be converted to a beef critter if it had a habit of kicking over the pail while being milked.

"Nice as pie," Something that went off well.

"He has Moxie," Means that someone has a lot of courage, or guts in spite of the odds. Moxie was an early bottled soft drink that was still commonly available in the 1950s, and exists today in limited areas. To many, it had a somewhat disagreeable flavor combining sweet and bitter. It was Grandma Bertha Wood's favorite beverage. That old gal sure had Moxie!

"Fit as a fiddle," A person in good health, or a piece of equipment in a good state of repair.

"Every Tom, Dick, and Harry," Everyone. It used to refer to a group of people that showed up unexpectedly, or to people willing to take credit for a task well done even if they had nothing to do with the outcome.

"Between a rock and a hard place," Described being faced with a decision between two equally undesirable options.

"You can lead a horse to water, but you can't make him drink," Often applied to students or others who were supplied with all the tools needed to get an education or do a task, but they did not take advantage.

"You have to take the bitter with the sweet," This expressed the opinion that if you want the benefits of something, you also need to be willing to accept the bad side.

"A closed mouth catches no flies," Keep your mouth shut if you want to stay out of trouble.

Speaking of flies, **"You can catch more flies with honey than with vinegar."** This suggested that you often could obtain better results by being nice to people than being mean.

"He's all hat and no cows," This one originated down around Texas and originally referred to what you might call an "urban cowboy." It came to refer to anyone more interested in looking the part, or taking the credit, than actually doing something.

"A man who never made a mistake never made anything," This pointed out that if you wanted to accomplish something, you could expect to make a few errors along the way.

"A new broom sweeps clean," This expressed the hope that when someone new was put in charge of something, things would get better.

"Blood is thicker than water," Family came first.

"You have to walk before you can run," This was used to point out that it was often necessary to take one step at a time and in the proper order.

"Don't count your chickens before they hatch," This had a lot of uses, but an important one was to point out that you shouldn't spend money you haven't yet earned. Remember a few years back when Congress was arguing about how to spend the 'peace dividend'?

"Empty cans make the most noise," People making the most noise about an issue often had the least to say worth hearing.

"Half a loaf is better than none," You don't always have to come in first. Be happy with what you have.

"Mind your P's and Q's," Do what you are supposed to do, and do it correctly. Pay attention to your own part of the task. This may have originally been "Peas" and "Cues" referring to a very old way of accounting by people not highly skilled in mathematics.

"You can put silk on a goat, but it is still a goat," People don't change. Once a crook, always a crook.

"Put on your thinking cap," Stop complaining, buckle down and figure out how to accomplish the task at hand.

"Rob Peter to pay Paul," Jessie would probably say that this is exactly what the government is doing a lot of these days. It certainly describes the Social Security system.

"Rome wasn't built in a day," Don't be in too much of a hurry to finish something. It is more important to do it correctly.

"Too many irons in the fire," Taking on too many tasks to do any of them well. This was blacksmith originated, meaning that if too many parts are heated in the forge at once, some will get too hot and be ruined before they can be tended to.

"You must strike while the iron is hot," It's important to take advantage of opportunities when they become available and not wait too long. Another blacksmith related saying. After removing a hot iron from the forge, if a blacksmith waits any time at all it will cool rapidly and he will not be able to properly hammer it into shape. I always get a kick out of the standard scene in many western movies where the blacksmith pulls a horseshoe out of the fire with tongs, then proceeds to carry on a conversation with someone. After the conversation is over, he starts pounding on the horseshoe. Wrong!

"The devil finds work for idle hands," Some types of people will tend to get into trouble if they aren't kept busy doing something constructive.

"The squeaky wheel gets the grease," The person making the biggest fuss often gets the most attention.

"Little pitchers have big ears," Be careful what you say that children might hear and repeat to others. (The handles on a pitcher (cream or milk) are called "ears."

"We don't value water until the well runs dry," We always value most that which is scarce. Or, we don't realize how important something (or someone) was until it is gone. Another variation was **"Potatoes would be worth more than gold if we didn't have any."**

"There is little point in going fast if you are on the wrong road," It's more important to do something correctly than quickly.

"When the cat's away, the mice will play," Somebody needs to be in charge and paying attention in order to keep others out of trouble.

"You are judged by the company you keep," Others will judge your character based on the people you choose to associate with. A similar expression was **"Birds of a feather flock together."** Another saying often accompanying these was **"A leopard can't change its spots."** Some tell us this is no longer true.

"Lock, stock, and barrel," The whole thing. Everything. These were the three major components of an early firearm, thus if you had all three you had a complete musket.

"Just a flash in the pan," This described something, or someone, that got off to a good start, but never finished the job. It was derived from an early flintlock firearm in which the spark from the flint and steel ignited a small amount of gunpowder in a small depression called the pan. That burning powder was supposed to send flame through a small hole to ignite the main charge inside the barrel, but it didn't always happen. Sometimes the priming charge in the pan ignited with a flash, but the gun never went "bang."

"Getting down to brass tacks." This referred to finding out the real facts about something. This expression probably had its origin in the purchase of fabric goods. When a buyer asked to buy, say five yards, of a fabric, it was common practice for the seller to simply use the extension of his arm as a quick measure of a yard. However, there were brass tacks imbedded in the counter that could be used to verify the amount of goods, if so requested by the buyer.

"The whole nine yards," An expression meaning the whole thing or everything available. This seems to be of more recent vintage than most of this list. The origin isn't clear. We know it isn't from football, or it would be "The whole ten yards." I always thought the yards were the common unit of measure. However, it might stem from a naval officer's description of the output of all nine ship yards building Liberty Ships in WWII.

"No ifs, ands, or buts," Do exactly as you're told. Don't offer an excuse for changing something or not doing it. This might also be a fairly recent saying with its origin in a 1947 Tennessee Williams play.

Those are just some of the many sayings that were in everyday use decades ago. There were times when two or more country New Englanders would be talking and nearly their entire conversation would be made up of these and similar sayings linked together.

Appendix C

LEYDEN AND THE 1704

DEERFIELD MASSACRE

For well over 100 years, it has been "common knowledge" that following the sacking and massacre at Deerfield in the winter of 1704, the French and Indians and their captives crossed the south-east corner of Leyden on the second day of their 300 mile journey north to Canada. This appendix takes issue with that route and suggests a much more plausible path that traversed the full length of what would become Leyden.

In the very early years of the 18th century, the Connecticut River, bisecting New England north to south, essentially defined the western boundary of English civilization in Massachusetts. The northern boundary was a few miles south of the modern day Massachusetts/Vermont line. The town of Deerfield, populated by less than 300 settlers, was located a little west of where the waters of the Deerfield River joined those of the Connecticut. Thus, it sat nearly in the corner formed by the intersection of these two wilderness frontiers.

A massive wilderness extended west from Deerfield, nearly to Albany. Located south of what would later become Greenfield, Deerfield was also at the southern edge of another wooded wilderness that stretched all the way to the St. Lawrence River in Canada. The wooded hills that would become the future Town of Leyden were part of that northern wilderness.

Those hills formed the sudden transition between the flat river bottoms to the south and the hills and mountains to the north.

By the late 1600s, France and Britain had been in a nearly continuous power struggle for decades. Although the wars were primarily European, they always spilled over into North America where the issue was which kingdom would be the dominant ruler in the New World. Some Native American tribes sided with the French, others with the English, and still others remained neutral, wishing that both groups of invaders would go away. Finally, weary of the struggles, the French and English signed a peace agreement ending King William's War in 1697. Unfortunately, the peace did not last long. By 1703, yet another European war had spread to North America. This time it involved Spain, as well as France and Britain. In Europe, it was known as the War of Spanish Succession. Here it was called Queen Anne's War. Anne was Britain's King William III's sister-in-law and had succeeded him to the throne.

As is the case with many wars, the exact cause of the new war was a bit murky. One key ingredient was King Louis XIV of France wanting to install his grandson, Philip d'Anjou, on the Spanish throne. If successful, that would link the fortunes of France and Spain in the New World. Britain saw that plan as a threat to them and their ever expanding English colonies.

When the Marquis de Vaudreuil became governor of New France (Canada), he felt that something needed to be done to stop the threat of northward expansion of the British settlements in New England. The French residents of New France were greatly outnumbered by the English in New England, so de Vaudreuil enlisted the aid of several native Indian tribes to make raids on the New England frontier settlements and farms. He was careful not to launch raids close to Albany for fear of offending the powerful Iroquois tribes. Areas in the east, near Boston, were too heavily populated with militia to risk any major attacks there. The Connecticut River Valley in between seemed to be ripe for an assault along with areas of Maine and northern New Hampshire.

As an isolated outpost on the northwestern frontier, over

the years, Deerfield had suffered several attacks, both at the village and in the fields nearby. These were typically assaults by a handful of Indians on just a few settlers. There had been raids on the village in 1693, and 1695. A year later, in 1696, another raid ended with four captives being carried off. The French-English treaty in 1697 calmed things down a bit, but by 1701, hostilities were beginning again. During 1703, there had been several French-encouraged ambushes and raids on New England villages and farms by members of various native tribes. As recently as October, 1703, there had been an ambush near Deerfield in which two residents had been killed.

During the summer and fall of 1703, the Deerfield settlers had spent endless hours growing and harvesting crops on the fertile river bottoms, putting up hay for their livestock, and cutting firewood in the nearby forested hills, against the oncoming winter. Reaction to occasional news or rumors of incidents with Indians, or minor raids on other villages and farms, were a lower priority than putting together the necessities of life in order that they might live through the winter to see the next spring. Only Sunday, the Sabbath, was exempted from the daily toils of everyday life. That entire day was set aside for hours of worship in the church ministered by Reverend John Williams. Prayers were offered in the Puritan way asking God to protect them and safely see them through the winter's harshness. Reverend Williams was a typical minister of the day. He was well educated, and in addition to being the focal point of the town's religion, he was also a major civic leader. His wife, Eunice, was a member of the very well placed Mather family of eastern New England, which produced numerous religious and intellectual leaders including, Increase Mather and Cotton Mather.

As early as May, and as recently as December, there had been rumors of a large gathering of Indian warriors along with some French military at Chambly, not far from Montreal. That seemed like a long ways away from the lower Connecticut River Valley, so the Deerfield residents apparently weren't too concerned. The town's 10-foot stockade fence had recently been repaired and rebuilt. That provided a measure of protection for those residing inside, although about half the town's homes were outside its walls. The winter had been very cold and snowy, leading many residents to believe that they were safe from attack, at least until spring. As an added safety measure, about 20 militia members from outside Deerfield were quartered there late in the winter.

The addition of the extra militia soldiers brought the total population of the town to about 295 in February of 1704. Most of the troops were housed in some of the 40-some private homes that made up the settlement. On the night of February 29, 1704, the soldiers slept soundly in warm houses, as did the families. Dogs slumbered by the dying coals in the hearths and all was still outside in the cold. A sentry had patrolled the streets earlier in the night, but in the small hours of the morning, he grew bored, tired and cold. Soon, he too took shelter leaving the village totally undefended except for the stockade walls.

A few days earlier, there had been a major snowstorm and drifts had piled high against the stockade fence on the north side of town. About two hours before dawn, a band of 200 to 250 Indians and about 48 French officers and soldiers approached the north gate. According to some sources, the Indian warriors included members of at least three different tribes: Abenakis, Hurons and Mohawks. They may also have been joined by a few Pennacooks. The Pennacooks' main village was located near modern day Concord, New Hampshire, and thus they lived much closer to the English colonists than the Indians from the St. Lawrence area. Because of their proximity to Massachusetts, the Pennacooks were very concerned about the potential for expansion of the English colonies into their homeland.

As the raiding party approached the gate, a few used the snow drifts as a ramp to easily climb over the unguarded stockade walls. Then they opened the north gate permitting their army to enter and savagely attack the sleeping residents of Deerfield in their homes.

The attacking party was several times larger than any previous group of raiders that had penetrated south into

Massachusetts. A full-scale assault on a village was not a typical raid. The usual Indian tactic involved only a few warriors that struck quickly at a very few victims and then withdrew. The tactics employed at Deerfield in February of 1704, bore much more of a resemblance to European warfare than that of Native American combat.

The army had trekked nearly 300 miles through the cold and snowy February weather from near Montreal, with the specific intent of attacking Deerfield. The forces employed had been gathering near Chambly since May and originally had planned to sack Deerfield during the summer. However, they had been redirected to the Quebec area in response to a false report of English warships at the mouth of the St. Lawrence River.

With the hindsight of over 300 years, it is difficult to understand why the attacking party was not detected until they had traveled all the way from the St. Lawrence to Deerfield and fell upon the town. Some New England villages, including Deerfield, had received several recent warnings of a buildup of French and Indian fighters to the north. Yet, the large raiding force of about 300 members traveled for weeks on a long, slow journey southward for 300 miles completely unnoticed. They must have left a broad, easily detected trail through the snow. The discovery of such a large war party would have have alerted the residents of Deerfield; and would likely have caused militia from neighboring towns to converge and intercept the force, or at least greatly fortify the town. The evening before the attack, the raiders had camped for the night just across the Deerfield River, about two miles from the stockade, again undetected by their intended victims. Apparently, Deerfield's civic and military leaders made use of neither English, nor friendly Indian, scouts in spite of Deerfield's vulnerable position at the corner of two frontiers and reports of an enemy buildup in the north.

In order to remain secretive on their trek south, the French and Indians had to avoid all settled areas and routes that the English, or English-friendly natives, might be using. Yet, according to a report written by the governor of New France shortly after the fact, the route taken by the attacking force was that most commonly used for a journey from Montreal to the central New England area. They traveled south along Lake Champlain, crossed over to the Connecticut River via the French River, and then partway down the Connecticut.

The closer they approached to their objective, the greater the French and Indians' need for secrecy. They fully expected the English to be at least a little watchful. Although it presented the fastest and easiest route, clearly they could not risk following the Connecticut River all the way to Deerfield. When they were about 25 miles from their objective, in order to minimize the chances of being detected, the raiding party left the river. First they cached a large portion of their supplies, sleds, and equipment near modern day Brattleboro, Vermont, and then turned into the hills. This location was not chosen at random. Had they followed the river much farther, steep hills would have made access to the north-south valleys more difficult. The raiders relieved themselves of the burden of hauling their supplies and equipment in order to make travel through the hills much easier, once they left the broad river valley. Once they hid their cache, they traded the easily traveled river for the concealment, but more difficult travel, offered by the hills that rise west of the river. The unpopulated, narrow valleys of Leyden, running north-south like arrows aimed at the heart of Deerfield directly to the south, served the raiders' purpose perfectly. Leaving the river at Brattleboro and traveling south through the low hills of Guilford and into Leyden greatly increased their chances of not being detected until it was too late.

Once inside the stockade, the raiders spread out and assaulted numerous homes simultaneously. It appears that the 10 to 20 French officers made little attempt to control the actions of the Indians that slaughtered men, women, and children in their beds. This inaction by the French military was repeated several times over the coming decades, most notably at Fort William Henry on the south shore of Lake George in 1757. There, Montcalm and his French forces watched as their

Indian allies murdered over 100 men, women, and children as the fort was being abandoned under the terms of surrender.

It may be significant that several raiders went directly to Reverend Williams' house as if one purpose of the raid was to capture him and/or his family. Two of the Reverend's young children, including a newborn infant, were slaughtered at the house and the rest of the family was taken captive. A militia member, sleeping upstairs, escaped through a window and ran south for help.

During the attack, a few other residents escaped and ran to Hatfield, about 12 miles away to summon aid. The killing, pillaging, and burning went on for over three hours as several well-armed and fortified homes put up a good fight and avoided the fate of many of the others. When it was over, more than 50 residents had been savagely murdered, many homes and barns were burned, and large amounts of the farming village's livestock and food supplies destroyed. Terrorism is not a modern invention.

As if the murdering, burning, and sacking was not enough, following the attack, about 112 captives including men, women, and children, were herded north through the fields and woods covered deeply with snow. Their destination was a group of Indian villages near Montreal, Canada, nearly 300 miles away through the wilderness. During the march north, over 20 captives, nearly all women and young children, would join their murdered neighbors in reddening the New England snows with all their life's blood.

The burning homes lit up the sky and word of the attack quickly spread to other towns. A few mounted militia men arrived from the south as the Indians were exiting the north gate and traversing the fields north of town. Giving chase, the militia was quickly driven back by the deep snow and the much larger band of Indians, but not before nine of the militia had been killed.

Many more militia arrived throughout the day, but it appears that no additional attempt was made to follow close on the heels of the raiders. It was obvious that the captors and their captives were headed north and they must have left a deep, broad trail through the snow that could have been easily followed. The large number of captives, on foot, must have caused the raiders to travel much more slowly than a mounted militia could have traveled. Yet, oddly, no attempt was made by the militia to get ahead of the group and set up an ambush, or even to follow closely behind. The captives were on their own to face whatever torment or mercy their captors might dole out to them. Just as the raiding party was undetected during its entire journey southward, that party, plus its captives, were unobserved, unmolested, and not followed on their way north. One can only wonder why.

The raiding party, however, was not at all confident that they would not be pursued or ambushed. They were fully aware of the gathering militia and of their own slow progress northward. After spending all of the first day traveling only a very short distance, they spent the first night on the slope of a hill southwest of present day Greenfield. The next day the Indians and their captives continued north along the west side of the Green River. Just south of the future Leyden town line, they crossed that river. In the 1950s, there was an original covered bridge and swimming hole close to their crossing point. From there, they moved up a hill into what is now Leyden. The river crossing and hill are well documented in the writings of John and Steven Williams, who wrote of their experiences several years later.

Only a few weeks before the attack, Reverend Williams' wife, Eunice, had given birth to their latest child. She had watched the baby be slain by an Indian at the door to her home, along with many other very young children. Still weak from childbirth, cold, and despondent, she fell into the water while crossing the Green River. Her Indian captor dragged her out, but she had great difficulty continuing. A short ways east of the river, at the foot of the hill, deciding that she was more trouble than she was worth, her captor slew her with his tomahawk. There exists a stone monument marking the spot where her body was found the next day by a group of Hatfield, and surviving Deerfield, militia men. Eunice was the third captive murdered since leaving Deerfield. One young girl had been killed earlier and the night before, some Indians had killed Williams' slave, Frank, purely for sport.

Unaccustomed to travel under such harsh conditions, other captives could also not keep up, and many more were to meet the same fate as Eunice Williams before the group reached Canada. Most of those who were murdered by the Indians along the way were women and very young children. Oddly perhaps, children between the ages of about five and thirteen were of special value to the Indians, maybe because they could easily be adopted into the tribe. Many of that group under about eight years of age were carried on the backs of their Indian masters or hauled on sleds.

Over the years, various explanations have been given for the taking of captives by the woodland Indians in the Northeast. Some claim that they wanted young people to adopt into their tribes to replace lost members. Other sources say that they were taken in order to obtain slaves to help with the work of their villages. Other reasons might include the French paying a bounty for special captives (Reverend Williams?) and Indians obtaining victims to be used for their fiendish tortures. It is quite possible that one objective was similar to the horse raids by the western Indians. In the west, a warrior's wealth and position in the plains and mountain tribes was often measured by the number of horses he possessed. There, wars and raids on neighboring tribes and settlements would be conducted in an attempt to steal horses to increase a warrior's wealth and prestige. The same sort of thing may have been going on in the northeast except with human captives instead of horses. It is easy to imagine that a warrior who went on an expedition and returned with captives would be held in higher esteem by the tribe than one who did not.

The modern day road from Greenfield crosses into Leyden not far from where the Indians and their captives crossed the Green River, and where Eunice Williams was murdered. In Reverend Williams' book, he wrote of climbing a "small mountain" soon after crossing the river. Those writings and the known location of Eunice Williams' death, clearly establish that the group almost certainly entered what would become Leyden at that point.

After their entry into Leyden, it seems well established that the Indians then traveled by some route to a location on the Connecticut River near modern day Brattleboro, Vermont, to retrieve the supply of food and equipment that had been cached there on their trip south. From there they followed the Connecticut River northward before splitting up into several bands near today's White River Junction, Vermont. The destination of one band with many captives, including Reverend Williams, was the Indian village named Kahnawake, near Montreal. Some captives, who made it all the way to Canada, were redeemed several years later. Reverend Williams and his son, Steven (the central character in Mary P. Wells Smith's book, *The Boy Captive of Old Deerfield*), returned to the Deerfield area after a few years in captivity and wrote of their experiences. However, some captives elected to remain in Canada, including Reverend Williams' daughter, Eunice, who was about eight years old when captured. She voluntarily lived her life with the Indians, briefly visiting the Deerfield area a couple of times later in life. She died in Canada, at the age of 89.

As a boy, I was intrigued by the stories of this tragedy and read everything I could find about it. In the 1950s, stories of the event continued to be handed down in local families, although it had happened 250 years earlier. Many long-time Leyden residents were as familiar with the history of the 1704 Deerfield Massacre, as if it had happened in their lifetime. Over the years, many volumes by many different authors have been written about the attack and the experiences of the captives. Some authors have tried to be as factual as possible. Other books are based at least loosely on the facts, and some are pure fiction. However, the original sources are mainly just the writings of Reverend Williams and his son, Stephen, upon their returns from captivity. Most of the books simply rehash what the Williams wrote with a few new "facts" thrown in.

Virtually all the books dealing with the trek north say very little, if anything, about that part of the journey from the point of Eunice Williams' death to the cache near Brattleboro. This would have occurred during the second and/or third day of their voyage. Some 19th century historians wrote that they crossed a corner of what would become Leyden and into Bernardston. That has been picked up and repeated by nearly every writer since. However, there seems to be no historical, archeological, geographical, or logical reason for the definition of this route.

Through much of the 1950s, the local Leyden historian, William T. Arms, was busy putting together his *The History of Leyden Massachusetts 1676 - 1959* in time for the town's 150th anniversary which was coming up in 1959. I became aware of his project through his wife, Marsha, who was a local photographer of note. After I promised not to waste a lot of her husband's time with my boyish questions, she arranged for me to meet with Mr. Arms at their home.

The Arms had done a tremendous amount of research for their upcoming publication. They had delved into original official records all the way to Boston, and had interviewed hundreds of people who had verifiable family records. However, when I began asking Arms a lot of specific questions about the route of the Indians and their captives through Leyden, he admitted that there wasn't a lot to go on. Their entry point into the town was well established by the location where Eunice Williams' body was found and the description in Reverend Williams' book. The next "known" location had been identified as being the deep gorge near where Couch Brook enters Fall River in Bernardston. However, he admitted that he was unaware of any verifiable documentation of the Couch Brook location.

Arms showed me the map he was drawing for inclusion in his book. In addition to the locations of original homesteads, it showed the locations of all the old roads and trails that he had identified. For the route of the Deerfield captives, he had simply connected what he called the two known points (Eunice Williams' death site, and the Bernardston gorge crossing) with a straight line. The line he drew went in a more or less northeast direction across the southeast corner of Leyden. I was curious why he thought they would have taken such a route. I pointed out that if the Indians, with their captives, had taken anything like that route, it would have required frequent arduous climbing and descent of steep hills. They would have had to traverse the entire East Hill (Leyden)/West Mountain (Bernardston) area, on foot, through deep snow, dragging over 100 unwilling captives and loads of plunder with them. With the threat of a possible militia party following them, or getting ahead to ambush them, and the slowness of travel due to the great number of captives inexperienced in winter travel through the forest, it seemed very unlikely to me that they would have selected anything like such a difficult route when much more easily traversed terrain was available.

It was clear that my questioning interested him. Arms and I had several good discussions of the logical possibilities for the actual route. Arms told me that the Bernardston location had grown out of information in the Williams' writings about a small child being killed and thrown into a deep gorge not long after Eunice Williams had been killed. The Couch Brook gorge in Bernardston seemed to match the description, and since it was known that at some point the Indians followed the Connecticut River northward, it seemed like a fit. It was claimed by local Bernardston tradition that the entire party crossed that gorge on a single log. That seemed to me like a bit of a stretch considering that nearly 300 captors, over 100 captives, and loads of plunder would have had to cross that log. All the while they would have been worrying about a possible pursuit party or rescuers coming up the river at them. I was far from convinced and continued to pound Arms with questions.

In response to my suggestion, Arms admitted that the gorge written about could just as well have been the deep natural cut at the south end of the Leyden Glen. And, its proximity to the location of Eunice Williams' murder seemed to fit much better with the timing indicated in the original sources. Since the Glen Brook flows north-south, no crossing of the gorge would have been required. They could simply have followed the west bank of the stream northward.

At the time I met with Arms, I had not yet read an original

copy of Reverend Williams' book, published in 1707, after his redemption from Canada. Since then I have read it several times. My copy of *The Redeemed Captive Returning to Zion* mentions the death of the child, but it does not say anything about it being thrown into a gorge. However, I understand that the book was a best seller in its day and went through several editions, all of which were not necessarily identical.

I hoped that Arms would do a bit of exploring with me out in the field to see if we could better define the route of the captives. However, he was quite involved researching many other aspects of Leyden's history. He was feeling pressure to get his manuscript completed and didn't have a lot of spare time to wander the woods with a boy who asked a lot of questions. The story of the captives' route really wasn't much more than a detail to be mentioned a half dozen times throughout his book. In the end he did decide to replace the map's original straight line with a lazy S pattern winding through the hills that form the east side of Leyden and the west side of Bernardston. But, his line still ended in Bernardston.

My curiosity was fired up, however, and I was determined to better define exactly the route taken by the Indians and their captives through Leyden. Being very familiar with the topography of the town, I set out to determine what would have been the most direct and easiest route from the Eunice Williams marker to Brattleboro, in the days before roads.

The first question to be answered was: Why did the Indians take their captives through any part of the Leyden hills in the first place? Did they really do that, or had Williams' text been misinterpreted for 250 years? Being distraught from the very recent murder of his wife and two children, did he really accurately note the topography? Certainly it would have been far easier and faster to have taken the route north from Deerfield directly along the frozen Connecticut River and avoided steep and difficult terrain altogether. The river route would have provided them with the opportunity to cover many more miles per day than any route through the hills. If there was a major north-south highway through central New England in 1704, it certainly was the Connecticut River. That same route is followed by Hwy 5 and 191 even today. So why did the Indians take their captives over a much more demanding route? And, if they really did enter Leyden, why would they have made things even more difficult by traversing across the highest, steepest hills from there in order to reach Bernardston? Finally, what might have been their reason for going to Bernardston at all?

The decision as to what route to take may have been made while they spent the night on Petty Plain, just across the Deerfield River from the plundered village. From there, they could have easily followed the Deerfield River downstream to the Connecticut and then turned north. Without a doubt that would have been the fastest and easiest way to go, but they did not. Instead they went up the Deerfield a short ways and then followed the Green River to the foot of the Leyden hills. Why?

The Connecticut River was clearly the easiest route, but it also may have been the route that possible avengers would expect them to have taken. The raiders must have been aware of the large buildup of militia that had begun in the ravaged village of Deerfield, soon after their departure for the north. There was a chance that militia was gathering at the mouth of the Deerfield River, expecting the raiders and their captives to appear there. The militia could have arrived there quickly from Deerfield and Hatfield, and it was a very logical place for an ambush. Even if they were not followed by the militia, if the Indians and their captives were anywhere along a major river, there was a very real possibility of being discovered by other travelers or settlers along the way. They had the same need for secrecy on the return trip that they had on their trek south.

The Eunice Williams' death site, and Reverend Williams' writings, firmly establishes that the group entered Leyden at the south end. Therefore, it seems logical that they would have used the hills to keep out of sight and shield themselves from flanking attacks until well away from the Deerfield area. They also needed a direct, route to their cache, and that meant traveling over easy ground, not climbing up and down a lot of steep hills. Thus, the Indians took to the narrow valleys in the Leyden hills which rise west of the river. It is very likely that their return route was the same one that they took when they made their way south undetected to attack Deerfield. In fact, 300 travelers making the trip south would have broken a broad trail through the snow making for easier travel on the return. They had left a large cache of food and supplies near present day Brattleboro, Vermont, rather than drag it through the hills. On the return trip, a high priority would have been to reach that cache quickly.

Assuming for the moment that the Couch Brook location in Bernardston is correct, and that the Indians wanted to go there for whatever reason, the question must be asked "Then why did they bother to go through the Leyden hills at all simply to arrive at the Connecticut River after several miles of difficult travel that could have been easily avoided?" They had passed this way only a couple of days earlier, so they certainly were familiar with the terrain. They were traveling on foot through winter snows with a lot of ill-equipped and inexperienced captives, many of whom were women and young children. There must have been at least some fear of pursuit prompting them to cover ground quickly. Why would they want to cross several big hills, only to drop down to the river at Bernardston? If they wanted to go to Bernardston for some unknown reason, it would have been much faster and easier, starting from their Green River crossing, to skirt around the south end of the Leyden hills through the Greenfield Meadows area on a nearly level route.

After much thought and evaluation of the terrain, I developed the hypothesis that the Indians and their captives never went to Bernardston at all. Rather, they traveled as straight north as possible toward their cache near Brattleboro, VT following a route that was relatively easy, with no high hills to climb or steep descents, with the easy availability of water the whole way. Not knowing the situation with possible pursuers, they needed a route that would shield them from discovery and ambush. The ideal route would have been a narrow, gently sloping valley with steep hills on either side to protect their flanks and hide them from suspicious eyes. Yet, the valley floor needed to be relatively wide to accommodate their group of

400 individuals without the need to walk single file or always wade in the stream of a narrow canyon. Tromping through the snow in the winter makes one quite thirsty. There also needed to be abundant water easily available along the entire route. In a word, they needed Leyden, end to end.

Had the French and Indians followed the Green River farther than they did, travel would have soon become very difficult through a narrow, rocky gorge. Then, to reach the Connecticut River, it would have been necessary to travel in an easterly direction, crossing several high ridges before reaching their cache north of the modern day Vermont border. It makes sense that the Indians crossed the Green River where they did to avoid getting into the canyon and having to cross those ridges. I climbed most of these ridges as a boy, in the summer, unencumbered by snowshoes and unwilling captives, and would not have cared to do so in the winter snows. And, crossing where they did, gave them an easy alignment with the south end of a long valley through Leyden that leads directly toward Brattleboro.

Without a doubt, the easiest, safest, and most direct route from the Eunice Williams murder site to their cache, would have been along the full length of the long valley that runs north-south through Leyden, from the Greenfield line to the Vermont border. It requires no climbing of steep hills or ridges, other than the one at the southern border of the town which was described by Reverend Williams. This valley is shielded on the west by the West Leyden ridge and the hill that today contains Leyden Center. The east side of the valley is protected by the high, steep-sided East Hill area. Those hills would shield the captors and captives from any party of avengers from the south that may have gone up the Connecticut River in hopes of cutting off the escape. Similarly, any pursuit up the Green River would have placed several high ridges between the raiding party and the pursuers. If militia followed directly behind, the valley provided numerous ideal locations from which the Indians could ambush them.

To enter the valley, first they had to climb the hill just north of the Greenfield line. Reverend Williams' book makes it very clear that this is exactly what they did. He describes the climb and his exhaustion upon reaching the top. In fact, it is the only mention he makes of climbing a hill or mountain for several days. That would seem to suggest, that once they had climbed the hill, travel was over much easier terrain for quite some distance. After climbing to the top of the hill, they could have continued directly north much as the Greenfield Road does today. Or, if they climbed only part way, they could have dropped down a little into what is called Leyden Glen along Glen Brook and then followed that stream north. The Glen would have provided ready water access and therefore was the likely route. In the 1950s, there was a narrow dirt road that followed the likely route into the Glen. Before the Greenfield Water Department built a reservoir there, the Glen contained a deep gorge through its center. Part of that gorge can still be seen below the dam. If it is true that a child was thrown into a gorge, the Leyden Glen gorge fills the bill perfectly and makes a lot more sense than the one on the other side of East Hill in Bernardston, and there was no need to cross it on a log.

Continuing north, they would have soon passed the future location of the single room, South School House. A little farther north, the valley widens out a bit and continues to near where the Pearl Rhodes Elementary school stands today. At this point the modern road divides, with the Greenfield Road going steeply up the hill to the left toward Leyden Center. The right branch passes the school and continues to follow the much more gentle terrain up the valley. The Indian's immediate destination was Brattleboro. Interestingly, this branch of the road is called the Brattleboro Road today. The Indians would have followed the much gentler terrain rather than climb a steep hill only to soon descend once more. The valley also contained the same stream they had already been following. Their route would have passed behind the school site and crossed the future location of the field where Old Home Day celebrations were held and baseball games were played in the 1950s. They would have had relatively easy traveling on gradually rising terrain with the steepness of East Hill sheltering them on their right and the ridge that now contains Leyden Center, protecting their left flank.

Somewhere along their route that day, the Indians stopped and held a council among themselves. There is no way of knowing if this occurred in Leyden or after they had passed into what is now Vermont. I would bet on Leyden, because of the protection afforded by the valley. According to the writings of captives, who made it back home after several years, the discussions were quite loud and vocal. It appears that the conference centered on what to do about Reverend John Williams. He had been lagging behind ever since his wife had been killed and had been doing a lot of talking with some of the other captives. Some of the Indians appeared to be concerned that he might be fixing to lead a revolt. He appeared to them to be a troublemaker and some in the council wanted to rid themselves of him by burning him at the stake, thereby removing his influence and setting an example for the rest of the captives. Others wanted to simply dispatch him with a tomahawk blow and not delay any longer, thereby giving a possible rescue party time to catch up.

A theory has been presented by some historians that the primary objective of the raid on Deerfield, may have been to capture Reverend Williams for the French to use in a prisoner exchange in order to free a French pirate being held in prison in Boston. As one of the most prominent leaders on the wilderness frontier, and with his connections to the influential Mather family, Williams' trading value would have been quite high. Whether this theory is true or not, we will never know, but for some reason Reverend William's life was spared and after a short rest the group traveled on.

Soon, they would have passed the start of the modern day Frizzell Hill Road, where it breaks off to climb East Hill. In the 1950s, this was the location of Barton's Garage, the only other place in Leyden where gasoline could be purchased, or a car repaired, other than at Henry's Leyden Garage. Shortly beyond that point, the valley widens a little and Zimmerman Hill Road drops down into it off the ridge from Leyden Center. The valley floor is quite flat there, at least it used to be. In the 1950s, it was a very productive hay meadow with some marshy, wet areas along the stream that hugs the eastern edge. Today, this area is filled with small ponds and overgrown with brush. In the 1950s, about 250 years after the Indians and their captives passed through, this was the location of Henry Glabach's farm. His farm included most of this part of the valley, as well as partway up the hills to the west and east. Jessie's parents, Frank and Bertha Wood, lived there and operated a small dairy on about 120 acres.

At the north edge of what was to be Henry's farm, the valley floor narrows a bit and changes from gradually sloping upward to the north to gradually sloping downward into Beaver Meadow. Beaver Meadow later became one of the first settled areas in the town. It is a relatively wide, open spot protected by the hills. Presumably, this was once the location of several beaver ponds, but beaver were very scarce animals in the 1950s, so I don't recall ever seeing any there. I know there once was an inn and store there. The building was still standing, in the late 1950s, and may be still. I was hired one summer to help with some remodeling in the rear kitchen area. We tore off the latter-day plaster and lath and uncovered the original pine paneling. That paneling consisted of wide pine boards running horizontally. The boards were obviously cut from original growth trees because many of the boards were almost totally knot free and ranged from 18 to almost 30 inches in width. I think the owner sold some of those boards to finance the renovation.

In the 1950s, this area was the location of the Dobias farm, a one-room school house, and a small cemetery largely overgrown with brush and weeds. The Chapin family lived back in the woods up the Alexander Road which eventually merged with the West Leyden Road if you followed it far enough.

Several small streams converge in Beaver Meadow to form Keets Brook which flows northeastward to eventually pass its waters to the Connecticut River in Bernardston. It is possible that the Indians and their captives followed the Keets Brook eastward from Beaver Meadow, but it is not likely. Just as at the south end of Leyden, one has to ask why would they would go east here, following a steep, narrow, rocky, twisting, turning stream into Bernardston, when they could have much more easily continued north through gentle terrain directly to the location of their cache.

The fact of the cache is quite certain since some redeemed captives reported that the Indians recovered supplies which had been stashed on their trip down to Deerfield. In addition to food and clothing, the cache contained numerous sleds that greatly facilitated and hastened the northward march from that point. The following morning they resumed their journey northward following the Connecticut River to its junction with the White River in Vermont. There, they split into two or three bands taking different routes for the remainder of their journey.

It is very likely that this north-south route through the valley in Leyden had been used by Indians for centuries as an alternative to following the Connecticut River. It was an easy route with good water all the way, no steep hills, and excellent concealment. Any time they wanted to avoid detection by enemies along the more heavily traveled river route, or hunt for game as they traveled, the Leyden route would have been ideal. In his book, Arms points out that, later in the 1700s, when the first settlers arrived in Leyden, most of them established homes and farms high on the hills and ridges for better protection from Indians. This would suggest that there was significant evidence of Indian travels in the valley below. It wasn't until the French and Indian wars in the area had ended after 1754, that settlement in the valleys was undertaken.

I have often wished that I had spent more time trying to locate Indian artifacts along the route I have described. From time to time I would do a little random digging just to see what I could find. My digging only produced two stones that might be arrowheads at the Old Home Day field, and one certain arrowhead in the woods to the north. One day, I accidentally found what I believe was the stone head of an Indian war club in the stream through the hay meadow on Henry's farm. When I was fishing, it caught my eye as an unusual looking black stone. It was in the shallow, rocky bottom of the small stream that flowed into the meadow below the house. The stone was coal-black and smoothly polished, totally unlike any others in the stream bed. It was rounded on one end, with the other end formed into a chisel shape.

I believe it is highly likely that Leyden's Native American background consists of much more than the occasional hunting party assigned to it by most historians.

Appendix D

A FEW LEYDEN RECIPES

The following, are a few of the many favorite recipes of Leyden cooks. All are copied from the *Leyden Cookbook Bicentennial Year*, editors: Katie Ainsworth, Jessie Glabach, and Anne MCarthy, with permission granted by the Leyden Historical Commission. The recipes are as they appear in the cookbook.

========================

The first two, are the recipes that have been used for over 70 years to make beef stew, and clam chowder, for sale at the Leyden Food Booth at the Franklin County Fair in Greenfield, MA. The originators of the stew and chowder recipes are not identified.

These are quantity recipes and you will want to cut them back. The bowl used for measuring vegetables held about five cups.

BEEF STEW

3 lbs. of stew meat, marrow bone if possible
1 bowl chopped onions
2 bowls of carrots, sliced in rings
3 bowls of potatoes, cut into small pieces

Cook the stew meat slowly, until tender. Add the carrots and cook until tender; then add potatoes. Season well with salt and pepper and cook until potatoes are done.

This stew may be re-heated, and it will be better the second time.

CLAM CHOWDER

1 bowl chopped onions
1/2 lb. margarine
Salt to taste
3 bowls potatoes
1 No. 5 can minced clams
2 quarts milk

Cook onions in margarine until yellow. Add all other ingredients except milk. Cook until potatoes are tender. Add milk, heat, and it's ready to serve. Formerly, salt pork was used, but many people disliked the pieces of pork.

==========================

The last two recipes are from the "world famous" blueberry suppers. Many different cooks made muffins and pies in their home kitchens for the suppers at the Town Hall. The recipes were not standardized. These are typical.

BLUEBERRY MUFFINS

"This is the recipe I use when I make muffins for the annual Blueberry Supper," Katie Ainsworth

1/3 cup salad oil
3/4 cup sugar
1 egg
1/3 cup dry milk
1 cup water
1 3/4 cups flour
3 tsp. baking powder
1 tsp. salt
1 to 1 1/2 cups blueberries

...eam together salad oil, sugar, and egg. Beat. Add dry ...our, baking powder and salt. Add water and blueberries. ...00 degrees, 15 to 20 minutes.

...SH BLUEBERRY PIE
...nown Contributor

...ry for 2-crust pie
...ps blueberries
... cup sugar
...4 cup flour
...innamon, cloves, salt to taste
1 tbl. Lemon juice
2 tbl. Butter

Line 9-inch pie pan with pastry; fill with berries tossed with ...ugar, flour, spices and salt. Sprinkle fruit mixture with lemon ...uice, dot with butter. Adjust top crust, slash to allow steam ...to escape. Bake in hot oven (400 degrees) about 35 minutes or ...until crust is browned and the filling bubbly.

Resources

Although the vast majority of the contents of this volume a[...]
based on the author's memories, the following sources a[...]
provided valuable input and guidance.

A Triple Celebration of Methodism in Leyden, Massachu[...]
October 6, 1966. Church Building 125 years, Congre[...]
100 years, Education Building Open House. Publis[...]
The Anniversary Committee. This booklet contains [...]
of the church, dated 1912, and of the original Tow[...]
It also contains another photo, dated 1900, of the[...]
showing the two front entrances. Neither photo [...]
a steeple on the church.

Abbott, Katharine M. *Old Paths and Legends of the New [...]*
Border Connecticut, Deerfield, Berkshire. G. P. Putn[...]
Sons The Knickerbocker Press, 1907.

Ainsworth, Katie; Glabach, Jessie; McCarthy, Anne, edito[...]
Leyden Cookbook Bicentennial Year. 1976.

Ainsworth, Katie. Longtime Leyden resident and very activ[...]
church member. Graciously provided numerous notes[...]
clippings, and a history of the Church's Food Booth at the[...]
Franklin County Fair.

Anderson, Fred. *The War That Made America.* Published by The[...]
Penguin Group, New York, 2005.

Anniversary Souvenir, The Meeting House, The Methodist Church Leyden, Massachusetts. Published by the Anniversary Committee 1941. Published to celebrate the 100th anniversary of the New Meeting House, and contains much history.

Annual Reports of Officers and Committees of the Town of Leyden, Massachusetts. For the year ending December 31, 1958. Every year, the town provided each household with a copy of the town report listing all the town's expenses for the previous year, the proposed budget for the next year, and all the issues to be resolved at the upcoming town meeting.

s, William Tyler. *History of Leyden, Massachusetts 1676 – 1959.* Originally published by The Enterprise and Journal, range, Massachusetts, 1959. A reprint is available from igginson Book Company, Salem, Massachusetts.

Samuel. *The Route of the French and Indian Army that cked Deerfield Feb. 29th, 1703-4, On Their Return March Canada With The Captives.* Published in *History and oceedings of the Pocumtuck Valley Memorial Association 80 – 1889* Vol. II. Deerfield, MA. 1898. Describes the ute in considerable detail, but contains little information bout their passage through Leyden.

ond, June Barton. One of Doug Barton's children, and classmate of the author at the Center School.

emos, John. *The Unredeemed Captive, A family Story from Early America.* Published by Alfred A. Knopf, New York, 1994. This is the story of Eunice Williams, captured in Deerfield as a very young child, who lived with the Indians in Canada until her death at the age of 89.

Fisher, Edith. Longtime Leyden resident, highly active in all town and church events, and founder of the Leyden Historical Commission.

Glabach, Jessie W. Numerous photo albums, scrapbooks, and notes she kept from the early 1920s until the 1980s. Unless indicated otherwise, the photos in this book were taken by her, or a family member. These materials are all in the possession of the author.

Glabach, William. Cousin and neighbor of the author during the time period of this book. Selectman and life-long Leyden resident.

Greenfield Recorder-Gazette. Every few years, the Greenfield newspaper would run a feature article on Leyden and or Henry and his shop. The author recently contacted representative of the newspaper, and learned that th no longer have these in their archives. Fortunately, Je kept clippings of each article in her scrapbooks.

Haefeli, Evan and Sweeney, Kevin. *Captors and Captive 1704 French and Indian Raid on Deerfield.* Publis the University of Massachusetts Press, Amherst. This is one of the best researched, and best w books on the topic.

Holmstrom, J. G. *Modern Blacksmithing, Rational Horses and Wagon Making.,* by Fredrick J. Drake & Co Can be read online at www.usagennet.org. Load blacksmithing tips of the trade.

Howes, Dottie. Wife of George Howes, and Leyden resid during the period of this book.

Kellog, Lucy Cutler. *History of the Town of Bernardstor* Published by Press of E. A. Hall & Co. 1902. Availabl to read online at www.archive.org. Containing much information about early Leyden, it was a major source for W. T. Arms in writing his book. Describes the supposed crossing of the log by the Deerfield captives.

Sesquicentennial Celebration Program. Town Hall, Leyden, Aug. 22 & 23, 1959.

Williams, John. *The Redeemed Captive Returning To Zion or A Faithful History of Remarkable Occurrences in the Captivity and Deliverance of Mr. John Williams.* Sixth edition. Published by Samuel Hall, Boston, 1795. Reprinted in 1908, as *The Redeemed Captive Returning to Zion or the Captivity and Deliverance of Reverend John Williams of Deerfield,* by *The H. R. Huntting Company, Springfield, Massachusetts.* The latter can be read online at www.archive.org.

Williams, Stephen W. *A Biographical Memoir of the Reverend John Williams, First Minister of Deerfield, Massachusetts.* C. J. J. Ingersoll, Greenfield, Mass. 1837. Author was a direct descendant of Reverend Williams. Includes: *Account of the Captivity of the Reverend Doctor Stephen Williams, Written by Himself.* The latter is from the journal kept during captivity by the young son of Reverend Williams.

Wikipedia.org was consulted for details and history of chestnut blight, gypsy moths, and tree diseases.

Photo: Henry Glabach working at the forge in his blacksmith shop. Photo taken in the late 1960s or early '70s. Courtesy of Greenfield Recorder-Gazette and Leyden Historical Commission.

Back Cover Photo: South side of the Leyden Blacksmith Shop with the church on the hill behind. Author photo from the 1970s.